Studies in Childhood and Youth

Series Editors
Afua Twum-Danso Imoh
University of Sheffield
Sheffield, UK

Nigel Thomas
University of Central Lancashire
Preston, UK

Spyros Spyrou
European University Cyprus
Nicosia, Cyprus

Penny Curtis
University of Sheffield
Sheffield, UK

This well-established series embraces global and multi-disciplinary scholarship on childhood and youth as social, historical, cultural and material phenomena. With the rapid expansion of childhood and youth studies in recent decades, the series encourages diverse and emerging theoretical and methodological approaches. We welcome proposals which explore the diversities and complexities of children's and young people's lives and which address gaps in the current literature relating to childhoods and youth in space, place and time.

Studies in Childhood and Youth will be of interest to students and scholars in a range of areas, including Childhood Studies, Youth Studies, Sociology, Anthropology, Geography, Politics, Psychology, Education, Health, Social Work and Social Policy.

More information about this series at
http://www.palgrave.com/gp/series/14474

Lydia Martens

Childhood and Markets

Infants, Parents and the Business of Child Caring

Lydia Martens
Keele University
Newcastle, UK

Studies in Childhood and Youth
ISBN 978-0-230-28425-8   ISBN 978-1-137-31503-8   (eBook)
https://doi.org/10.1057/978-1-137-31503-8

Library of Congress Control Number: 2018943279

This Palgrave Macmillan imprint is published by the registered company Macmillan Publishers Ltd. part of Springer Nature
The registered company address is: The Campus, 4 Crinan Street, London, N1 9XW, United Kingdom

Preface

The materials discussed in this book have their embryonic beginnings in a series of convivial conversations with Sue Scott and Dale Southerton in cafés in Durham. Coming together with backgrounds in sexuality, risk, consumption and intimate everyday lives, we discussed the relative absence of children in the sociology of consumption, and the importance of bringing these varying sociologies together. It soon became clear that we were not the only ones asking questions like this, and in fact, some—including Viviana Zelizer, Ellen Seiter and David Buckingham—had already developed work on the location of children and families in economic and mediated life, the moral questions this was giving rise to, and the ubiquitous enmeshing of the private and the public. It is clear that the past 15 years have seen significant acceleration in debates on children, childhood and consumer culture. This is witnessed, for instance, in the global participation of a research community in the successful International and Pluridisciplinary Child and Teen Consumption conference, which, as the brain child of Valerie Inés de la Ville, commenced in 2004 and has since taken place bi-annually at different locations in Europe. This book engages with these evolving debates. In particular, it grapples with the question how, through theoretical innovation, scholarship can prevent itself from becoming tied up with the strong moralities that dominate the topic of children's consumption and the location of children in consumer culture. My argument is that the scholar's task, in the first instance, is not to moralise, but to understand how common everyday moralities come about, and to explore what the consequences are. Empirically, this book is about the youngest of children—babies and toddlers, and even those yet to be born, their carers, and the business of child caring that has evolved to service the goods and services that allow child caring to be performed. This focus has been selected purposefully, as young children, the question of children's age, and the problematic of the generational relations that inform both the moral debates and the location of children in consumer culture are either absent, or have remained hidden from view. The theoretical approach adopted in this book brings these relationalities out and into the open. As you commence reading, be prepared to read about how the mundane world of early childhood and new families gives rise to an amazing array of cultural productions and achievements, with the capacity to shape the worlds of children, families and business.

Keele, Staffordshire, UK   Lydia Martens

Acknowledgements

This book has been informed by, and matured during many conversations, held over coffees and teas, and during meal times, at conferences and in seminars, and during visits to commercial events. I feel very grateful that so many people have willingly participated in exchanges with me, some of which were short, others more lengthy, and some demanding substantial time input. All have helped the arguments developed in this book on their way.

Especially noteworthy are the many conversations I have held with colleagues from the British and European Sociological Association consumption networks. In the European consumption network, I am grateful towards so many people, not all of whom can be named, but who have over the years made this network the friendly and welcoming home it is for informal, engaging and encouraging discussions on European consumption research. Special thanks go to Bente Halkier, Tally Katz-Gero, Terhi Anna Wilska, Eivind Jacobsen, Unni Kjaernes, Laura Terragni, Margit Keller, Dale Southerton and Monica Truninger, for motivation, inspiration and for your friendship. Thank you so much, Bente, for providing me with your honest comments and suggestions for improving the arguments. In fond memory of Kaj Ilmonen, who not only taught us about the importance of consumption research, but also about the absolute necessity of collegiality. You remain in our memory.

Deep and sincere appreciation goes to Sue Scott and Alan Warde. You have both been excellent mentors, co-researchers and co-authors over the years, and above all, very good friends. Alan, you have always shown the way with your distinct approach to sociological thinking and reasoning, and your kind and considerate manner of engagement. Sue, your support and advice has often been forthcoming in understated ways, most readily delivered over cups of tea and coffee, in cafes and on the couch, during discussions in kitchens, around dinner tables and on walks. Thank you both for being there.

I offer a heartfelt thank you to the colleagues with whom I worked on the ESRC seminar series Motherhood, Markets and Consumption. Pauline Maclaran, Margaret Hogg, Stephanie O'Donohoe, Lorna Stevens, Linda Scott and Mary Jane Kehily, your unfailing enthusiasm, the engaging and thought-provoking seminars that you organised in your host institutions, and the excellent team-work you delivered in pulling publications together, taught me a lot about how collaborative work can be both efficient and thoroughly enjoyable. Special and warm thanks go to Pauline Maclaran, your friendly coaching and absolute generosity of spirit have made working with you a pleasure. In the Child and Teen Consumption network, I am grateful to David Buckingham, Valerie Inés de la Ville, Dan Cook, Vebjørg Tingstad, Tora Korsvold, Olivia Freeman, Helene Brembeck, Malene Gram and many others. Particular and heartfelt thanks go to Anna Sparrman, Minna Ruckenstein and Pascale Garnier, for joining me in a special symposium session to discuss the book at the 8th CTC conference in Angoulême, and for providing valuable feedback on the book.

At Keele, I would like to thank my supportive colleagues, and especially Emma Head, Rebecca Leach, Emma Surman, Liz Parsons and Farzana Shain. Thank you, Emma Head, for participating in many conversations with a shared interest, and for sharing resources over the years. I am grateful to Keele and to my colleagues for giving me research time to make progress with this book. In working towards the finishing line, I would like to thank Amelia Derkatsch for guiding the completion process and for being so patient with me. The editors of the Palgrave series on Children and Youth: Penny Curtis, Afua Twum-Danso Imoh, Nigel Thomas and Spyros Spyrou, thank you for reading through drafts and providing useful comments. Writing academically means participation in a continuous journey, with multiple directions, and in a community of practice. Any faults remaining are my own.

Thanks are due to the many exhibitors and people working at the consumer exhibitions and trade shows that I visited, for agreeing to talk with me, and some for offering post exhibition talking time. Christine and Matt from Clarion Events were helpful in 'personalising' my work at The Baby Show. And special thanks go to Emma Casey and Liz Ellis. Liz helped out when I joined The Baby Show in Birmingham as an exhibitor, and participated in conversations with new and prospective parents. Emma trialled 'shopping with people' with me when she was pregnant with her first child and I enjoyed our shared investigations of baby slings and cloth nappy systems. Finally, I would like to thank the prospective and new parents, who agreed to talk with me about their intimate experiences of pregnancy and parental becoming through the lens of consumption and consumer culture, for generously offering their time and for their interest in the study. Some held strong moral views about the consumer world in which they were spending time; others were more inclined to enjoy themselves on their day out. But the stories of all were laced with a strong dose of intimacy and familial love and appreciation. Growing new life clearly brings people together.

Love and intimacy are important themes in this book, and they are equally important on a personal level. My sisters, Jacqueline and Monique, have listened to endless stories about the many challenges of living life as an academic. They have also rejoiced with me when hard work has paid off. To Carina and Eva, for giving me first hand experience of the process of growing up, for making me a parent, and for finding good Japanese animated films to watch together. To Steven, for bringing music into my life and for always being there for me. I love you all! I dedicate this book to my parents, Jan and Jeanne Martens, for giving me all those years of care and love, and for walking and becoming alongside me.

Contents

List of Figures

List of Tables

1

Introduction

In the early stages of developing this project on young children and consumer culture, I visited the warehouse sized out-of-town retailing site of Mothercare, called *Mothercare World*. Mothercare is a well-known international brand name in retailing[1] in the life course trajectory that includes pregnancy, birth, and the early years of a young child's life. On arrival, the appeal to this client group was immediately apparent. The façade of the building that housed the store stood out from the other warehouses nearby by visually telling the visitor that this was a place for and about young children. The building had a cream-coloured frontage, and dominating the central entrance was a giant petrol-green coloured porch, featuring a large clock, with smiling sun and moon faces and a huge 'Mother Earth' right in its centre. The hourly dial was curvy and yellow, and, in bright orange spiky letters underneath the clock, was an announcement that visitors were entering 'the world' of Mothercare. The warehouse itself felt cool and comfortable when I entered from the warmth of a sunny summer's day, and its aesthetic organisation again

---

[1]From the Mothercare website http://www.mothercareplc.com/who-we-are/at-a-glance.aspx, accessed on 16 October 2016.

© The Author(s) 2018
L. Martens, *Childhood and Markets*, Studies in Childhood and Youth,
https://doi.org/10.1057/978-1-137-31503-8_1

announced the centrality of the young child. Organised on two levels, with the first floor starting halfway down, the vista was dominated by a giant green tree, reaching all the way from the floor to the roof. A huge face with rolling eyes, alternately opening and closing, was located in the middle of the tree, and couched on either side were two staircases. These invited children into the upper floor, where the store's toy selection was housed, with the ground floor filled with the serious stuff of childcare—from Moses baskets for new-borns, to mattresses, bedding and travel systems. In the centre of this ground floor space, and sandwiched between the tills at the front entrance and the giant tree in the middle, was an oval shaped department with clothing for new-borns and babies. This area stood out for its soft pastel colours. A cascade of orange-speckled butterflies circled above, whilst soft toned background music transported me into the tranquillity of an imagined baby nursery.

Those in search of the goods and services that facilitate the practices and emotional experiences of pregnancy and early-years childcare soon discover that a distinct collection of commercial providers form a rather unique market of products, services and resources aimed at them. This market includes specialist retailers, out-of-town shopping warehouses, specialised shopping isles in high street chemists and city centre department stores, and common brand names, such as Mothercare, Boots, and Babies-R-Us, soon start to flow easily off the tongue in conversations that need not necessarily be about shops and shopping. This commercial landscape can be called unique because, as expressed by the prospective parents I spoke with during my research, this is a world about which many claim ignorance before the idea of having a baby started to turn into reality. With products ranging from those with a quick turn-over rate, like weaning foods and disposable nappies, to more durable and one-off items, such as potties and car seats, now sold through a range of terrestrial and online retailing settings, the unique quality of this world is further accentuated by the fact that most of the products and services found here are, quite literally, for the care of the young child in the fold of family life.

Caring for a young child is made possible by a broad range of often very mundane and everyday goods and services. As commodities, these goods and services come with a price tag, and are designed, produced and marketed by what, in this book, I call *the business of child caring*, and bought by new and prospective parents, and other interested adults. I argue that it is the practice of child caring that brings together commercial agents, new and prospective parents, and a range of other people, organisations and entities, including the notion of childhood. In the interactions between these entities, understandings of the young child are realised, and used in the service of pecuniary value creation and in parental reasoning of what it is that they are looking for when shopping for a growing family. My argument is that it is these understandings of the young child that provide the underlying rationale for *why* and *how* young children need to be cared for. This book also presents an investigation of how the business of child caring is organised. It explores how the possibilities and opportunities for commercial action and value-creation are enabled and curtailed by cultural understandings of young children. Amongst other things, I will seek answers for why businesses that operate in this terrain are so careful, and why some new parents express concern for the environment when they shop for their young offspring, when others invest in silver charms that have the form of their baby's tiny hands and feet, and yet others keep referring back to the content of their purse. Researching the business of child caring is also important because consumption scholars, including those specialising in children and childhood, have not shown much interest in young children (Brownlie and Leith 2011; Cook 2008; Martens 2005; Martens et al. 2004; Sjöberg 2013). One of the aims of this book is therefore to locate young children and the business of child caring more clearly into broader debates on children, childhood and consumer culture.

Researching Children and Consumer Culture

Recent years have seen a call for change in the direction of scholarship on children, childhood, consumption and consumer culture (e.g. Buckingham 2009, 2011; Buckingham and Tingstad 2010; Sparrman et al. 2012; Taylor 2013; Woolgar 2012). In the emergence of this call, the highly moralistic character of debate in this area has been high-lighted as a problem. Woolgar bears witness to this:

> As a newcomer to the field of child studies and child consumption, I am struck first by the intensity of debates and feelings about questions of consumption associated with children, and, second, by the strength of the assumptions about the nature and identity of the key actors at the heart of these debates, and especially, of course, the child. Notions of what is right for children fuel debates in policy, academia, the media and pop-ular culture; debates that seem to gain much of their momentum from entrenched assumptions about what is good for children, what children need, what is in children's best interests – in short what, after all, a child *is*. (2012: 33)

The arena of children, childhood and consumer culture is clearly a highly generative cultural terrain (Cook 2012), giving rise to urgent new social 'problems' such as the emerging debates, in the past 20 years, on childhood obesity and the sexualisation of childhood cul-ture (Buckingham 2009). These debates are illustrative of the ease with which protagonists can position themselves in binary camps, enacting understandings of the child that are incompatible, and that reflect the broader cultural narrative of incompatibility of the market, culturally defined as profane, from the intimacy of family life and sacred famil-ial personae, like children (Zelizer 1985). Arguably, the idea of *the child consumer* takes on a central location in these debates, becoming symp-tomatic of the polarisation between the empowered and powerless, and the competent and incompetent/vulnerable child (Buckingham 2009, 2011; Buckingham and Tingstad 2010; Cook 2005, 2012; Sparrman et al. 2012).

In *The Commodification of Childhood*, Dan Cook (2004) argues that *the child consumer* is a historical invention, brought into being by entrepreneurs during the twentieth Century as they sought to expand consumer demand. *The child consumer* is thus a discursive and cul-tural construct, with a history (2004: 5). Accepting *the child consumer* as a discursive figure is useful for clarifying that it should not be con-fused with actual flesh and blood children, or, as Cook has it, sentient beings with unique biographies. As such, the characteristics with which *the child consumer* is endowed can be, and have been, twisted and turned in accordance with the moral and political intentions of its narrators, who, of course, need to be acknowledged as always adults, identifying as parents, or organised into interest groups representing a range of bodies with diverging interests, but always with the proclaimed best interests of the child at heart (Buckingham 2011). These easily gravitate towards entrenched moral positions. *The child consumer* is, for instance, frequently sketched as a child with an 'insatiable desire for things, its knowledge about products, its tastes, its conspicuous display, and its seemingly unquestioned identification of self with commodities' (Cook 2004: 5). To describe the child as having insatiable desires, excellent knowledge of products, distinct and individual tastes, and accepting consumption, or better still, consumerism, as a taken for granted priority in life, is of course to associate children with an overly negative and controversial set of assumed qualities of what engagement in consumer culture entails. In her ethnographic study with children aged 10, and living in a poor work-ing-class African American neighbourhood in the US, Elizabeth Chin (2001: 6) relates how this negative image of *the child consumer* is further amplified when merged with understandings of race and poverty:

> … the pressures of fantasy worlds projected by television, advertising, and the downtown mall collide with the profoundly anti-fantastic experi-ence of being both economically strapped and black in the United States. From the outside, this mixture of consumer culture and poverty has long been viewed as dangerously combustible, resulting in crazed pathological consumers who kill for sneakers and are addicted to brands.

David Buckingham concludes that 'the figure of the child consumer is framed and constructed in … ways, which … marginalize or prevent other ways of thinking about the issue' (2011: 6). Hence, there has been a growing consensus for the need to move 'beyond the moralistic and sentimental views about children's consumption that tend to dominate the public debate' (2011: 2), and some arguments for how this may be achieved. One way forward is summed up in Buckingham and Tingstad (2010), which is to present varied empirical case studies that unearth the often complex and contradictory realities of lives that children live, and that demonstrate that the contexts of children, consumption and consumer culture are varied (Buckingham and Tingstad 2010; Chin 2001; Martens et al. 2004; Martens 2005). Situated empirical investigations are indeed important, and this book represents an example of this, but I would stress also that there is a risk that the insights developed through such studies can come to 'sit alongside' accounts that continue to successfully drive the moral and political populist agendas that are in need of critical appraisal.

For reasons discussed in Chapter 2, I argue that moving beyond moralistic and sentimental views about children's consumption is not so straightforward. In fact, conducting research on children and consumer culture is wrought with challenges, not least because of the immediate demands made on scholars to engage with the morally intense debates and feelings that characterise the field. They are called upon to take a position, and a critical one at that. This is signalled, for instance, when Buckingham (2011: 226) 'defends' the approach he adopts in *The Material Child*, stating that this may be read as endorsing the interests of marketers. But what kind of critical analyses can be offered, and indeed, what does it mean to present such an analysis? The polarisation of which Buckingham speaks, and the idea of *the child consumer*, harbour and hide conceptual knots and ways of thinking that make it hard to get at the complex underlying relations. This book attempts to develop a critical analysis that grapples with these underlying complexities by working with an analytical framework that facilitates understanding of the relations between markets, young children, childhood, parents/mothers, adults, sales conventions, products and product narratives, child caring and other cultural understandings. In doing so, I build upon recent arguments for the uptake of alternative theoretical approaches (e.g. Sparrman et al. 2012; Woolgar 2012; Nairn and Spotswood 2015). There are useful theoretical tools out there with which this economic-cultural world, and its complex human and post-human relations, and conceptual knots, can be explored, and my hope is that this study will encourage other researchers to follow suit. The book's concentration on the young child and the business of child caring is conducive for developing such an alternative framework. At once, it decentres *the child consumer* and insists on the inclusion of generational practices in order to understand how this economic and intimate world works. It also touches on the all-important matter of the broader cultural significance of children in today's affluent consumer societies, and how this relates to the matter of monetary value creation.

Young Children in Consumer Culture

Stimulated by my earlier argument that research on children and consumer culture should pay more attention to diversity amongst children (Chin 2001; Martens et al. 2004; Martens 2005), I set out to examine the market that services practices of child caring, young children and their families. I developed insight by speaking with staff representing commercial players, and new and prospective parents, and by observing interactions in market environments. I also gathered a wealth of textual materials, and included this in my work. I discuss the research further towards the end of Chapter 3. In truth, where it concerns the youngest of children, babies, toddlers, and those yet to be born, scholarly commentary is relatively sparse. It is almost as if there is little expectation that much can be learned about children and consumer culture by focussing on young children. Thus, whilst research on children and consumer culture has been quite buoyant, with some exceptions (e.g. Cook 2000, 2004; Cross 2002, 2004a; Freeman 2009, 2012; Lim 2015; Martens 2009, 2014; Plowman et al. 2010; Sjöberg 2013; Saltmarsh 2009; Takahashi 2015), the same cannot be said for analyses of the significance of the youngest of children in consumer culture. This work is notable for showing how young children often become 'barely visible' bystanders in the recently expanding debate on mothering, motherhood and consumer culture (e.g. O'Donohoe et al. 2013; Taylor et al. 2004), in which the transition to motherhood forms an important sub-theme (AbiGhannam and Atkinson 2016; Afflerback et al. 2014; Barnes 2015; Boyer and Spinney 2016; Burningham et al. 2014; Clarke 2004; Fuentes and Brembeck 2016; Kehily 2014; Martens 2009; Ponsford 2014; Theodorou and Spyrou 2013; Thomas 2017). I return to this peculiarity in Chapter 2. So how have young children and consumer culture been conceptualised?

In his analysis of the establishment and expansion of the children's wear industry in the US over time, Dan Cook (1995, 2000, 2004, 2012) draws on Viviana Zelizer's (1985) analysis of the historical transformation in how children are socially viewed in the industrialising worlds of the nineteenth and twentieth centuries. The emergence of the priceless or precious child in everyday culture saw a shift from children being appreciated for their economic worth in family life, towards a state that is 'extra-commercium' (Cook 2004: 8) or 'outside' economic life. The priceless child, following Zelizer, is valued for its sacred and emotional qualities, and has taken up a cultural position that is opposite to that of the profane space of the market. The problematic Cook addresses is how, given this distancing of the child from economic life, entrepreneurs interested in expanding markets responded. The location of 'the child' in sacred space, he argues, was resolved through two major strategies for monetary value creation. The first was to target child carers directly, with mothers positioned as the 'moral core' 'between child and market' (2004: 11). This strategy was to:

> Define or redefine commodities as beneficial and functional for children. "Beneficial" goods can fall under various rubrics, including those which are "fun" or "educational," which promote "personal expression" or aid in "development." "Child Development," first popularized in the '20s and '30s with the aid of popular, national media such as *Parents* magazine, has served as the quintessential mode for the adjudication of what may be legitimized as beneficial to children. (2004: 11)

The second strategy Cook (2004) discusses is the emergence of *the child consumer*, introduced earlier. This figure is interesting particularly for the definition of children 'as full *persons* who are, in a relatively unproblematic way, desirous of goods' (2004: 11). This idea of *the child consumer* is close to the contemporary neoliberal image of the 'adult' consumer as having the capacity to have preferences and desires, and the right to choose amongst alternatives in a market place (Warde 2014).

Overlaying these two strategies is a further one: this is the alignment of pecuniary value with the practice of child-related age grading. This is a prominent theme in Cook's early work, where he carefully attends to the ways in which distinct age-related child categories, including 'the toddler' (Cook 2000, 2004) and 'the tween' (Cook 2004; Cook and Kaiser 2004), emerge in and through the development of marketing practices during the twentieth Century. The connection between children's age and development is also a theme in historical analyses of children's toys (Cross 1998), when in the contemporary context, keen interest has been shown in what may be called the Baby Einstein phenomenon (Quirke 2006; Thomas 2007; Wall 2005), and the growth in modern educational technologies targeted at young children (Plowman et al. 2010). In the research conducted for this book, the practice of age-grading the young child and the foetus, but also the staging of the life course around early childhood, were very prominent as methods for organising sales materials and realizing economic value (see e.g. Chapter 8).

A subtly different analysis to that proposed by Cook, is presented by Gary Cross (2002, 2004a, b). Analysing US marketing literature of the early twentieth Century, Cross finds evidence of the use of the young child's desiring look, and in particular its wonderment, in marketing to parents. Cross calls this practice 'wondrous innocence' and juxtaposes this with what he calls 'sheltered innocence', which encapsulates the 'ascetic' modernist and rational developmentalist understanding of childhood that is present in child-rearing manuals and consumer culture, and that perhaps best approximates the first of Cook's strategies.

> Instead of stressing the modern developmentalists' formula of protection and preparation, this third approach exposed the child to 'delight' and delayed maturation. It celebrated the child's individuality while rejecting the adult's rational and prudential vantage point. Instead, the adult embraced the 'wonder' of childhood as an escape from the disappointments of market society and modernity. (2004a: 184)

Wondrous innocence works by tapping into the emotional experiences of parenthood and adulthood. In Cross' analysis, adulthood presents a 'jaded' existence in which adults are no longer capable of experiencing the wonderment offered by consumer culture on their own accord. By bestowing children with consumer goods that induce wonderment in the child, parents turn to their children to gain such experiences. The nuances of the analysis presented by Cross are interesting. It may, for instance, be argued that it is the parental pursuit of wondrous innocence that stimulates the consumer socialisation of the young child, not least because it is the need of adults for wonderment that fills the lives of young children with the objects of consumer culture. In this way, young children also grow up learning that pleasure, enjoyment, and consumption, go well together. Ultimately, Cross' analysis intimates that the binary opposition between the sacred and the profane does not lead to singular strategies for the generation of pecuniary value, and indeed, that this opposition may not be universally enacted. It is important to remember, though, that these analyses draw on historical textual sources that come from marketing literatures.

If it is agreed that *the child consumer* 'fits' the older agentive child better than the younger child, then the two strategies proposed by Cook may also be read as age-related strategies. He argues that these strategies 'commingle without much moral approbation' (2004: 11), though as argued above, part of the challenge of conducting research on children and consumer culture are the binary oppositions that so easily map onto the idea of *the child consumer*. Cook also acknowledges that the idea that the child can be desirous of things demands a more active parental response (2004: 69). There is some uncertainty, then, as to whether these pecuniary value creation strategies can easily operate in tandem, and in relation to all children, regardless of their age. It is frequently argued that child development and child age do not map onto one another in easy ways, and there is also the commercial practice of fuzzying the 'age' of children, where it remains unclear exactly what age the child is that marketers speak of (Cook and Kaiser 2004). The recently recurring suggestion that marketers approach children at increasingly younger ages (Buckingham 2011: 1) also works as an example of how uncertainties about the age of children can serve as a useful narrative device for those intend on criticising children's consumer culture (see also the discussion of Thomas (2007) in Chapter 2). My view is that the significance of the age of children, and its relation to the idea of the child as a consumer, with individual tastes and preferences, is an empirical one. This opens up for consideration the possibility that showcasing *the child consumer*, and the specific qualities it is given, may vary in time and space. Thus, whilst Cross (2004a) discovered a celebration of 'the child's individuality' in US marketing literature in the early twentieth Century, this does not necessarily mean that we may expect to find the same 'child' in contemporary sales narratives. The question that needs to be pursued is in what ways, if at all, *the child consumer* 'can be' shown in commercial texts that discuss (young) children.

Additional questions are revealed when reading across this work. Cross suggests that pecuniary value creation may be realised in ways other than proposed in Cook's analysis. Behind the pecuniary value creation strategies explored by Cook stands 'the child' and 'its interests', whereas in the analysis offered by Cross, 'the child's interests' take second stage behind the emotional needs of adults. Cook's analysis confirms that the matter of children, consumption and consumer culture is *about children*, when Cross highlights the importance of generational saliences and practices. Cross' analysis also makes us attentive to the idea that pecuniary value creation practices are not uniform, always working in the same direction. Thus, in the examples given above, we learn that monetary value may be made by *stimulating* children to grow up, but also by *delaying* that process. One of the starting points of this book on childhood and markets is acknowledgement of the fact that 'the market' is multifaceted, telling a complex story where it concerns the ways in which young children and new families are approached, and monetary value is created. One peculiarity that I hope this book will provide some amends to is that whilst the combined works of Cook and Cross have been well received in debate on childhood and consumer culture, their analyses of how pecuniary value may be realised in relation to *young* children does not appear to have been taken much further. Drawing on empirical research conducted in the UK, I endeavour to broaden their historical work on US marketing practices out with this study of the contemporary business of child caring. Following Sparrman and Sandin (2012) and Cook (2012), my concern is with how young children and new parents are situated in the consumer worlds of affluent societies, and how the value of infants and monetary value are co-realized in these worlds.

The Growing Emotional Significance of Young Children

At the heart of debate on children, childhood and consumer culture, including the challenges that have just been discussed, is the question of the emotional and societal significance of children (Meyer 2007; Zelizer 1985). I already touched on Zelizer's (1985) work, which traces the historical transformation of the cultural significance of children from one of economic import towards one of emotional consequence. Zelizer, of course, traces this change over the nineteenth and into the twentieth Century, with an interesting link to the economic sphere through the insurance market. Victoria Alexander (1994) explores fluctuations in the emotional-societal salience of children during the twentieth Century, through an analysis of the comparative presence of children and families in advertising. In doing so, she sees 'the market' merely as a 'response mechanism' of societal-cultural change, rather than as constitutive of this. Nevertheless, her article gives evidence of the emerging scholarly debate, during the 1980s, and to which Zelizer's work forms an important contribution, on the emotional and societal significance of children. Given her analysis stops at the year 1990, one question is whether the emotional and societal salience of 'the child' has changed since then? Moreover, if so, can this be seen as related to changes in consumption and consumer culture?

Contemporary commentators have argued that children's emotional worth has become more pronounced in recent years, but the question is in what respects this is a societal phenomenon? Daniel Miller's (1998) analysis in the *Theory of Shopping*, for instance, signals the growing importance of children in family life, seeing the prioritisation of their needs and desires over those of other adults in the family, including fathers and husbands, who where sketched as taking precedence in earlier studies (see e.g. Charles and Kerr 1988; DeVault 1991). In relation to this, Allison Pugh argues that:

> ...children are ever larger in their worlds, their joys and pleasures reverberating, their needs and predilections even at times dominating their environments. ... Children's symbolic presence has swelled to new dimensions. (2009: 19)

Yet, she insists that this growing emotional worth of children has a domestic quality. She argues there is evidence that outside the domestic sphere, the importance of children has been diminishing. Drawing on Barry Thorne's (1993) notion of 'the privatization of childhood,' she makes reference to the fact that children appear to have less space outside their homes to call their own. At the same time, the argument continues, the American state is withdrawing from childhood, prioritising its limited resources to support a growing elderly population. She also emphasises the increasing numbers of children who are living in poverty in the United States: something that is shared by some affluent societies, including the UK, though not others. We may agree with Pugh that the state has been withdrawing financial support from children and families. At the same time, substantial public resources (monetary and symbolic) still go into a range of child care infrastructures, including health, child protection, and education. Though suggestive of commodification (e.g. Kenway and Bullen 2001), the picture is nevertheless complex (e.g. Sandin 2012). And then there is the matter of children's emotional value at a cultural level, which is surreptitiously linked to other issues, such as 'nature' and the environment, where public concern has also been growing in recent years (e.g. Taylor 2011, 2013). Noteworthy here is that childhood appears to have become an important 'reference point' for the voicing and discussion of a range of moralistic issues and concerns (e.g. Meyer 2007).

Pugh's argument on the domestication of children's emotional worth could be read as indicative of the growing salience of a neo-liberal market society, that brings together a process of the individualisation of responsibility, within the context of consumer choice and information (e.g. Cairns et al. 2013), and connects neatly with arguments in motherhood sociology on intensification (see Chapter 2). It may be that one of the twists in these arguments is that 'childhood' is in a process of transfer, from the state to the marketplace, with the science-medical complex moving alongside this (Martens 2009, see also Chapter 8). Yet, as suggested in the analysis presented by Cross (2002, 2004a, b), childhood scholars have proposed other ways of interpreting the relationship between markets, value creation, adults, and the emotional worth of children. Such contrasting explanations have not been brought together, and perhaps it would be worthwhile doing so. Whilst this book does not offer a historical analysis, the approach that is adopted and discussed in the chapters ahead will offer food for thought in order to reflect further upon questions like this.

At a Glance

The arguments presented in this book start with setting out the adopted framework and the rationale behind it. I argued earlier that moving scholarship on children, childhood and consumer culture beyond the moralistic and sentimental approaches, identified by Buckingham (2011) as so common and problematic, demands some rethinking. In the first chapter, I argue that there is a need for awareness of the challenges that confront those wishing to follow the call for advancement. Several exist. On the one hand, a set of conceptual knots, including commonly occurring binary oppositions like the sacred and the profane, and discursive practices like those of childhood, steer scholarly thinking in specific ways. On the other hand, there is a problem with scholarly performativity. Chapter 2 concentrates on the *performativity* in debate on children and consumer culture of the binary opposition of the sacred and the profane. Various forms of performativity are highlighted, and I concentrate especially on one form, which I call entity-focused territorialisation. In relation to the focus in this book on young children, this is the development of tracks of scholarship around the entities of 'the child', 'motherhood' and 'parenting', 'consumption' and 'the market'. Territorialisation also has implications for the possibilities of thinking, especially beyond the agendas that are manifested in each of these terrains. In response to these challenges, I propose to draw on theories of practice and performance to analyse what makes child caring such an important and emotionally charged social practice, and how it is located at the centre of interactions between different people, organisations and more-than-human entities. In Chapter 3, I explain why I draw on Theodor Schatzki's argument that practices are social entities that are organised by a teleoaffective structure, principles and instructions, and understandings. The teleoaffective structure of a practice includes the ends or purposes of why one would carry out a practice and, linked to this, the emotional consequences of carrying a practice. In the book, I explore what elements make up the teleoaffective structure of child caring, and how these elements are performed in the interactional contexts of market environments. I argue that a range of entities can perform or carry this practice, and that includes commercial actants. As the teleo-affective structuration of child caring happens in and through repeated performances of different actants, and also results in institutionalised phenomena, I draw on insights from science and technology studies and feminist theory to argue that the analysis should be guided by a horizontal methodology. Chapter 3 finishes with a discussion of this methodology and the methods that guided the research.

In Chapter 4, I introduce the business of child caring and start to explore the ways in which interactional sales practices are organised. The discussion focuses on the consumer exhibition, and I use this event as representative of the broader business of child caring. Drawing on my ethnographic work and interviews with new and prospective parents, the consumer exhibition is discussed in some detail. I draw out a number of characterising features that mediate the sales-buyer interface and I explore different modes of exhibition. On the basis of an analysis of product leaflets and website content, I also comment on the 'product content' of childcare and identify six pathways of child caring. Each of these pathways, I argue, is supported by a set of products and services that point to and inform the teleoaffective structure of this practice. This brings together four main qualities of the young child: those of loveable, vulnerable, pure and the 'need' for nurturing and leads into the second part of the book (Chapters 5–7), which attends to the teleoaffective structuration of child caring. The argument that I develop in the book is that the generational practices that form the discourse of childhood are played out in the teleoaffective structuration of child caring, through the convergence around specific ways of knowing the young child.

My analysis of teleoaffective structuration purposefully starts with the quality of the young child as *loveable*, because the loving quality of the young child serves as the 'anchor' for other elements in the teleoaffective structure. Chapter 5 therefore presents an analysis of the aesthetic organisation of the commercial environments that were explored. The chapter demonstrates the role aesthetic organisation plays in the shaping of the particular understanding of 'the young child' as loveable. Elements of the aesthetic of early childhood outlined in this chapter, and found in the commercial world of young children and child caring, include the use of colours and colour schemes, the definition of 'cute' objects, designed as playmates for children and used as affective devices targeting adults, and conventions in the visual representation of young children. I close with a discussion on the use of certain kinds of objects in practices of personal life lovemaking. In and through these various practices, 'the young child' is known as lovable, not only in the privacy of family life, but as a signifier in a broader generational and symbolic culture of childhood. Chapter 6 moves onto the enactment of *protecting* as another main teleoaffective element of child caring. I examine how this teleoaffective priority is produced and maintained in the commercial world through the theme of infant safety and the constitution of 'the young child' as vulnerable in embodied ways. Through the juxtaposition of vulnerability as either enigmatic or unpredictable, performances of the young child as *vulnerable* also make age-related knowledge and sales practices visible. Infant vulnerability opens up a plethora of opportunities for the sale of products, where the product and sales narratives borrow from techno-medical-science input. This is illustrated through discussions of products that are marketed as countering infant flat head syndrome and sudden infant death syndrome. Chapter 6 finishes with a discussion of how child caring acquires affective importance through the entanglement of *vulnerability* with the young child's ascribed *lovable* and *pure* qualities. Here, I draw on parental narratives. Infant purity and practices of purification are discussed in Chapter 7. Purification is conceptualised as a set of ritualised practices performed on babies *and* products, *and* in material-embodied and symbolic ways, creating a range of material and symbolic orders that keep the pure child pure. In the first part of the chapter I present an analysis of the recently growing interest in re-usable nappies. This gives insight into the hybridity of early parenting in the sense that practical, embodied, environmental and symbolic concerns are brought together by parents in their reasoning about the planned use of nappies. The second part of this chapter presents an analysis of the purification work performed in sales narratives to render products natural and normal, thus enhancing their suitability as components in child caring practices. This discussion, in which infant feeding tools serve as an empirical case study, heralds the shifting focus from the process of teleoaffective structuration to a consideration of the implications of the teleoaffective order of child caring. In short, in the second part of Chapter 7, I discuss the moralisation of child caring products in sales narratives.

The final two chapters in the book continue with questions that stay close to the moral significance of child caring, and the implications for the performance of this practice. Chapter 8 focuses on child caring pedagogies and asks how new and prospective parents locate themselves in relation to the moralities of this practice. The discussion starts with a phenomenon I have called the marketisation of child caring pedagogy, in which, through features such as pedagogic merging and the brand-company website, I explore how larger commercial players position themselves as child caring educators. Following the argument in Chapter 3 that practices may be carried by different entities and that this is characterised by the pursuit of specific interests, here I focus on the question what the process of pedagogic marketisation conveys about the position and positioning of commercial interests in the field of child caring. I then move onto the second part of the chapter, where, based on interviews with new and prospective parents, I present a three-fold typology of parental moral-selving (Barnett et al. 2005: 30). I conclude by thinking through how effective the marketisation of pedagogy is in governing the consumption and the process of parental becoming of prospective and new parents. In the final chapter, I present an analysis of how the practices of commercial organisations are infused with the moral concerns of child caring. First, I highlight examples of how the moral concerns of child caring appear as salient in the practices of commercial players. I discuss an episode of moral disruption around the chemical compound Bisphenol A; the transformation of which into a safety concern created commotion in the business of infant feeding tools during my fieldwork. This is followed by reflection on how moral worth manifests itself through gossip and in the institutionalisation of product standards. I close the chapter by questioning how the organisational features of commercial communicative practices, including techno-medical-science density; the pedagogical content; and the management of 'the face' in exchange interactions, may be read as institutionalised responses to the discourse of childhood that undergirds the teleoaffective structure of child caring.

Bibliography

AbiGhannam, N., and L. Atkinson. 2016. Good green mothers consuming their way through pregnancy: Roles of environmental identities and information seeking in coping with the transition. *Consumption Markets & Culture* 19 (5): 451–474.

Afflerback, S., A.K. Anthony, S.K. Carter, and L. Grauerholz. 2014. Consumption rituals in the transition to motherhood. *Gender Issues* 31 (1): 1–20.

Alexander, V.D. 1994. The image of children in magazine advertisements from 1905 to 1990. *Communication Research* 21 (6): 742–765.

Barnes, M.W. 2015. Fetal sex determination and gendered prenatal consumption. *Journal of Consumer Culture* 15 (3): 371–390.

Barnett, C., P. Cloke, N. Clarke, and A. Malpass. 2005. Consuming ethics: Articulating the subjects and spaces of ethical consumption. *Antipode* 37 (1): 23–45.

Boyer, K., and J. Spinney. 2016. Motherhood, mobility and materiality: Material entanglements, journey-making and the process of 'becoming mother'. *Environment and Planning D: Society and Space* 34 (60): 1113–1131.

Brownlie, J., and V. Leith. 2011. Social bundles: Thinking through the infant body. *Childhood* 18 (2): 196–210.

Buckingham, D. 2009. The impact of the commercial world on children's well-being. Independent assessment for the department of children, schools and families and culture, media and sport. Available at http://webarchive.nationalarchives.gov.uk/20130401151715/http://www.education.gov.uk/publications/eOrderingDownload/00669-2009DOM-EN.pdf.

Buckingham, D. 2011. *The material child*. Cambridge: Polity Press.

Buckingham, D., and V. Tingstad (eds.). 2010. *Childhood and consumer culture*. Basingstoke: Palgrave Macmillan.

Burningham, K., S. Venn, I. Christie, T. Jackson, and B. Gatersleben. 2014. New motherhood: A moment of change in everyday shopping practices? *Young Consumers* 15 (3): 211–226.

Cairns, K., J. Johnston, and N. MacKendrick. 2013. Feeding the 'organic child': Mothering through ethical consumption. *Journal of Consumer Culture* 13(2): 97–118.

Charles, N., and A. Kerr. 1988. *Women, food and families*. London: Routledge.

Chin, E. 2001. *Purchasing power: Black kids and American consumer culture*. Minneapolis: University of Minnesota Press.

Clarke, A. 2004. Maternity and materiality: Becoming a mother in consumer culture. In *Consuming motherhood*, ed. J.S. Taylor, L.L. Layne, and D.F. Wozniak, 55–71. Rutgers, NJ: Rutgers University Press.

Cook, D.T. 1995. The mother as consumer: Insights from the children's wear industry, 1917–1929. *The Sociological Quarterly* 36 (3): 505–522.

Cook, D.T. 2000. The rise of 'the toddler' as subject and as merchandising category in the 1930s. In *New forms of consumption. Consumers, culture, and commodification*, ed. M. Gottdiener, 111–130. Lanham, MD: Rowland and Littlefield.

Cook, D.T. 2004. *The Commodification of childhood: The children's clothing industry and the rise of the child consumer*. Durham, NC: Duke University Press.

Cook, D.T. 2005. The dichotomous child in and of commercial culture. *Childhood: A Global Journal of Child Research* 12 (2): 155–159.

Cook, D.T. 2008. The missing child in consumption theory. *Journal of Consumer Culture* 8 (2): 219–243.

Cook, D.T. 2012. *Pricing the priceless child*—A wonderful problematic. In *Situating child consumption: Rethinking values and notions of children, childhood and consumption*, ed. A. Sparrman, B. Sandin, and J. Sjöberg, 53–60. Lund: Nordic Academic Press.

Cook, D.T., and S. Kaiser. 2004. Betwixt and between: Age ambiguity and the sexualization of the female consuming subject. *Journal of Consumer Culture* 4 (2): 203–227.

Cross, G. 1998. *Kids' Stuff: Toys and the changing world of American childhood*. Cambridge, MA: Harvard University Press.

Cross, G. 2002. Valves of desire: A historian's perspective on parents, children, and marketing. *Journal of Consumer Research* 29 (3): 441–447.

Cross, G. 2004a. Wondrous innocence print advertising and the origins of permissive child rearing in the US. *Journal of Consumer Culture* 4 (2): 183–201.

Cross, G. 2004b. *The cute and the cool: Wondrous innocence and modern American children's culture.* New York: Oxford University Press.

DeVault, M. 1991. *Feeding the family.* Chicago: Chicago University Press.

Freeman, O. 2009. "The Coke side of life"—An exploration of pre-schoolers' constructions of product and selves through talk-in-interaction around Coca-Cola. *Young Consumers* 10 (4): 314–328.

Freeman, O. 2012. I do like them but I don't watch them. In *Situating child consumption: Rethinking values and notions of children, childhood and consumption*, ed. A. Sparrman, B. Sandin, and J. Sjöberg, 157–176. Lund: Nordic Academic Press.

Fuentes, M., and H. Brembeck. 2016. Best for baby? Framing weaning practice and motherhood in web-mediated marketing. *Consumption Markets & Culture* 20 (2): 153–175.

Kehily, M.J. 2014. For the love of small things: Consumerism and the making of maternal identities. *Young Consumers* 15 (3): 227–238.

Kenway, J., and J. Bullen. 2001. *Consuming children: Education-entertainment-advertising.* Maidenhead/Philadelphia: Open University Press.

Lim, S.M.Y. 2015. Early childhood care and education in a consumer society: Questioning the child–adult binary and childhood inequality. *Global Studies of Childhood* 5 (3): 305–321.

Martens, L. 2005. Learning to consume—Consuming to learn: Children at the interface between consumption and education. *British Journal of Sociology of Education* 26 (3): 343–357.

Martens, L. 2009. Creating the ethical parent-consumer subject: Commerce, moralities and pedagogies in early parenthood. In *Critical pedagogies of consumption: Living and learning in the shadow of the "shopocalypse"*, ed. J.A. Sandlin and P. McLaren. New York: Routledge.

Martens, L. 2010. The cute, the spectacle and the practical: Narratives of new parents and babies at the baby show. In *Childhood and consumer culture*, ed. D. Buckingham and V. Tingstad. Basingstoke: Palgrave Macmillan.

Martens, L. 2014. Selling infant safety: Entanglements of childhood preciousness, vulnerability and unpredictability. *Young Consumers* 15 (3): 239–250.

Martens, L., D. Southerton, and S. Scott. 2004. Bringing children (and parents) into the sociology of consumption: Towards a theoretical and empirical agenda. *Journal of Consumer Culture* 4 (2): 155–182.

McNamee, S., and J. Seymour. 2013. Towards a sociology of 10-12 year olds? Emerging methodological issues in the 'new' social studies of childhood. *Childhood* 12 (2): 156–168.

Meyer, A. 2007. The moral rhetoric of childhood. *Childhood* 14 (1): 85–104.

Miller, D. 1998. *A theory of shopping*. Cambridge: Polity Press.

Murcott, A. 1993. Purity and pollution: Body management and the social place of infancy. In *Body matters: Essays on the sociology of the body*, ed. S. Scott and D. Morgan, 122–134. London: Falmer.

Nairn, A., and F. Spotswood. 2015. "Obviously in the cool group they wear designer things": A social practice theory perspective on children's consumption. *European Journal of Marketing* 49 (9/10): 1460–1483.

O'Donohoe, S., M. Hogg, P. Maclaran, L. Martens, and L. Stevens (eds.). 2013. *Motherhoods, markets and consumption: The making of mothers in contemporary western cultures*. London: Routledge.

Plowman, L., J. McPake, and C. Stephen. 2010. The technologisation of childhood? Young children and technology in the home. *Children and Society* 24 (1): 63–74.

Ponsford, R. 2014. "I don't really care about me, as long as he gets everything he needs"—Young women becoming mothers in consumer culture. *Young Consumers* 15 (3): 251–262.

Pugh, A.J. 2009. *Longing and belonging: Parents, children, and consumer culture*. California: University of California Press.

Quirke, L. 2006. "Keeping young minds sharp": Children's cognitive stimulation and the rise of parenting magazines, 1959–2003. *Canadian Review of Sociology and Anthropology* 43 (4): 387–406.

Saltmarsh, S. 2009. Becoming economic subjects: Agency, consumption and popular culture in early childhood. *Discourse: Studies in the Cultural Politics of Education* 30 (1): 47–59.

Sandin, B. 2012. More children or better quality: Pricing the child in the welfare state. In *Situating child consumption: Rethinking values and notions of children, childhood and consumption*, ed. A. Sparrman, B. Sandin, and J. Sjöberg, 61–70. Lund: Nordic Academic Press.

Schatzki, T. 1996. *Social practices: A Wittgensteinian approach to human activity and the social*. Cambridge: Cambridge University Press.

Schatzki, T. 2002. *The site of the social: A philosophical account of the constitution of social life and change*. Pennsylvania: Pennsylvania State University Press.

Sjöberg, J. 2013. *In the eye of the market: Children and visual consumption*. Linköping: Linköping University Electronic Press.

Sparrman, A., and B. Sandin. 2012. Situated child consumption: Introduction. In *Situating child consumption: Rethinking values and notions of children, childhood and consumption*, ed. A. Sparrman, B. Sandin, and J. Sjöberg, 9–32. Lund: Nordic Academic Press.

Sparrman, A., B. Sandin, and J. Sjöberg (eds.). 2012. *Situating child consumption: Rethinking values and notions of children, childhood and consumption.* Lund: Nordic Academic Press.

Takahashi, M. 2015. Young children and consumer media cultures in Japan: Mothering, peer relationships, social identities and consumption practices. Doctoral thesis, Norwegian Centre for Child Research (NOSEB), Norwegian University of Science and Technology, Trondheim. Accessed online at https://brage.bibsys.no/xmlui/bitstream/handle/11250/293288/Mayumi_Takahashi_PhD.pdf?sequence=1.

Taylor, A. 2011. Reconceptualising the 'Nature' of childhood. *Childhood* 18 (4): 420–433.

Taylor, A. 2013. *Reconfiguring the natures of childhood.* London: Routledge.

Taylor, J.S., L. Layne, and D.F. Wozniak. 2004. *Consuming motherhood.* New Brunswick: Rutgers University Press.

Theodorou, E., and S. Spyrou. 2013. Motherhood in utero: Consuming away anxiety. *Journal of Consumer Culture* 13 (2): 79–96.

Thomas, S.G. 2007. *Buy, buy baby: How big business captures the ultimate consumer—Your baby or toddler.* London: Harper Collins Publishers.

Thomas, G.M. 2017. Picture perfect: '4D' ultrasound and the commoditisation of the private prenatal clinic. *Journal of Consumer Culture* 17 (2): 359–377.

Thorne, B. 1993. *Gender play: Girls and boys in school.* New Brunswick, NJ: Rutgers University Press.

Wall, G. 2005. Is your child's brain potential maximized? Mothering in an age of new brain research. *Atlantis* 28 (2): 41–50.

Warde, A. 2014. After Taste: Culture, Consumption and Theories of Practices. *Journal of Consumer Culture* 14(3): 279–303.

Woolgar, S. 2012. Ontological child consumption. In *Situating child consumption: Rethinking values and notions of children, childhood and consumption,* ed. A. Sparrman, B. Sandin, and J. Sjöberg, 33–52. Lund: Nordic Academic Press.

Zelizer, V.A.R. 1985. *Pricing the priceless child: The changing social value of children.* Princeton: Princeton University Press.

2

Researching Children, Childhood, and Consumer Culture

Introduction

This chapter examines the *performativity* of scholarly practices around the binary opposition of the sacred and the profane, and asks the question how such performativity presents challenges for the advancement of critical analyses of children, childhood and consumer culture. My focus is on a kind of performativity that I call *incompatibility work*. Everyday cultures, as is well known, are defined by sets of strong, culturally defined, binary oppositions (e.g. Derrida 1976; Kopytoff 1986; Taylor 2013; Zelizer 1985), and in relation to children and childhood, the opposition between the profane and the sacred, culture and nature, and competent and incompetent, are common. Binary oppositions work as 'vehicles' for locking in specific understandings of common cultural categories, such as 'the child' and 'the market', which in turn serve incompatibility arguments. Incompatibility work is thus heavily focused on entities and on the definition, maintenance and defence of *their* characteristics (Woolgar 2012). Arguably, because of the politically infused moralities that are so dominant, participation in research on children, childhood and consumer culture demands engagement

© The Author(s) 2018
L. Martens, *Childhood and Markets*, Studies in Childhood and Youth,
https://doi.org/10.1057/978-1-137-31503-8_2

with the very real presence of incompatibility work in everyday culture. There is, at the same time, the challenge of how to maintain a level of analytical distance to such common cultural practices. As explained by Haraway (2004: 47), it is all too easy to 'repeat and sustain our entrapment in the stories of the established disorders', as no-one stands outside culture, and scholars are hailed by the cultural practices they set out to investigate and understand in the same way as others are. Even so, it should not be assumed that, even amongst scholars, there is agreement that maintaining such a distance is necessarily seen as a priority, as alternative interests influence practices and argument development. However, for those wishing to advance analyses of children, childhood and consumer culture theoretically, there is an important task in reflecting upon how actively, and in what ways, everyday cultural practices that confirm the distinction between the profane and the sacred, and the ways of thinking and knowing that are furthered in and through these practices, are repeated, maintained and enacted in and through academic debate, and to reflect upon the consequences of this.

Scholarly debate on children, childhood and consumer culture evidence three models of rendering entities incompatibility. I first and briefly discuss *simple* forms of enactment, represented by what may be called *moral entrepreneurship*, and that have already been the target of much recent criticism (Buckingham 2009, 2011; Buckingham and Tingstad 2010). Including contemporary neo-Marxist critiques of consumer culture, which work actively to distinguish the profanity of commercial culture from the sanctity of intimate life in order to build a critique of capitalism, I call the second form *bad capitalism*. Here, political purchase is achieved through the maintenance of incompatibility between apparently unchangeable and uniform entities of 'the market' and 'the' family, mother, or child. In these two versions, incompatibility work is done in an explicit way, meaning that no attempt is made to distinguish the task of analysis from the practices of everyday culture. The third form of scholarly performativity is arguably the more challenging of the three, as it is tied up with the temporal trajectories of programmes of scholarly work, in what may be termed *the territorialisation around entities*. What I mean by this is the development of scholarly terrains of practice where research programmes have diverged to focus in on the entities of 'the child', 'motherhood' and 'parenting culture', 'consumption' and 'the market'.[1] Here, incompatibility work happens in more subtle ways in the sense that territorialisation frames the focus of research, and this results in degrees of invisibility and disinterest in questions that cut across territories, or indeed, that challenge the key terms of debate in these territories. Note that discussion on *bad capitalism* is embedded in the section on territorialisation.

Simple Forms of Incompatibility Work

Those familiar with the literature on children's consumer culture will know that the most common way of starting a conversation on this topic is an elucidation of the deeply moralistic, emotionally laden and controversial quality of the issues that are held to be at stake. As explained by Woolgar (2012), moral purchase is achieved by holding stable specific understandings of entities, such as child, consumption and market. This happens in simple versions of incompatibility work, where this ontological practice is presented in the form of rhetorical arguments in which specific associations and relations between entities are made. Simple forms of incompatibility work may also be seen as *moral entrepreneurship*. There is a growing body of popular texts, ranging from 'issue' books written by popular experts, through to catchy journalism in weekend newspapers that connect this practice with pecuniary value creation. A critical analysis of moral entrepreneurship may be found in Buckingham's work (2009), where Sue Palmer's (2006) *Toxic Childhood* and Martin Lindstrom's (2003) *Brandchild* are discussed as examples of how incompatible understandings of the consuming child are enacted through the adoption of different stances in the debate. These examples are not dissimilar to the contrasting methods of childcare that are presented in popular parenting books (see e.g. Thomson et al. 2011).

---

[1]See also Pyyhtinen (2016), for an equivalent practice that he calls subjectification.

In relation to the youngest of children, and following in the footsteps of *Toxic Childhood*, a good example of moral entrepreneurship is Susan Gregory Thomas' (2007) book *Buy, Buy Baby*. Moral reprobation is clearly a salient sales tactic in the book, demonstrated for instance through its two 'disturbing' sub-titles: '*How big business captures the ultimate consumer – your baby or toddler*' and '*How consumer culture manipulates parents and harms young minds*', but also in the write-up on the book's back cover, where the problematic of the child consumer is rendered more problematic, the *younger* the child is:

> In this groundbreaking book, Thomas pinpoints a dangerous economic and cultural shift: kids are becoming consumers at alarmingly young ages and are suffering all the problems of rampant consumerism usually faced by adults – from anxiety to hyper-competitiveness to depression. (2007: back cover)

In a rhetorical style in which a succession of simple associations are enacted, the reader's attention is drawn to 'the facts' that young children are consumers at 'alarmingly young ages,' that this is highly problematic, and also that to be a consumer in today's world inevitably means the experience of the detrimental impact of 'rampant consumerism'. This is typically explained with reference to advertising and branding, as illustrated in the early pages of the book:

> … Today's infants are crawling and toddling billboards for America's big brand names … all developmental milestones of early life are punctuated by brand names. Babies don't travel in plain old strollers; they ride in Maclarans, Graycos, or high-end Bugaboos. Their car seats have Eddie Bauer labels. Their nipples are Nuks, their bottles are Playtex or Avent. Their diapers are Huggies with Disney Winnie the Pooh or Pampers with Sesame Street characters. (Thomas 2007: 2)

In such brief text passages, common sense understandings of 'the child', 'consumption' and 'child consumption' are voiced, without the offer of any further analysis. As explained by Buckingham (2011), the world that is sketched here is simple in a multitude of ways, not least in its understanding of children and consumer culture. At the same time, caring adults are assumed to be absent, irrelevant or apparently incompetent (Martens 2005). Forms of moral entrepreneurship do not aim to develop critical analyses in scholarly ways. Instead, they are arenas in which the opposition between the sacred and the profane is enacted in an active and explicit way, with the resulting moral stories offering popular reading for those looking to confirm their own views and value systems (Seiter 1993).

Entity-Focused Territorialisation

The commercial world of products and services, which speaks to the life course phase that features pregnancy, the birth of first children, the establishment of new families, the development of motherly and fatherly subjectivities, and the process of children 'growing up', calls into focus different sociological 'frames of reference' (Buckingham 2011), or areas of research and debate. Prime candidates for inclusion are: children and childhood studies; the bodies of scholarship on parenting, motherhood and fatherhood; and sociologies of consumption and markets. This is the first point of interest—that there now are these four terrains calling for attention, begging the question how these are utilized and brought together in analyses. Also, at least three of these territories—those of consumption, childhood and mothering/parent-hood—are relatively juvenile. In the remainder of this chapter, I offer a discussion of these four scholarly territories. My aim is not to provide comprehensive overviews of each, but to explore how 'their' research agendas have evolved over time, and in relation to the cultural opposition of the sacred and the profane. I have thus set these four territories out in relation to the profane and the sacred in Fig. 2.1. As the discussion develops, I pay attention to how these agendas have been brought together in analyses of consumption, consumer culture, and intimate life.

Figure 2.1 sketches the common cultural practice of locating matters of intimate life in the terrain of the sacred, with markets and consumption in the profane. The ways in which the debate and research agendas

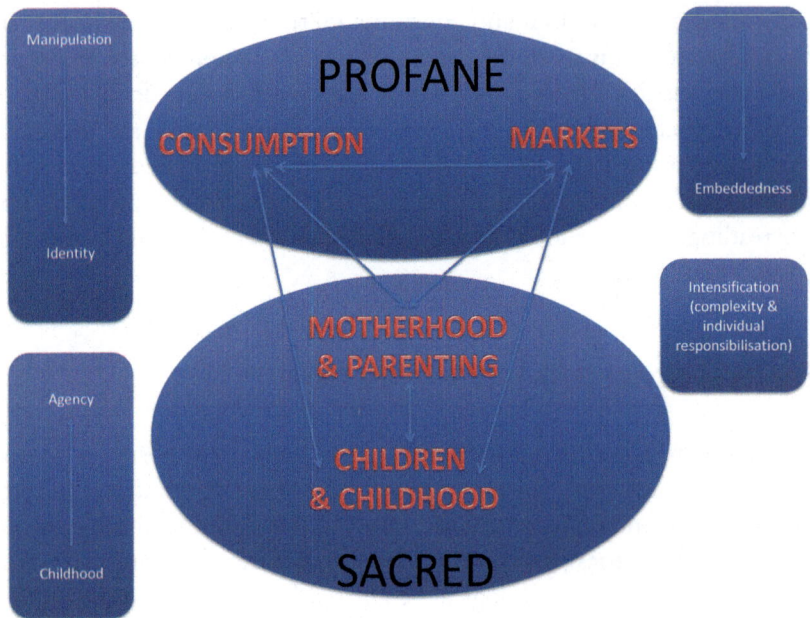

Fig. 2.1 Scholarly territories and their agendas in relation to the sacred and the profane

within these territories relate to this opposition varies. In relation to the territory of consumption, for instance, I argue that the conceptualisation of consumers as manipulated by markets attends to matters of the profane whilst rendering the sacred insignificant. Much recent sociology of consumption, however, has been concerned with intimate matters, such as consumer identity, and with the social relations of consumption practices (Warde 1994, 1997), shifting consumption towards a concern that is more closely related to the sacred. The argument presented in this book is that theories of practice offer a way of locating this scholarly project outside this opposition, making it possible to examine how this opposition is performed in everyday practices. I start with a brief discussion of the territories of consumption and the market, before moving on to discuss the agendas that constitute research on mothering & motherhood and children & childhood studies.

The enactment of 'the market' as profane has been a prominent historical narrative in critical analyses of economic life that focus on consumption and markets (e.g. Slater 1997). Guided by critical analyses of capitalism that examine the ways in which the exchange of goods and services is organised in this mode of production, consumers were sketched as manipulated in early interpretations of consumer culture (Featherstone 1991; Miller 1995a). The *production of consumption* approach is an example of *bad capitalism*, where the opposition between 'capitalism' and 'consumers' is maintained especially through the rigid categorisation of consumers as ignorant and consumption frivolous. This research tract foregrounded an interest in commercial sales practices and in processes of standardisation in cultural goods as a consequence of the dominance of profit motives (Adorno and Horkheimer 1997). The growth of the sociology of consumption, in the 1990s, alongside the growing interest in consumption across the humanities and social sciences (Miller 1995b), turned attention to the meanings of consumption practices and rituals, and resulted in a phase of cultural analysis that focussed on questions of consumer diversity and identity. This move may be seen as a shift in the location of concerns in this scholarly territory away from the profane, because these questions are more clearly about consumers and the cultural meanings that inform consumption (Miller 1987; Warde 1997). The recent turn to theories of practice in consumption sociology may be seen as moving away from the binary opposition of the sacred and the profane in more ways than one. The growing interest in the practical accomplishment of everyday life (Halkier 2010; Warde and Southerton 2012; Warde 2014) shifts the theoretical focus away from a primary concern with cultural theories and categories, and even locates consumption in a position relative to social practices. In the next chapter, I will argue that theories of practice provide useful tools for thinking across and beyond the entity-focused territories discussed here. However, I also argue that, given practices are socially known in the form of categories or entities, like other entities 'they' also have performative 'powers'.

In economic sociology, the question of the moral embeddedness of the market in wider social and cultural life has dominated debate for some time, witnessing a revival in what has been termed the 'new economic sociology' (Stehr et al. 2006; Sayer 1999, 2000, 2006). In early work in this programme of research, we see enactment of the bounded categories of 'economic,' 'social', 'cultural' and 'political', distinguishing spheres of life. This locates 'the market' in the cultural terrain of 'the profane', and, as pointed out by Zelizer (2012), little interest is shown in questions relating to the intimate. Yet, the growing interest in markets, culture and morality works to bring 'the sacred' into the frame, and in fact, battles with the categorical oppositions that have been so common in theories of markets. For instance, Fourcade and Healy (2007) emphasise the morally infused qualities of scholarship on markets, and in the final section of their review, they discuss examples of recent work where the focus shifts from thinking about the market as an entity with specific qualities, towards examination of the work or practices through which purified renditions of 'the market' come about. Bounded entities, such as the profane and the sacred, are not rejected as such, but the analysis is limited to how these become enacted in and through historical and culturally situated practices. The work of Kopytoff (1986) and Zelizer (1985) is illustrative for the presentation of carefully developed case studies that show how crucial cultural practices are in the constitution of the moral subjects and objects of economic life. In addition, the work of Michel Callon (1998) and colleagues is interesting for furthering analyses of how moral boundaries are managed through the work of framing. By asking questions about how market environments are assembled in and through practices that bring together a range of actants, including socio-technical assemblages (e.g. Knorr Cetina and Bruegger 2002), Fourcade and Healy (2007: 305) argue that these science and technology inspired approaches open 'the black box of morality' and dissect 'the cultural and technical work necessary to produce, to sustain, or—conversely—to constrain the market'.

The practice-based theories that inform recent scholarship on consumption and markets offer tools for maintaining analytical distance from the categories of culture, including the binary opposition of the profane and the sacred, whilst not ignoring the clear relevance of these cultural practices in everyday life. Such approaches acknowledge and favour cultural complexity, and examine how specific cultural and material fixities are outcomes of practices, in which multiple actants and their relations are implicated. At the same time, they demonstrate a good measure of *self-consciousness* and reflexivity, for instance, by recognising, conveying and exploring the performativity of scholarly constructs and knowledge. Developing the early accounts of Callon (1998), this is especially clear in recent science and technology analysis of financial markets (e.g. Kjellberg and Helgesson 2007).

One of the peculiarities that confronted this study is that the youngest of children are relatively invisible in debate on children, childhood and consumer culture (Martens et al. 2004; Martens 2005; though see Freeman 2009, 2012; Korsvold 2013; Saltmarsh 2009; Sjöberg 2013). At the same time, recent years have seen substantial research activity on mothering, motherhood and consumer culture (e.g. Cook 2013; Kehily and Martens 2014; Maclaran et al. 2011; O'Donohoe et al. 2013). Young children appear to have become less visible (e.g. Brownlie and Leith 2011; McNamee and Seymour 2013) as, respectively, 'the mother'/'parent' and 'the agentive child' are foregrounded in these territories. From the perspective of territorialisation, this warrants some attention, and I therefore continue with a more elaborate discussion of the scholarly territories and research agendas that have evolved around motherhood and parenting, and children and childhood, and how this is drawn upon in reflections on children and consumer culture.

Growing the Territory of Mothering/ Motherhood Studies

Mothering, motherhood and parenting are relatively new kids on the block in social and cultural studies. This begs the question how territorialisation around these entities has occurred, what research problems have been pursued, and whether and how these developments perform the binary opposition of the sacred and the profane? Of particular interest is the shift over time in focal categories. From the 1960s to the present, there was a shift first from 'the housewife' to 'woman', followed by a shift from 'woman' to 'mother'.[2] These shifts need to be acknowl-edged as related to a set of concurrent and interrelated developments, including the impact of feminism on academic debate, the changing social and cultural valuation of children discussed in the introduction, and broader cultural processes known as individualisation and respon-sibilisation, and that in turn are often collapsed under the banner of neo-liberalisation.

The shift from 'the housewife' to 'woman', and subsequently to 'mother', may be traced in academic debate through evolving research agendas, inspired by feminist critiques of gender differences, power and inequalities. Oakley's research on the housewife and housework in the late 1960s was symptomatic of a new second wave feminist aware-ness that rallied against the housewife and domesticity, whilst simul-taneously introducing sociology to the importance of unpaid work in family life and how this was organised (Oakley 1974, 1990). Feminism thus stimulated the shift from 'the housewife' to 'woman', with the lat-ter soon replacing the former as the most commonly used category in feminist-inspired scholarship. Second wave feminism was also intrigued by mothering and motherhood, not least because of the question of intergenerational (dis)continuity, which linked to the political quest for change in women's lives, giving rise to various theoretical iterations, including psychoanalytical interests in the mother-daughter relationship (e.g. Chodorow 1978; Umansky 1996) and the emotional qualities of mothering (Adams 1983; Lawler 2000). This scholarship had a clear political focus, as it reflected, for instance, on the relationship between the public and the private, where the public sphere was understood as an interconnecting complex of state, scientists and experts. Witness the evolving debates on the scientisation of motherhood (Apple 1987, 2006), on the growing presence and influence of an expert culture (Ehrenreich and English 1979; Furedi 2001; Hardyment 1995; Lawler 2000); and on diversities amongst mothers and in mothering (Gillies 2006). Whilst Kawash (2011) speaks of a silence in feminist studies on

---

[2]It may be argued that there has been a concomitant addition of 'mothering' and 'parenting' to social scientific research that previously focused mostly only on families.

motherhood in the first decade of the twenty first Century, in the UK, interesting work continued to be produced, including the transition into motherhood (Miller 2005) and the making of contemporary mothers (Thomson et al. 2011).

Motherhood and *Bad Capitalism*

One of the noteworthy curiosities when reviewing feminist work on mothering and motherhood is the relative absence of consumption, consumer culture and markets (Martens 2009; Taylor et al. 2004). The public sphere was in the first instance understood as composed by the state and the medical-science complex (e.g. Murphy 2003), and this has continued in contemporary debate on 'patenting cultures' (e.g. Lee et al. 2014). Capitalism, however, was subjected to scrutiny, and an excellent example here is the emerging debate, during the 1990s, on the intensification of motherhood. Led by American feminist sociologists Sharon Hays (1996) and Arlie Hochschild (Hochschild with Machung 1989), this focused first on women's paid and unpaid work. In later work, encapsulated especially in a series of evocative pieces that examine 'the commodity frontier' and the phenomenon of 'renting-a-mom' (Hochschild 2003, 2005), the focus shifted to a version of *bad capitalism*, in which 'the market' and 'the intimate sphere' are performed as strongly bounded and oppositional. One of the motivations for this debate was an interest in the question how the values that second wave feminism had furthered were playing into the hands of capitalism, creating opportunities for new markets and causing, so Hochschild (2003, 2005) argues, 'cooling' in intimate life. Taylor (2004: 3) sums this oppositional mode of argumentation in relation to the entities of motherhood and the market up as follows:

> Motherhood is supposed to be a special kind of human relationship, uniquely important because uniquely free of the kind of calculating instrumentality associated with the consumption of objects. It stands for "love", in sharp contrast to "money" ... Thus construed, motherhood offers a powerful model of human relationships that stand in opposition

to the logic of the marketplace and has provided a vitally important grounding for social critiques, both conservative and feminist.

Hays and Hochschild appear to offer alternative explanations of relations between 'the market', motherhood, the profane and the sacred. In both accounts, mothers are located in between 'the market' and 'the intimate sphere', in a position of moral responsibility and guardianship (see also Cook 2004: 11). Yet, whilst Hays (1996) and Hochschild with Machung (1989) examine the challenges mothers face in performing dual roles as working mothers, in Hochschild's later work (2003, 2005), there is the worry that mothers and intimate care are disappearing altogether as, through the commercialisation of intimate life, capitalism closes the gap between the sacred and the profane. Consequently, in Fig. 2.1, I have placed mothering and parenting in the space of the sacred, but located in between children/childhood and markets/consumption. It is work of this kind that heralds the shifting focus from work to consumption—though consumption is without doubt sketched as work—and that favours a broader understanding of 'the public sphere' in reflections on mothering and parenting. The arguments presented by Hays and Hochschild may be seen as forms of *bad capitalism*, in that common cultural understandings of 'the market' and 'the intimate sphere' are mobilised into a critique of capitalism.

Motherhood, Consumption, and Intimate Life

While Janelle Taylor, in the introduction to *Consuming Motherhood* (2004), points to the historical opposition between the values of markets and motherhood, Alison Clarke and others have been interested in exploring evidence of a growing appreciation amongst mothers of the affordances offered by the market for the conduct of intimate life (Clarke 2007; Miller 1998; Warde 1997). It is suggested that this opposition may be waning. Following the lead of consumption sociology, scholars have gone on to examine the ways in which mothering cultures and identities are forged in and through consumption practices. An example is Clarke's (2007) discussion of mothers' organisation of their children's birthday parties, which argues that mothers create normalised and localised mothering cultures through the adoption and acceptance of parties that are orientated around consumption. The relations between mothers, commodities and sales cultures also offer insights into variations and similarities of experiences of intimacy across the life course. Layne (2000), for instance, comments on the consumption rituals engaged in by mothers of stillborn babies, through which loss, memory and mothering identity are entangled, whilst others focus on the transition into parenthood and the challenges this entails (e.g. AbiGhannam and Atkinson 2016; Afflerback et al. 2014; Barnes 2015; Boyer and Spinney 2016; Burningham et al. 2014; Clarke 2004; Fuentes and Brembeck 2017; Kehily 2014; Martens 2009; Ponsford 2014; Theodorou and Spyrou 2013; Thomas 2015). Studies of older children indicate how mothers and children actively negotiate around fashion (Boden et al. 2004; Appleford 2014), whilst Hogg and colleagues (2004) comment on the experiences of mothers in 'empty nest' families. These accounts share an acknowledgement of the emotional import of personal lives (May 2011; Smart 2007).

Even so, the recently growing scholarship on mothers, consumption and consumer culture is also characterised by a reverberation of the contradictions that markets, sales narratives, and commodities bring to personal lives. Consumption practices are, for instance, seen as illustrative of how mothering is diverse in terms of its experiences, and especially, in terms of the contradictory ways in which mothers are positioned in relation to the market. Work by Pugh (2004, 2009) and others deliver important insights into how differential access to monetary resources organises the ways in which mothers can participate in consumer culture (e.g. Banister et al. 2015; Casey 2007; DeVault 1991; Ponsford 2014). These studies build upon commentaries on working class mothering (Gillies 2006), but in ways whereby consumption is foregrounded (Martens and Casey 2007). Yet, by moving the debate on the intensification of motherhood from the 1990s into the contemporary context, through a focus on consumption, market culture and neo-liberalisation, many recent studies also appear to sketch mothering as a 'uniform' predicament. In a neo-liberal environment, consumption comes to stand for the adoption of individual responsibility by mothers, who guide their caring work through the acquisition of information and the wielding of choice (Cairns et al. 2013). This literature investigates a set of interesting and related themes, amongst which is the question of responsibilisation. This has an established track record in motherhood studies, where growing 'good mothers' came to be seen as dependent on the circulation of pedagogical resources delivered through a medical-science expert culture (e.g. Apple 1995, 2006; Arnup 1994; Ehrenreigh and English 1979; Hardyment 1995; Lawler 2000). Whether and how 'the market' has made inroads into the delivery of parental pedagogy, and the consequences of this, remain important and outstanding questions (Martens 2009; Thomson et al. 2011, and see Chapter 7). Consumer culture certainly demonstrates the knack of identifying and multiplying 'problems' for those guarding intimate life. It does, of course, offer a plethora of products and services by way of solution to these problems, but with an absence of any kind of clear consensus (Thomson et al. 2011: 133; Warde 1997). Not surprising, then, is the common observation that consumer culture intensifies mothering because it points to a myriad of risks, dangers and concerns that need to be attended to (Coutant et al. 2011; Afflerback et al. 2013). Noteworthy here is the clustering of commentaries on problem areas, including environment and pollution (AbiGhannam and Atkinson 2016; Burningham et al. 2014; James 1993), child safety hazards and monitoring (Nelson 2008, 2010), child development in the early years (Vincent and Ball 2007; Vincent and Maxwell 2016), and infant feeding (Boyer 2010; Boyer and Boswell-Penc 2010; Keenan and Stapleton 2013; Lee 2008).

Arguably, these themes gain in salience in relation to the transition into motherhood and parenting, which forms an important subtheme in the field (Kehily 2014; Martens 2010; Miller 2010, 2005; Thomson et al. 2011). In the current age, it is argued, new motherhood identity is understood and formulated increasingly in relation to consumption practices (Thomson et al. 2011) and indications are that the corresponding market for pregnancy and early childhood/parenthood is a growth area. Mary Jane Kehily (2014) argues that shopping and the acquisition of knowledge and familiarity with child-care lore, products and services, is part of the process of becoming a parent. Brusdal and Frønes (2013) offer an explanation for how the shift to smaller families, changing demographics in terms of parental age, and relative wealth at the birth of the first child, has stimulated a growing climate of consumerism in Norway. Finally, the growing 'technological quality' of early parenthood is inspiring critical reflection and moral reprobation, whether it concerns ultrasound technologies and their commoditisation (Taylor 2004, 2008; Thomas 2015), the breast pump (Boyer and Boswell-Penc 2010), baby monitoring technologies (Nelson 2008), or immunisation (Brownlie and Leith 2011), whilst innovations in reproductive technologies have also generated some science and technology inspired work (e.g. Thompson 2005).

In this section, I have explored how scholarship has territorialised around the entities of mothering, motherhood and parenting in recent times, and how the research questions that have defined this scholarship have shifted from primarily feminist ones—for instance, in relation to the mother-daughter relationship—to a politics of concern about the predicaments of mothering/parenting, in which consumption and consumer culture have become increasingly common reference points. This body of work conveys a strong sense of the moral and social complexities and (in)justices of mothering and parenting in contemporary affluent societies, and as such, it is very much a project that is inward looking, and thus fails to address questions that cut across the territories discussed here. There is little sense of this work engaging with the culture of the profane and the sacred in a way other than to confirm the incompatible quality of this binary opposition—responsibilisation argumentation confirms the idea that mothers or child carers form the moral core in between the profane space occupied by 'the market' and the sacred space of familial intimacy (Cook 2004). In addition, there is a continuing line of argumentation in which economic and market practices are altogether absent and where the public sphere continues to be conceptualised as a space populated only by the state and the medical/science complex.

Growing the Territory of Children and Childhood Studies

The new social studies of children and childhood (NSSC) may be acknowledged as a response to, and enactment of, the growing emotional and cultural importance of 'the child' in contemporary affluent societies. From its inception in the 1990s, the NSSC has built a research agenda around a primary concern: to give voice and agency to children (e.g. James and Prout 2015; Kraftl 2013). The assertion of children's consequence may be recognised as a political project (e.g. Moran-Ellis 2010; Prout 2011) that attempts to shift 'the child' away from the realm of the sacred, where cultural practices that at least to some extent reflect the growing emotional consequence of 'the child' in everyday culture, continue to render children innocent and ignorant (e.g. Taylor 2013). I have reflected this in the location of children and childhood in relation to the profane and the sacred in Fig. 2.1, with child agency arguments pushing away from the sacred.

Suzanne Shanahan (2007: 413) has argued that children and childhood studies has been marked by ambiguity because of 'unclear definition and operationalisation of childhood itself'. The sociological ambivalence towards childhood, she continues, derives 'from the tendency in the literature to blur the analytical distinction between research on children and childhood' (2007: 408). In discussing the operationalisation of childhood, Shanahan implicitly acknowledges that childhood has different analytical properties, though these are not spelled out. Even so, her argument is important as it pays witness to the fact that children and childhood scholars are finding it hard to keep a handle on the distinct qualities of childhood in their work. These were discussed in early discussions in the NSSC (e.g. Alanen 2001; James et al. 1998; Qvortrup 1993; Scott et al. 1998), and fusing these arguments, at least three analytical understandings of childhood may be identified. First, as the commonly held understanding of childhood suggests, childhood is operationalised in lay terms as a personal and autobiographical experience, as when children and adults talk or think about their own childhood (Alanen 2001: 12; Scott et al. 1998). Second, the concept of childhood works as a category to demarcate a specific trajectory of the human life-course, and as such is contrasted with other age-related cultural categories, such as youth, adulthood, and old age. The third distinct analytical property of childhood recognises 'its' structural qualities. Thus, Qvortrup (1993) has favoured an understanding of childhood as a structural phenomenon, whilst James and James (2001) have conceptualised childhood as a social space. Alanen, in turn, argues that childhood is a discursive formation 'through which ideas, images and 'knowledges' of children and childhood are conveyed in society' (2001: 12–13), requiring analyses that are distinct from 'research with children', and that take on the task of deconstructing discursive formations such as 'cultural ideas, images, models and practices of children and childhood' (2001: 13).

Having (re)introduced these three distinctive analytical properties of childhood, it becomes clear that the ambiguity Shanahan highlights is a result, at least in part, of the fact that this multiplicity is hidden behind the singular façade of the first property: that of childhood as a personal and autobiographical experience. It is this slipperiness that makes childhood such a challenging concept for scholars. On the one hand, it impedes analyses of these distinct analytical qualities. On the other, the conceptual knottiness of childhood makes it hard to examine the relations between these different analytical qualities. Thus, research that prioritises children's agency is a scholarship that has primarily investigated children's personal and biographical experiences. As explained by Shanahan (2007), this is quite a different endeavour to research that focuses on childhood, leading to different 'scholarly camps' in the NSSC: those that focus alternately on children and on childhood. This paves the way for a consideration of two challenges: first, how the slippery quality of the discourse of childhood works to absent *its* generational practices and the young child, and second, the problem of social constructionism.

Absenting Young Children and the Generational Practices of Childhood

In the search for the agentive child and the concern with locating children and childhood in the realm of social studies, the NSSC has been questioned for creating absences. Recent discussions question the absenting of young children and adults (Brownlie and Leith 2011; Johansson 2012; McNamee and Seymour 2013). Examining the content of three main journals in the field of children and childhood studies, McNamee and Seymour (2013) show how young children have a marginal presence in the emerging and evolving social science debate on children and childhood of the past 20 years. Brownlie and Leith suggest that young children challenge the primacy of child agency, and relate this to the cultural proximity of young children with their bodies:

> It is perhaps the very conflation of babies with their bodies – the framing of them as 'biobundles' (Gottlieb, 2000) – that has contributed to their relative absence from the sociology of childhood which, understandably, has been concerned to foreground children's agency and competence. (2011: 197)

By locating the agentive child in the foreground, gaps arise around questions that do not cohere with the priorities set out in the research territory. This includes the absenting of adults and generational relations and saliences. In children and childhood studies, Johansson concurs, adulthood flickers in and out of view, making 'catching sight of it' problematic (2012: 102). A series of recent papers has started to address these absences, by focussing on young children and their interrelations with carers, and by asking what such studies might have to offer social science knowledge of children and childhood (Brownlie and Leith 2011; Lupton 2013a, b; Rosen 2014; Taylor 2011).

The young child calls attention to the interrelatedness of the categories of child and adult, or childhood and adulthood. However, to argue, as Alanen (2001: 11) does, that 'childhood is an essentially generational phenomenon' carries a salience that is greater than the intergenerational relations of direct kin. Taylor (2011: 420) suggests that these broader generational saliences point to the co-occurrence of two features of the generational practice of childhood: the emotional condition of the status of adulthood in modern societies and unequal relations of power. It is the latter that is ultimately addressed in the specific concerns of the NSSC, giving rise to its pre-occupation with children's agency and voice (Kraftl 2013). Drawing on earlier work in childhood (Jenks 2005) and agreeing with Cross (2004a, b) and others, Honeyman (2005: 3) explicates this as follows:

> I seek to demonstrate the great but underestimated extent to which we impose "childhood" on those we define as children according to biased standards of adult nostalgia and desire. These standards and impositions reveal a slow backlash from the Age of Reason embedded in both romantic and modern notions of childhood: a need to escape the burden of rationalist epistemologies, their demands for hyperliterate knowledge, and the responsibilities of power.

These sentiments are rooted in oppositional conceptual work implicating and linking childhood and adulthood. There is some agreement that common cultural meanings of childhood are constructed in and through their opposition with adulthood (e.g. Honeyman 2005; Johansson 2012; Shanahan 2007):

> In the West, adults have generally insisted that childhood is innocent (or ignorant in the Puritan tradition), pre-sexual, irrational, and unschooled, … all these definitions can really tell us is that we construct childhood as such in order to protest that adulthood is experienced, sexual, rational, and schooled. (Honeyman 2005: 3)

This constitution of childhood in opposition to adulthood is another way in which the cultural practice that positions the sacred in opposition to the profane, is performed. As the generational practices that envelop children's cultures, and inform understandings of childhood, are important themes in my argument, I have reason to argue that these be pushed more into the foreground.

Childhood and Social Constructionism

The slipperiness of the practice of childhood and the ambiguity that Shanahan (2007) speaks of point to a further challenge: the uses to which the method of social constructionism can be, and has been, put. There is another conundrum in children and childhood studies, illustrated in Shanahan's review, in that analyses of childhood often return to a distinct set of primary cultural characteristics, whilst simultaneously being heralded as variable. By accentuating temporal and cross-cultural variations in childhood or amongst children, social constructionism is the method used to remonstrate against the cultural homogeneities of childhood. Thus, one apparently immutable, because historically continuous, understanding of what children in The West are like—the notion of childhood innocence—appears as a central thread in historical reflections (Aries 1962; Davis 2011; Higonnet 1998; Smith 2011) and contemporary debate (e.g. Meyer 2007; Taylor 2011).[3] This has simultaneously been countered by arguments based in social constructionism, used to further the idea that the meanings of childhood or 'what a child is' varies over time and space. As pointed out by Prout (2005) and Woolgar (2012), social constructionist arguments of this kind have a tendency to create oppositions in their own right.

One question that arises is how this conundrum slips into arguments on the relationship between markets and childhood. Cook (2004), for instance, acknowledges the structural-generational qualities of childhood by referencing Qvortrup and Zelizer. Thus, on the one hand, childhood is sketched as culturally highly generative:

> Childhood generates bodies as well as meanings which grow, interact, and transform to the point of creating new childhoods, new meanings, and quite often new markets, and in the process effectively ensuring the movement and transformation of exchange value beyond any one cohort or generation. (Cook 2004: 2)

---

[3]Childhood innocence is, for instance, discussed in relation to contemporary media coverage and the sexualisation of children's mediated consumer culture (e.g. Meyer 2007; Taylor 2010). Childhood innocence also sits at the bedrock of commentaries on childhood, markets and consumption (e.g. Zelizer 1985; Cross 2002, 2004a, b).

At the same time, children's lack of agency is highlighted for the possibility of making any sort of claims about children and what they are like:

> The uncertainty of children's agency renders defensible all sorts of claims and counterclaims about who children "are" and what children "want," allowing most anyone to frame the child in any number of ways … In their passing state of dependency, young children in particular offer no initial or enforceable resistance to definition by others. Individual children, as well as the category of childhood itself, thereby serve as ready vehicles for the expression of any number of identities, values, and histories. (Cook 2004: 15)

Apparently contrasting assertions like these create confusions. Yet both have been used to conceptualise the relationship between markets and childhood, with the latter opening the analysis up to *bad capitalism* as a consequence of positing 'the market' as all powerful in its generative capacity. The approach developed and adopted in this book is aimed at moving beyond this type of argumentation. It does so by attending to the cultural work that happens around childhood (in the third sense) at the intersections between markets, products and parents. It works with, rather than against, the idea that childhood is 'a thoroughly social phenomenon,' and thus an outcome, at any point in time and space, of social practices (Alanen 2001: 11), whilst also acknowledging that childhood is 'a perpetually emergent social structure whose qualities are always in part attributable to the agents who populate it' (Shanahan 2007: 423). Whilst not refuting the possibility of understandings of childhood shifting and changing over time, as the research on this project progressed, the analysis became focused on a set of recurring key understandings of the young child. Consequently, I have pursued the question how a limited set of generationally informed key understandings of childhood becomes sedimented in and through a varied range of performances in market environments, making it possible to attend not only to an analysis of the structuration of childhood, but also to a questioning of the implications of childhood as a structure.

Conclusion: Moving Beyond the Challenges

This chapter has addressed the problematic of why advancing analyses of children, childhood and consumer culture is challenging. I have concentrated on the question of scholarly performativity and evidence of forms of incompatibility work around the binary opposition of the sacred and profane. In doing so, I focussed substantially on the process of scholarly territorialisation. Scholarship that is relevant to studies on children, childhood and consumer culture appears to have progressively converged into a set of distinct research agendas around the primary entities of markets, consumption, mothering/parenting, and children and childhood. These different 'frames of reference,' which have been drawn upon in varied ways in research on children, childhood and consumer culture, were discussed in relation to the strong cultural binary opposition of the sacred and the profane to address the question in what way this binary opposition has been performed through territorialisation, and in these territories over time.

It may be argued that the development of these research pathways has distinct benefits. Amongst these is that voice is given to questions that are clearly of social importance. But territorialisation also comes with problems. One of these is the problem of investigative segregation, which is not dissimilar to the problem of absenting described by Nimmo (2011) as a practice that characterises texts. Several examples of absenting within and across these territories were discussed, not least of which was the problematic of absenting young children and the generational consequence of the discourse of childhood. My argument chimes with those of others. For instance, Viviana Zelizer concurs:

> … my two intellectual 'homes' – childhood studies and economic sociology – remain remarkably alien to each other. … Moreover, economic sociologists have focused their efforts on studies of production mostly by firms and corporations, oddly marginalizing the analysis of consumption. Meanwhile, noting 'the missing child in consumption theory', Dan Cook (2008) has shown how specialists in theories of

consumption outside the self-defined field of economic sociology have remained largely blind to children's involvement. (2012: 74–75)[4]

And in relation to the growing debate on mothering and motherhood, Steph Lawler (2000: 4) pointed out some years ago how children are essentially hidden in accounts, when there is a need to acknowledge and explore mutual interconnections:

> Analyses of … mothering and the mother-daughter relationship have proceeded on the assumption that childhood is a 'given'; that it does not need to be subject to intellectual scrutiny. 'Mother' as a social category is constituted in relation to the prior category 'child': what children are considered to need for development is used to define 'good mothering' …

It seems necessary to repeat observations like this in a context where scholarship appears to be blinkered by the territorial concerns that go with 'the patch', and where there seems to be a forgetfulness of prior conclusions. This, I believe, is one of the salient take-home messages of Shanahan's (2007) review, and explains why I have dwelt on her argument.

Territorialisation around entities further runs the risk of confirming the importance of cultural explanations that are directly related to the specific research agendas that are explored, to the exclusion of others. A consequence is the formulation of explanations that lack attention to complexity (Law 2004). A related problem occurs when these agendas are brought together for the purpose of developing 'quick and easy' critiques of capitalism. I called this *bad capitalism*, and it is characterised by the creation of black boxes of mutually incompatible entities. The entities that frequently recur in debate on children, childhood and consumer culture demonstrate other forms of performativity, too. The most important of these in this chapter is the discourse of childhood, which hides *its* performative practices behind a façade of the singular meaning of a child's personal biographical experience. This has posed problems in

---

[4]See also Martens et al. (2004) for an argument of the lack of mutual engagement between the sociologies of consumption and childhood.

children and childhood studies, and may also lead to unclear conceptualisation of the relations of childhood and markets. The capacity of the discourse of childhood to hide the generational practices that give rise to key cultural meanings is of particular interest for the analysis of this book.

In the next chapter, I outline the approach that was developed and adopted for this study on young children and consumer culture. I opted to work with theories of practice and more-than-human theoretical inspiration, in order to develop an analysis of practices of pecuniary value creation that engage with the practice of child caring through cultural work on understandings of 'the young child.' It will be argued that this theoretical approach will facilitate comprehension of the complex relations between the growing emotional importance of the child in Western culture, childhood and its generational practices, the experiences and practices of parenting, organised interactions in markets, as well as the strong moralities that have characterised debate on children, childhood and consumer culture.

Bibliography

AbiGhannam, N., and L. Atkinson. 2016. Good green mothers consuming their way through pregnancy: Roles of environmental identities and information seeking in coping with the transition. *Consumption, Markets and Culture* 19 (5): 1–24.

Adams, P. 1983. 'Mothering', *m/f* 8: 40–52.

Adorno, T., and M. Horkheimer. 1997. *The dialectic of the enlightenment*. London: Verso.

Afflerback, S., S.K. Carter, A.K. Anthony, and L. Grauerholz. 2013. Infant feeding consumerism in the age of intensive mothering and risk society. *Journal of Consumer Culture* 13 (3): 387–405.

Afflerback, S., A.K. Anthony, S.K. Carter, and L. Grauerholz. 2014. Consumption rituals in the transition to motherhood. *Gender Issues* 31 (1): 1–20.

Alanen, L. 2001. Introduction. In *Conceptualizing child-adult relations*, ed. L. Alanen and B. Mayall. London: RoutledgeFalmer.

Apple, R.D. 1987. *Mothers and medicine: A social history of infant feeding, 1890–1950*. Madison: University of Wisconsin Press.
Apple, R.D. 1995. Constructing mothers: Scientific motherhood in the nineteenth and twentieth centuries. *Social History of Medicine* 8 (2): 161–178.
Apple, R.D. 2006. *Perfect motherhood: Science and childrearing in America*. New Brunswick, NJ: Rutgers University Press.
Appleford, K. 2014. Like mother, like daughter: Lessons in fashion consumption, taste and class. *Families, Relationships and Societies* 3 (1): 153–157.
Arendell, T. 2000. Conceiving and investigating motherhood: The decade's scholarship. *Journal of marriage and family* 62 (4): 1192–1207.
Aries, P. 1962. *Centuries of childhood; a social history of family life*. Translated from the French by Robert Baldick. New York: Knopf.
Arnup, K. 1994. *Education for motherhood: Advice for mothers in twentieth-century Canada*. Toronto: Toronto University Press.
Banister, E.N., M.K. Hogg, K. Budds, and M. Dixon. 2015. Becoming respectable: Low-income young mothers, consumption and the pursuit of value. *Journal of Marketing Management* 32 (7–8): 652–672.
Barnes, M.W. 2015. Fetal sex determination and gendered prenatal consumption. *Journal of Consumer Culture* 15 (3): 371–390.
Boden, S., C. Pole, J. Pilcher, and T. Edwards. 2004. New consumers? The social and cultural significance of children's fashion consumption.
Boyer, K. 2010. Of care and commodities: Breast milk and the new politics of mobile biosubstances. *Progress in Human Geography* 34 (1): 5–20.
Boyer, K., and M. Boswell-Penc. 2010. Breast pumps: A feminist technology, or (yet) "more work for mother"? In *Feminist technology*, ed. L. Layne, S. Vostral, and K. Boyer. Urbana: University of Illinois Press.
Boyer, K., and J. Spinney. 2016. Motherhood, mobility and materiality: Material entanglements, journey-making and the process of 'becoming mother'. *Environment and Planning D: Society and Space* 34 (6): 1113–1131.
Brownlie, J., and V. Leith. 2011. Social bundles: Thinking through the infant body. *Childhood* 18 (2): 196–210.
Brusdal, R., and I. Frønes. 2013. The purchase of moral positions: An essay on the markets of concerned parenting. *International Journal of Consumer Studies* 37 (2): 159–164.
Buckingham, D. 2009. The impact of the commercial world on children's well-being. Independent Assessment for the Department of Children, Schools and Families and Culture, Media and Sport. Available at http://

webarchive.nationalarchives.gov.uk/20130401151715/www.education.gov. uk/publications/eOrderingDownload/00669-2009DOM-EN.pdf.

Buckingham, D. 2011. *The material child*. Cambridge: Polity.

Buckingham, D., and V. Tingstad (eds.). 2010. *Childhood and consumer culture*. London: Palgrave Macmillan.

Burningham, K., S. Venn, I. Christie, T. Jackson, and B. Gatersleben. 2014. New motherhood: A moment of change in everyday shopping practices? *Young Consumers* 15 (3): 211–226.

Cairns, K., J. Johnston, and N. MacKendrick. 2013. Feeding the 'organic child': Mothering through ethical consumption. *Journal of Consumer Culture* 13 (2): 97–118.

Callon, M. (ed.). 1998. *The laws of the markets*. Oxford: Blackwell Publishers.

Casey, E. 2007. Gambling and everyday life: Working class mothers and domestic spaces of consumption. In *Gender and consumption: Material culture and the commercialisation of everyday life*, ed. E. Casey and L. Martens, 123–140. Aldershot: Ashgate.

Chodorow, N.J. 1978. *The reproduction of mothering: Psychoanalysis and the sociology of gender*. London: University of California Press.

Chin, E. 2001. *Purchasing power: Black kids and American consumer culture*. Minneapolis: University of Minnesota Press.

Clarke, A. 2004. Maternity and materiality: Becoming a mother in consumer culture. In *Consuming motherhood*, ed. J.S. Taylor, L.L. Layne, and D.F. Wozniak, 55–71. Rutgers, NJ: Rutgers University Press.

Clarke, A. 2007. Making sameness: Motherhood, commerce and the culture of children's birthday parties. In *Gender and consumption: Material culture and the commercialisation of everyday life*, ed. E. Casey and L. Martens, 79–98. Aldershot: Ashgate.

Cook, D.T. 2004. *The commodification of childhood: The children's clothing industry and the rise of the child consumer*. Durham, NC: Duke University Press.

Cook, D.T. 2008. The missing child in consumption theory. *Journal of Consumer Culture* 8 (2): 219–243.

Cook, D.T. 2012. Pricing the priceless child—A wonderful problematic. In *Situating child consumption: Rethinking values and notions of children, childhood and consumption*, ed. A. Sparrman, B. Sandin, and J. Sjöberg, 53–60. Lund: Nordic Academic Press.

Cook, D.T. 2013. Introduction: specifying mothers / motherhoods. *Journal of Consumer Culture* 13 (2): 75–78.

Coutant, A., V.I. de la Ville, M. Gram, and N. Boireau. 2011. Motherhood, advertising, and anxiety: A cross-cultural perspective on danonino commercials. *Advertising & Society Review* 12 (2): 1–19.

Cross, G. 2002. Valves of desire: A historian's perspective on parents, children, and marketing. *Journal of Consumer Research* 29 (3): 441–447.

Cross, G. 2004a. Wondrous innocence print advertising and the origins of permissive child rearing in the US. *Journal of consumer culture* 4 (2): 183–201.

Cross, G. 2004b. *The cute and the cool: Wondrous innocence and modern American children's culture*. New York: Oxford University Press.

Davis, R.A. 2011. Brilliance of a fire: Innocence, experience and the theory of childhood. *Journal of Philosophy of Education* 45 (2): 379–397.

Derrida. 1976. *Of grammatology*, trans. G.C. Spivak. Baltimore, MD and London: Johns Hopkins University Press.

DeVault, M. 1991. *Feeding the family*. Chicago: Chicago University Press.

Ehrenreich, B., and D. English. 1979. *For her own good: 150 years of the experts' advice to women*. London: Pluto.

Featherstone, M. 1991. *Consumer culture and postmodernism*. London: SAGE.

Fourcade, M., and K. Healy. 2007. Moral views of market society. *Annual Review of Sociology* 33: 285–311.

Freeman, O. 2009. "The Coke side of life"—An exploration of pre-schoolers' constructions of product and selves through talk-in-interaction around Coca-Cola. *Young Consumers* 10 (4): 314–328.

Freeman, O. 2012. I do like them but I don't watch them. In *Situating child consumption: Rethinking values and notions of children, childhood and consumption*, ed. A. Sparrman, B. Sandin, and J. Sjöberg, 157–176. Lund: Nordic Academic Press.

Fuentes, M., and H. Brembeck. 2017. Best for baby? Framing weaning practice and motherhood in web-mediated marketing. *Consumption Markets & Culture* 20 (2): 153–175.

Furedi, F. 2001. *Paranoid parenting*. Chicago: Chicago Review Press.

Gillies, V. 2006. *Marginalised mothers: Exploring working class experiences of parenting*. London: Routledge.

Gottlieb, A. 2000. Where have all the babies gone? Toward an anthropology of infants (and their caretakers). *Anthropological Quarterly* 73 (3): 121–132.

Halkier, B. 2010. *Consumption challenged: Food in mediated everyday lives*. Farnham: Ashgate.

Haraway, D. 2004. Ecce homo, ain't (ar'n't) I a woman and inappropriate/d others: The human in a post-human landscape. In *The Haraway Reader*, 47–62. New York and London: Routledge.

Hardyment, C. 1995. *Perfect parents: Baby-care advice past and present.* Oxford, UK: Oxford University Press.

Hays, S. 1996. *The cultural contradictions of motherhood.* New Haven: Yale University Press.

Higonnet, A. 1998. *Pictures of innocence: The history and crisis of ideal childhood.* London: Thames & Hudson.

Hochschild, A., with A. Machung. 1989. *The second shift: Working families and the revolution at home.* New York: Penguin.

Hochschild, A.R. 2003. *The commercialization of intimate life: Notes from home and work.* Berkeley: University of California Press.

Hochschild, A.R. 2005. "Rent a mom" and other services: Markets, meanings and emotions. *International Journal of Work Organisation and Emotion* 1 (1): 74–86.

Hogg, M.K., C.F. Curasi, and P. Maclaran. 2004. The (re-)configuration of production and consumption in empty nest households/families. *Consumption, Markets & Culture* 7 (3): 239–259.

Honeyman, S. 2005. *Elusive childhood: Impossible representations in modern fiction.* Columbus: Ohio State University Press.

James, A. 1993. Eating green (s). In *Environmentalism: The view from anthropology*, ed. K. Milton, 205–218. London: Routledge.

James, A., and A.L. James. 2001. Childhood: Toward a theory of continuity and change. *The Annals of the American Academy of Political and Social Science* 575 (1): 25–37.

James, A., and A. Prout (eds.). 2015. *Constructing and reconstructing childhood: Contemporary issues in the sociological study of childhood.* London: Routledge.

Jenks, C. 2005. *Childhood.* London: Routledge.

Johansson, B. 2012. Doing adulthood in childhood research. *Childhood* 19 (1): 101–114.

Kawash, S. 2011. New directions in motherhood studies. *Signs* 36 (4): 969–1003.

Keenan, J., and H. Stapleton. 2013. 'It won't do her any harm' they said, 'or they wouldn't put it on the market'. In *Motherhoods, markets and consumption: The making of mothers in contemporary western cultures*, ed. S. O'Donohoe, M. Hogg, P. Maclaran, L. Martens, and L. Stevens, 71–87. London: Routledge.

Kehily, M.J. 2014. For the love of small things: Consumerism and the making of maternal identities. *Young Consumers* 15 (3): 227–238.

Kehily, M.J., and L. Martens. 2014. Introduction. "New parents and young children in consumer culture." Special issue, *Young Consumers* 15 (3).

Kjellberg, H., and C.F. Helgesson. 2007. On the nature of markets and their practices. *Marketing Theory* 7 (2): 137–162.

Knorr Cetina, K.K., and U. Bruegger. 2002. Traders' engagement with markets: A postsocial relationship. *Theory, Culture & Society* 19 (5–6): 161–185.

Kopytoff, I. 1986. The cultural biography of things: Commoditisation as process. In *The social life of things: Commodities in cultural perspective*, ed. A. Appadurai. Cambridge: Cambridge University Press.

Korsvold, T. 2013. *Scandinavian early childhood and consumer culture. E-book.* Bergen: Fagbokforlaget.

Kraftl, P. 2006. Building an idea: The material construction of an ideal childhood. *Transactions of the Institute of British Geographers* 31 (4): 488–504.

Kraftl, P. 2013. Beyond 'voice', beyond 'agency', beyond 'politics'? Hybrid childhoods and some critical reflections on children's emotional geographies. *Emotion, Space and Society* 9: 13–23.

James, A., C. Jenks, and A. Prout. 1998. *Theorising childhood.* Oxford: Polity Press.

Law, J. 2004. *After method. Mess in social science research.* London and New York: Routledge.

Lawler, S. 2000. *Mothering the self: Mothers, daughters, subjectivities.* London: Routledge.

Layne, L.L. 2000. 'He was a real baby with baby things': A material culture analysis of personhood, parenthood and pregnancy loss. *Journal of Material Culture* 5 (3): 321–345.

Lee, E. 2008. Living with risk in the age of "intensive motherhood": Maternal identity and infant feeding. *Health, Risk and Society* 10 (5): 467–477.

Lee, E., J. Bristow, C. Faircloth, and J. Macvarish. 2014. *Parenting culture studies.* London: Palgrave Macmillan.

Lindstrom, M., with P. Seybold. 2003. *Brandchild.* London: Kogan Page.

Lupton, D. 2013a. Infant embodiment and interembodiment: A review of sociocultural perspectives. *Childhood* 20 (1): 37–50.

Lupton, D. 2013b. Precious, pure, uncivilised, vulnerable: Infant embodiment in Australian popular media. *Children and Society* 28 (50): 341–351.

Maclaran, P., L. Martens, S. O'Donohoe, L. Stevens, and M. Hogg. 2011. (Re)Creating cultural models of motherhoods in contemporary advertising. Special issue, *Advertising and Society Review* 12 (2).

Martens, L. 2005. Learning to consume—Consuming to learn: Children at the interface between consumption and education. *British Journal of Sociology of Education* 26 (3): 343–357.

Martens, L. 2009. Creating the ethical parent-consumer subject: Commerce, moralities and pedagogies in early parenthood. In *Critical pedagogies of consumption: Living and learning in the shadow of the "shopocalypse"*, ed. J.A. Sandlin and P. McLaren. New York: Routledge.

Martens, L. 2010. The cute, the spectacle and the practical: Narratives of new parents and babies at the baby show. In *Childhood and consumer culture*, ed. D. Buckingham and V. Tingstad. London: Palgrave Macmillan.

Martens, L., and E. Casey. 2007. Afterword: Theorising gender, consumer culture and promises of betterment in late modernity. In *Gender and consumption: Material culture and the commercialisation of everyday life*, ed. E. Casey and L. Martens, 219–242. Aldershot: Ashgate.

Martens, L., D. Southerton, and S. Scott. 2004. Bringing children (and parents) into the sociology of consumption: Towards a theoretical and empirical agenda. *Journal of Consumer Culture* 4 (2): 155–182.

May, V. (ed.). 2011. *Sociology of personal life*. London: Palgrave Macmillan.

McNamee, S., and J. Seymour. 2013. Towards a sociology of 10–12 year olds? Emerging methodological issues in the 'new' social studies of childhood. *Childhood* 12 (2): 156–168.

Meyer, A. 2007. The moral rhetoric of childhood. *Childhood* 14 (1): 85–104.

Miller, D. 1987. *Material culture and mass consumption*. Oxford: Basil Blackwell.

Miller, D. 1995a. Introduction. In *Acknowledging consumption: A review of new studies*, ed. D. Miller. London: Routledge.

Miller, D. (ed.). 1995b. *Acknowledging consumption: A review of new studies*. London: Routledge.

Miller, D. 1998. *A theory of shopping*. Cambridge: Polity Press.

Miller, T. 2005. *Making sense of motherhood*. Cambridge: Cambridge University Press.

Miller, T. 2010. *Making sense of fatherhood: Gender, caring and work*. Cambridge: Cambridge University Press.

Moran-Ellis, J. 2010. Reflections on the sociology of childhood in the UK. *Current Sociology* 58 (2): 186–205.

Murphy, E. 2003. Expertise and forms of knowledge in the government of families. *The Sociological Review* 51 (4): 433–462.

Nelson, M.K. 2008. Watching children: Describing the use of baby monitors on Epinions.com. *Journal of Family Issues* 29 (4): 516–538.

Nelson, M.K. 2010. *Parenting out of control: Anxious parents in uncertain times*. New York: New York University Press.

Nimmo, R. 2011. Actor-network theory and methodology: Social research in a more-than-human world. *Methodological Innovations Online* 6 (3): 108–119.

Oakley, A. 1974. *The sociology of housework*. Bath: Robertson.

Oakley, A. 1990. *Housewife*. London: Penguin.

O'Donohoe, S., M. Hogg, P. Maclaran, L. Martens, and L. Stevens (eds.). 2013. *Motherhoods, markets and consumption: The making of mothers in contemporary Western cultures*. London: Routledge.

Palmer, S. 2006. *Toxic childhood: How the modern world is damaging our children and what we can do about it*. London: Orion.

Ponsford, R. 2014. "I don't really care about me, as long as he gets everything he needs"—Young women becoming mothers in consumer culture. *Young Consumers* 15 (3): 251–262.

Prout, A. 2005. *The future of childhood*. London: Routledge.

Prout, A. 2011. Taking a step away from modernity: Reconsidering the new sociology of childhood. *Global Studies of Childhood* 1 (1): 4–14.

Pugh, A.J. 2004. Windfall child rearing: Low-income care and consumption. *Journal of Consumer Culture* 4 (2): 229–249.

Pugh, A.J. 2009. *Longing and belonging: Parents, children, and consumer culture*. California: University of California Press.

Pyyhtinen, A. 2016. *More-than-human sociology*. London: Palgrave Macmillan.

Qvortrup, J. (ed.). 1993. *Childhood as a social phenomenon*. Vienna: European Centre.

Rosen, R. 2014. 'The scream': Meanings and excesses in early childhood settings. *Childhood* 22 (1): 39–52.

Saltmarsh, S. 2009. Becoming economic subjects: Agency, consumption and popular culture in early childhood. *Discourse: Studies in the Cultural Politics of Education* 30 (1): 47–59.

Sayer, A. 1999. Valuing culture and economy. In *Culture and economy after the cultural turn*, ed. L. Ray and A. Sayer, 53–75. London: Sage.

Sayer, A. 2000. Markets, embeddedness and trust: Problems of polysemy and idealism. Published by the Department of Sociology, Lancaster University, UK, at http://www.comp.lancs.ac.uk/sociology/papers/Sayer-Markets-Embeddednes-and-Trust.pdf.

Sayer, A. 2006. Approaching moral economy. In *The moralization of the markets*, ed. Nico Stehr, Christoph Henning, and Bernd Weiler. New Brunswick: Transaction.

Scott, S., S. Jackson, and K. Backett-Milburn. 1998. Swings and roundabouts: Risk anxiety and the everyday worlds of children. *Sociology* 32 (4): 689–705.

Shanahan, S. 2007. Lost and found: The sociological ambivalence toward childhood. *Annual Review of Sociology* 33: 407–428.

Sjöberg, J. 2013. *In the eye of the market: Children and visual consumption*, 247. Linköping: Linköping University Electronic Press.

Slater, D. 1997. *Consumer culture and modernity*. Cambridge: Polity Press.

Seiter, E. 1993. *Sold separately: Parents and children in consumer culture*. Bloomington: Indiana University Press.

Smart, C. 2007. *Personal life*. Cambridge: Polity.

Smith, K. 2011. Producing governable subjects: Images of childhood old and new. *Childhood* 19 (1): 24–37.

Stehr, Nico, Christoph Henning, and Bernd Weiler (eds.). 2006. *The moralization of the markets*. New Brunswick: Transaction.

Taylor, A. 2010. Troubling childhood innocence: Reframing the debate over the media sexualisation of children. *Australasian Journal of Early Childhood* 35 (1): 48–57.

Taylor, A. 2011. Reconceptualising the 'nature' of childhood. *Childhood* 18 (4): 420–433.

Taylor, A. 2013. *Reconfiguring the natures of childhood*. London: Routledge.

Taylor, J.S. 2004. Introduction. In *Consuming motherhood*, ed. J.S. Taylor, L. Layne, and D.F. Wozniak. New Brunswick: Rutgers University Press.

Taylor, J.S. 2008. *The public life of the fetal sonogram: Technology, consumption, and the politics of reproduction*. New Brunswick: Rutgers University Press.

Taylor, J.S., L. Layne, and D.F. Wozniak. 2004. *Consuming motherhood*. New Brunswick: Rutgers University Press.

Theodorou, E., and S. Spyrou. 2013. Motherhood in utero: Consuming away anxiety. *Journal of Consumer Culture* 13 (2): 79–96.

Thomas, G.M. 2015. Picture perfect: '4D' ultrasound and the commoditisation of the private prenatal clinic. *Journal of Consumer Culture* 17 (2): 359–377.

Thomas, S.G. 2007. *Buy, buy, baby: How consumer culture manipulates parents and harms young minds*. Boston: Houghton Mifflin Harcourt.

Thomson, R., M.J. Kehily, L. Hadfield, and S. Sharpe. 2011. *Making modern mothers*. Bristol: Policy Press.

Thompson, C. 2005. *Making parents: The ontological choreography of reproductive technologies*. Cambridge: MIT press.

Umansky, L. 1996. *Reconceiving motherhood: Feminism and the legacies of the 1960s*. New York: New York University Press.

Vincent, C., and S.J. Ball. 2007. 'Making up' the middle-class child: Families, activities and class dispositions. *Sociology* 41 (6): 1061–1077.

Vincent, C., and C. Maxwell. 2016. Parenting priorities and pressures: Furthering understanding of 'concerted cultivation'. *Discourse: Studies in the Cultural Politics of Education* 37 (2): 269–281.

Warde, A. 1994. Consumption, identity-formation and uncertainty. *Sociology* 28 (4): 877–898.

Warde, A. 1997. *Consumption, food and taste: Culinary antinomies and commodity culture*. London: Sage.

Warde, A. 2014. After taste: Culture, consumption and theories of practice. *Journal of Consumer Culture* 14 (3): 279–303.

Warde, A., and D. Southerton (eds.). 2012. *The habits of consumption*, vol. 12. Helsinki: Helsinki Collegium in the Humanities and Social Sciences.

Woolgar, S. 2012. Ontological child consumption. In *Situating child consumption: Rethinking values and notions of children, childhood and consumption*, ed. A. Sparrman, B. Sandin, and J. Sjöberg, 33–52. Lund: Nordic Academic Press.

Zelizer, V.A.R. 1985. *Pricing the priceless child: The changing social value of children*. New York: Basic Books.

Zelizer, V. 2012. A grown-up priceless child. In *Situating child consumption: Rethinking values and notions of children, childhood and consumption*, ed. A. Sparrman, B. Sandin, and J. Sjöberg, 71–80. Lund: Nordic Academic Press.

3

Child Caring and Market Interactions

Introduction

In the previous chapter, I argued that the development of critical analyses of children, childhood and consumer culture is confronted by challenges. For instance, it may be argued that the focus on *the child consumer* diverts attention away from the question of pecuniary value creation, and how this is realised in and through practices in which the value of children is also, at the same time, performed. In addition, as I argued in the introduction, little interest has been shown in the practices nurtured by commercial organisations to grow pecuniary value in relation to young children. My starting point in this chapter is agreement with Sparrman and Sandlin (2012: 15) that, in order to understand value(s):

> ... one needs to abandon the idea of applying theories of value to people, and instead *turn to practices to see how value is being made*. (Italics my emphasis)

© The Author(s) 2018
L. Martens, *Childhood and Markets*, Studies in Childhood and Youth,
https://doi.org/10.1057/978-1-137-31503-8_3

But when it comes to young children, new parents and consumer culture, what practices need to be considered and what theoretical underpinnings will support the analysis? As argued in the introduction, crucial in an analysis of young children and consumer culture is the practice of child caring. I add that it is in and through specific performances of this practice, in the organised interactions of markets, that the value of the young child and pecuniary value are co-realized. Another practice for consideration has therefore been the interactional practices that can be found in market settings.

In this chapter I explain the approach to practices that I have developed to organise my analysis. Theories of practice have become relatively common tools used in scholarship on mundane consumption practices in the routines of everyday life (Gronow and Warde 2001; Ilmonen 2001; Halkier 2001). Good summary articles exist, some of which herald the usefulness of theories of practice for understanding consumption (Gram-Hanssen 2011; Røpke 2009; Shove et al. 2008; Warde 2005), with others demonstrating applications of these tools in consumption research (Halkier et al. 2011; Magaudda 2011; Truninger 2011), and providing theoretical overviews and adaptations (Shove et al. 2012; Southerton 2013; Warde 2014). Warde (2014: 286) sums up the appeal of theories of practice for consumption scholars:

> Theories of practice seem appealing for the study of consumption because they promise to make a double correction to previous work; first, by providing an alternative framing to models of individual choice, whether based upon the sovereign or the expressive individual, and, second, by uncovering and exploring phenomena normally concealed in cultural analysis ... against the model of the sovereign consumer, practice theories emphasise routine over actions, flow and sequence over discrete acts, dispositions over decisions, and practical consciousness over deliberation.

I have drawn extensively on Theodor Schatzki's theory of practices (1996, 2002), especially his argument that practices are organised by a teleoaffective structure, principles and instructions, and understandings. Because of the questions that confronted me as I tried to understand the business of child caring, and the organisation of the interactional market contexts in which my research was conducted, the discussion that follows is informed by two concerns. First, in the previous chapter, I recognised and questioned the performative qualities of textual practices, including the reproduction of binary oppositions that undergird incompatibility work, and the discourse of childhood, which, amongst other things, hides 'its' quality as a generational practice. Likewise, I argue here that the practice of child caring has performative qualities, in the sense that the normativities and understandings that 'it' brings together make 'us' think about the practice in specific ways. The challenge that confronts the scholar is then similar to that discussed previously: how to think about practices analytically 'outside' the common understandings of the practice (see e.g. Martens 2012; Martens and Scott 2017). This has implications for *who* and *what* is typically thought about when considering the question how a practice is carried. I therefore start this discussion with the question of how child caring is carried. Next, I attend to the teleoaffective qualities of child caring, and see these qualities as 'structured' in and through knowledge practices that understand the young child in ways that give the practice of child caring its *reason d'etre*. As child caring can be carried by different entities and in different contexts, the structuration of the practice's organisational elements therefore needs to be acknowledged as a politically infused process (Halkier 2010). For this reason, I continue to draw on insights from science and technology studies, and other post-structuralist theories, to guide the analysis with a *horizontal* methodology that does not prioritise some actants (e.g. prospective parents and their narrative performances) over others (e.g. the combined textual materials that exist for a branded product). I close the chapter with a discussion of the empirical research on which the arguments presented in the book draw.

Carrying the Practice of Child Caring

To develop my analysis of how pecuniary value and the value of young children are co-realized in the business of child caring, I have drawn on Schatzki's philosophical analysis of practices as social entities, and on the sociology of consumption that works with this ontology. My work may be seen as part of the third generation of practice theory scholarship (Postil 2010), where the promotion of a practice theoretical approach 'is directed to … considering how various themes arising from the heterogeneous sources of … theoretical development might be employed to address problems of description, interpretation and explanation of social processes and behaviour in a particular domain' (Warde 2014: 285). I accept, following Schatzki (1996, 2002) and others (Schatzki et al. 2001; Shove et al. 2012; Warde 2005), that practices are the primary entities that make up the social, and that the starting point of analysis is therefore practices, not human subjects.

Child caring may be described as an integrated practice that harbours a range of projects, from feeding through to reading bedtime stories, and shopping. I use the practice concept of *child caring* in preference to *child rearing*, which is more commonly used in American idiom (see e.g. Hays 1996; Pugh 2009), and which speaks of growing and developing the child. Child *caring* points more explicitly to the relational qualities of caring that undergird this practice, and that positions children as 'cared for', with 'others' doing the work of caring. Like childhood, the concept of child caring speaks of the generational saliences of the relations that constitute 'caring', though as signalled earlier, my argument is that these are saliences that move beyond those intimate relations of child and parent. When considering practices, an important question to consider is how the projects that make up the practice cohere is ways that make these recognisable as 'belonging' to the same practice. In Chapter 4, I illustrate how these projects, or practice pathways, share the same teleoaffective priorities.

Theories of practice are clear that in order for a practice to exist, 'it' has to be practiced, performed, or 'carried out' (Schatzki 1996; Warde 2005; Shove et al. 2007), but who or what can carry practices? There is a tendency in applications of practice theory in consumption sociology to understand practice carriers as persons, and usually those persons to which the common-sense understanding of the practice points. In relation to child caring, the common sense understanding is that parents carry this out, with other human carers, like the child care nursery nurse or the grandparent, coming second place. As witnessed in decades of scholarship on family life and motherhood, these persons are also those that are socially held responsible for child caring. But the imagination does not stretch much beyond this. In his recent review of scholarship on consumption and theories of practices, Warde (2014) picks up on this, implying that there is a need to move beyond 'individual behaviour':

> Currently, practice-theoretic accounts most often analyse individual behaviour, albeit as performances rather than voluntary, deliberative personal choices. Yet, they pay little attention to the creation of norms, standards and institutions, which produce shared understandings and common procedures. Sometimes, machines and artefacts dictate common procedures. (Warde 2014: 295)

The argument I further here is that carrying the practice of child caring can be done by different kinds of entities, be these individuals, institutions, or artifacts, like the baby feeding bottle or the car seat. This suggests that commercial organisations can be carriers of the practice of child caring also. Acknowledging commercial organisations as carriers of child caring is a way of opening the black box of 'commerce' or 'the market', providing access to the relational qualities that are evident and examining closely what has been conceptualised as the process of 'de-commodification' (Kopytoff 1986; Sayer 2003). From the perspective of an everyday culture in which 'the market' is located in the realm of the profane, and in opposition to that of the sacred, this idea is certainly highly controversial. Of course, to argue that commercial organisations enact child caring is not to deny that 'making a profit' is the primary priority in their performances. However, my argument is that their profit-making ventures in relation to this area of practice could not exist without the simultaneous enactment of child caring. In thinking through the benefits and challenges of theories of practice, it has been argued that everyday performances are more often than not forms of multi-practice-ing (Shove et al. 2012; Southerton 2013; Warde 2014), and in this project, commercial organisations are always and at the same time enacting at least two practices: those of selling and child caring.

Multi-practice-ing raises important questions about how, in performance, the potentially contradictory priorities and standards of these different practices are negotiated. In relation to child caring, the cultural problematic of the sacred and the profane can be seen to be such a contradiction (Cook 2004). Given child caring is itself a composite set of projects, it is also possible, as pointed out by Halkier (2011, 2013), that there are 'internally' contradictory priorities, raising similar questions (see also Warde 1997). Moreover, as practices are performed by different kinds of carriers, it is very possible that different carriers 'perform' different priorities, thus also giving rise to variation and contestation.

In relation to new parents, child caring is characterised by peculiarities that are worth exploring in some detail. One of these is that new parents enter the practice of child caring all the time; another is that the priorities of this practice change substantially, and at a quick pace, over a short period of time. As product websites and early parenting magazines are keen to remind readers, within the time period of, say three years, most new parents will go through the distinct experiences of pregnancy, birth, care for a small baby, a crawling infant and then an active toddler. Each of these phases is of relatively short duration, and contemporary child bearing patterns mean that this process is not oft repeated more than two times, though research suggests that becoming a grandparent can again mean a period of carrying this practice (Edwards and Mumford 2005).[1] In the previous chapter, I discussed how motherhood sociologists have been particularly interested in what is called the transition into parenthood, analysing this process of becoming as a transformation of the self (e.g. Burningham et al. 2014; Miller 2005; Taylor et al. 2004; Thomson et al. 2011). From a practice theory perspective, the transition into parenthood is the problematic of becoming a carrier of the practice of child caring. When pregnant, new parents do not yet engage in many of the embodied childcare practices about which they hear when they prepare themselves during pregnancy and which kick in

---

[1] The UK Office for National Statistics that that in 2014, 38% of live births were first births, 36% were second births and 16% were third births. https://www.ons.gov.uk/peoplepopulationand-community/birthsdeathsandmarriages/livebirths/bulletins/birthsbyparentscharacteristicsinenglandandwales/2014, accessed on 18 March 2017.

as a day-to-day reality only when a baby is 'in situ'. This brings an interesting twist to an analysis that is located in practices, for even though pregnancy assumes its own set of good parenting practices, amongst which is a prerogative to find out about the kind of things that will need to be done once a baby is born, the prospective and new parents I spoke with during my fieldwork were shopping for tools and services to be used in practical performances with which, at the time of purchase, they had little to no hands-on experience.

Schatzki (1996, 2002) acknowledges that there are different ways of knowing a practice, and he makes a distinction between agents that carry a practice by conveying only conceptual understanding, as opposed to those that also convey practical understanding. The example he draws on (1996: 92–93) is that of playing a musical instrument and he argues that some people may convey a 'nonparticipatory propositional understanding' of how an instrument ought to be played, without actually being able to play it. Understanding of how to play the flute, he argues, conveys a rounded understanding, but for my purpose what is of interest is that nonparticipatory propositional understanding may be used to carry the practice. It is thus possible to enact the conceptual understanding that organises a practice-as-entity, without enacting the practical-embodied elements to which the practice's organisational elements point. Commercial organisations can carry the practice of child caring in this way. As I explain further below, this works in and through the embodied, technical and organisational qualities of sales practices, and does not typically involve the wiping of a baby's bottom in any physical sense of the word. Thus, even when commercial agents do not 'look after' real life babies, they can and do 'look after' the conceptual qualities of the practice-as-entity through which the practice is a shared understanding. Of course, some individual sellers or employees of commercial organisations share in the practical understanding of child caring as parents, and are thus also carriers of child caring as commonly understood.

When prospective and new parents enrol into the practice of child caring at this stage of the life course, this process is also guided by conceptual reconnaissance that may involve shopping, in terrestrial or online settings, and that may involve reading magazines and talking to a friend over coffee. The process of becoming a new parent, or, to put it more finely, the process of moving through the different 'stages' of the life course of early parenting, is also always in some way forward looking, concerned with planning and the need to gain familiarity with the care practices and the tools for the next stage of early child care (Miller 2005; Thomson et al. 2011).[2] Arguably, this 'need' arises from the practice-as-entity that child caring is, that is embedded in broader societal relations, and that, as discussed in Chapter 8, profit making organisations keenly try to exploit to organise this process of becoming. One of the take-home messages is that distinguishing between 'practice-as-entity' and 'practice-as-performance' (Shove et al. 2012) can produce confusion, as the elements of a 'practice-as-entity' that organise the practice need to be performed, but this does not necessarily have to be done in and through the type of practical performance to which the practice-as-entity points.

Amongst commercial organisations, and the products they produce, there are also continually new entrants and those that exit, for instance, when companies go out of business, when they withdraw a brand-product from the market, or when there is a shift into new sales areas. During this research, for instance, the well-known UK baby feeding tool brand Avent merged with the global domestic technologies giant Phillips, followed by the development and integration of new feeding technologies such as breast pumps and sterilising equipment into a product portfolio. At the same time, commercial practices give rise to long-lasting and durable entities, like successful brand-products that have turned into household names. Of course, the durability of brand-products is itself an active historical accomplishment in which the underlying product, as well as the meanings behind the brand, may change over time, but where the brand name, and possibly its icon, conveys a sense of temporal continuity (Arvidsson 2005). Finally, when

---

[2]This is not so different from the practice of inconspicuous consumption, discussed by Sullivan and Gershuny (2004), which theorises about the purchase of goods stimulated by dreaming or imagining participation in family/home based leisure pursuits for which there really is no time. Prospective parents plan and purchase products before these can be put into practice, some of which may, in the end, never get used.

thinking about commercial entities as carriers of the practice of child caring, it is important to recognise these carriers as often quite large organisations, composed of diverse practice domains (finance, design, production, sales), and in which the ways in which child caring is carried will no doubt vary. The research for this book was limited to practices of selling products and services. For these reasons, commercial organisations are, on the whole and in comparison with parents, more seasoned carriers of the practice of child caring. At the same time, they tend to be specialists, operating in specialised niche areas of, for instance, health, food or mobility, that represent projects or pathways in the practice of child caring (see Chapter 4). Looking across the field of child-caring, different commercial practitioners will develop kinds of specialist knowledge of 'the child' and 'how it needs to be cared for' that relate to their area of practice. Together, these segments of knowledge slot into the understanding of child caring, to which those working in sectors other than the economy also contribute.

Teleoaffective Structuration and the Politics of Practice

Schatzki's ontology offers useful tools for analysing what makes a practice a social entity. He argues that a practice is a nexus of actions, of sayings and doings, which are organised or linked in specific ways:

> Three major avenues of linkages are involved: (1) through understandings, for example, of what to say and do; (2) through explicit rules, principles, precepts, and instructions; and (3) through what I will call "teleoaffective" structures embracing ends, projects, tasks, purposes, beliefs, emotions, and moods. (1996: 89)

Alternative concepts have been put forward in consumption research for summing up what makes practices social, and Gram-Hanssen (2011: 65) provides a schematic overview. I have stayed close to Schatzki's formulation, as the linkages he suggests, especially the teleoaffective structure and the principles and instructions, are particularly useful for an understanding of the emotional and moral priorities of child caring. Schatzki argues that the teleoaffective structure:

> is a range of normative and hierarchically ordered ends, projects, and tasks, to varying degrees allied with normativized emotions and even moods. By normativity, I mean, first, oughtness and, beyond this, acceptability. The indefinite range of end – project – task combinations contained in the practice's teleoaffective structure and realised in participants doings and sayings are either ones the participants ought to realise or ones that it is acceptable for them to do so. A practice always exhibits a set of ends that participants should or may pursue, a range of projects that they should or may carry out for the sake of these ends, and the selection of tasks that they should or may perform for the sake of those projects. (Schatzki 2002: 80)

The ends, purposes and emotions of the practice of child caring are bound up with understandings of the young child. The fundamental underlying reason for caring for a child is that this child is important, and in addition, that it is an entity that is in need of being looked after. Moreover, if the end or purpose of child caring is the child and its wellbeing, than the projects or pathways (see Chapter 4) of child caring follow on from this, but demand further understanding of this child, in order to identify why and how it needs to be cared for. Arguably, the more there appears to be at stake and the more entrenched the underlying understandings, the more the normativities of the practice turn into strong moral concerns. The central location of the young child in the teleoaffective structure of child caring connects with the discussion in the introduction on the growing emotional importance of the child. This emotional importance informs the teleoaffective qualities of child caring. The question that will be addressed in subsequent chapters (5–7) is how the teleoaffective qualities of child caring are structured in the fields of practice that I examined.

Zelizer's (1985) argument suggests the possibility of change, over time, in how children are valued, and this calls attention to the causes of change. Change in practices has also been of substantial interest to consumption scholars (Halkier et al. 2011; Gram-Hanssen 2011; Shove et al. 2012; Warde 2014), though for different reasons. In this context, the idea that consumption is contested is interesting for 'bridging' practices as performed in domestic contexts with broader, often mediated and morally/politically motivated, interventions (Halkier 2010; Keller and Halkier 2014; Vihalemm et al. 2015). The practice-as-entity of child caring thus connects with the scholarship discussed in Chapter 2, and that point to the highly moral and political quality of practices that involve children. It does this, for instance, through the question how the teleoaffective qualities, and the principles and instructions of this practice, come about. Even though it appears as if the projects and emotional saliences of the practice are stable, theories of practice insist that practices as entities are always dynamically performed.

It is a likely proposition that child caring has undergone change as the cultural salience of children has moved from one of economic import to one of emotional consequence (Zelizer 1985). An economically active child gives the impression of less dependency, and thus as not so much in need of 'care'. The emotionally important child, on the other hand, has seen the expansion of caring work within and beyond the family; into education, social care, and a range of other medical-health care provisions (Apple 1995; Zelizer 1985). In fact, the period of cultural transformation initiated the specialisation and institutionalisation of knowledge practices of the child, into communities of practice such as social work (Ferguson 2008) developmental psychology (e.g. Jenks 2005; Lee 2005; Prout 2005), and education. The interconnections between the three practices of child caring, knowing the child, and sales practices, and their relative importance, may be traced over time. In the late nineteenth and into the twentieth Century, Rima Apple (1987, 2006) argues, motherhood underwent a process of scientisation, which may be seen as a shift in childcare lore that was embedded in local social networks, and characterised by the sharing of knowledge across generations and between peers, to the growing presence and dominance of medical/science/psychology forms of knowledge and expertise (Lawler 2000). As discussed in Chapter 2, the debate on the intensification of mothering engages with these social developments, but does not offer much clarity about the role of commerce in this process. Apple's work has been an important exception for demonstrating how medical/science/psychology knowledge making and commerce did always interact. The question I asked in the introduction: (whether and) how the growing emotional importance of children is related to the growing presence and prominence of a consumer culture in the twentieth century, may be translated into the problematic of how *influential* commercial practice carriers are in relation to other carriers of the practice of child caring. It is in relation to the performance of the normativities of this practice that the politics of practice become especially visible, and, as pointed out by Halkier (2010), it is here that researchers need to look for contrasting and contested narratives amongst practice carriers.

Researching Market-Based Interactions and Child Caring

Consumer and trade shows are commercial events that take place in exhibition centres, and that are temporally specific, typically lasting only a few days. Trade shows are events intended for commercial organisations and are typically marketed as international events. An example is the Harrogate International Nursery Fair,[3] which is a UK-based trade show. Consumer exhibitions invite consumers/visitors to comingle with commercial practitioners and their organisations. In the UK, such shows are either national events that take place in one of the major exhibition centres around the country, or regional affairs. The Baby Show and The Baby and Toddler Show are examples of national events; the East Midlands Baby and Toddler Show is an example of a regional event. Investigations into shopping and retailing have focused on inner city and out-of-town shopping centres and malls (Jackson et al. 2005), department stores (e.g. Falk and Campbell 1997; Nava 2000), supermarkets (Miller 1998; Humphery 1998), the corner shop (Everts and Jackson 2009; Everts 2010), local markets (Cook 2008; vom Lehn 2014), the car boot and other second hand sales environments (Gregson and Crewe 1997). Scholarly interest in exhibitions has been limited to

---

[3]http://www.nurseryfair.com/, accessed on 27 April 2017.

historical analysis, especially of the 'great' exhibitions of the industrialising era, which were celebrations of modernity and advancements in ideas and technologies for display (Williams 1991).

Between 2005 and 2014, I spent time visiting these events, and made repeated journeys to the national consumer exhibition The Baby Show, and its Scottish equivalent. Targeting the same life course phase as retailers specialising in pregnancy, the early years and new families, The Baby Show is organised by the events organisation company Clarion Events, which specialises in 'high value, difficult-to-engage markets'[4] through the creation of 'environments that stimulate consumers to interact with our clients'. The Baby Show moves around the big national exhibition centres in the UK on a yearly basis, stopping off in Birmingham, London, and Manchester for three-day periods that include the weekend. During the course of my research, the Scottish event first moved from Clarion Events to QD Events, and, under the name of The Baby and Toddler Show, is now organised by the Ocean Media Group. Altogether, I visited The Baby Show and the national Scottish shows on 15 occasions, spending a total of 45 days at these events. My bursts of fieldwork may best be described as focused or short-term ethnography (Knoblauch 2005; Pink and Morgan 2013), in the sense that:

> … the researcher does not spend a lengthy and continuous period of time in the field but visits the field for short periods at various intervals. During those short periods of data collection, the researcher gathers a large amount of diverse data, including field observations, audio /video recording, photographs, written documents and other material. She/he is not primarily concerned with understanding how actions are embedded in a wider social and cultural context but with explicating the organisation of practice. (vom Lehn 2014: 1450)

I participated in consumer exhibitions as a visitor and exhibitor, as a researcher and a mother of young children. This provided insights

---

[4]From the company's website: http://www.clarionevents.com/?page=whatwedo, consulted on 26 January 2008.

into the varying roles adopted by the people and organisations present, whilst my autobiographical reality came into play through reflections between my mothering experiences and my observations (Ellis and Bochner 2000). I spent time at consumer exhibitions walking around, talking with and observing visitors, exhibitors and their interactions, and paying attention to the exhibitions of products and services, and how these were organised. Like other visitors, as I moved along, I accepted product leaflets, information brochures and freebees that were offered when passing stands, and used these in later analysis work. I also purchased products that were of particular interest when talking at stands. An analysis of the organisation of exhibitions follows in the next chapter.

It soon became clear that the consumer exhibition offered access to the broader commercial world of pregnancy, birth, early childhood and new families. Such events bring together a range of commercial organisations, from small entrepreneurs through to the large brand-companies, their representatives, along with childcare 'experts' and health care professionals. In addition, a range of different people with diverging and converging interests attend, including parents, prospective parents, babies and young children, family members, other interested adults, charities and some researchers. These elements together produced a spectacle that included brands, niche products and boutique items, visitors, freebees, services, displays, entertainment, and childcare advice (Martens 2010). Listening into the plethora of medical, health, scientific, educational, safety, care, memory, fun, cute, needs and must-haves content, consumer exhibitions gave access to the complexities that connect child caring, the parent and the young child, with products, services and their descriptions in sales narratives. Visiting consumer exhibitions was thus useful as a setting for listening into the cacophony of voices that come from this market setting, and one of the purposes of visiting these exhibitions became exactly that: to use my time there to observe and to develop questions for further investigation after attending these shows. One of the ways in which I managed the complexity of these commercial events during the fieldwork was to concentrate on one facet of child caring at any time. In this way, I focused on the themes of safety, food and eating, and education, and then continued the work started at the exhibition by later investigating the websites of the companies I had encountered there. I also interviewed prospective and new parents. These parts of the investigation are discussed further below.

Markets, Organised Interactions and More-Than-Human Relations

My research at consumer and trade exhibitions served another purpose, which was to develop insight into the organisation of seller/buyer interactions. When encountering the business of child caring, it soon becomes apparent that much of it comes in the form of textual materials. Think, for instance, about parenting magazines, brands and advertising, products and their packaging, and the recent growth in online sales environments (Fuentes and Brembeck 2017). Whether walking through the aisles of Babies-R-Us or Boots, the customer is confronted more with mediated resources rather than opportunities for face-to-face contact. The packaging of products is a technology that serves multiple functions, from keeping the product pristine and new after customer handling, through to distinguishing the product from its competitors with distinct aesthetics, branding and the provision of product information. If all else fails, the contemporary customer can always refer to the online website of the brand-company, listed in the small print on the back, and check parenting Internet sites for product feedback and recommendation.

There is little doubt that the commercial world of early childhood and infant care has, over the past 15 years, manifested itself in a new online presence in the form of voluminous website content and web-based retailing. Brand-company websites are relatively new kids on the block of commercial literature, taking their place amongst other, more established, modes of commercial communication, such as advertisements, brands, magazines, advice literature, information brochures and product packaging, whilst simultaneously incorporating these modes of communication. Today, no product or service in this commercial terrain can apparently exist without a web presence. One of the things that drew me to trade and consumer exhibitions was an expectation that

I would find face-to-face interactions there, between real-life sellers and buyers, so that 'proper' ethnography could ensue. But this expectation soon turned into a puzzle, which was that the interactions between sellers and buyers were punctuated and mediated substantially by post-social tools and technologies, to the extend that it was often uncertain 'who' or 'what' did the selling.

Selling and buying may be acknowledged as distinct practices. But, as categories they map onto, and confirm, the binary opposition between sellers and buyers, retailers and shoppers. Yet, I was interested in finding out what kinds of interactional environments businesses of child caring create. Initially, I thought Goffman's notion of the encounter might be useful, especially given his definition of it as a *focused gathering*, during which 'people effectively agree to sustain for a time a single focus of cognitive and visual attention, as in a conversation' (1961: 8). The dictionary entry, moreover, pointed to the face-to-face qualities of encounters.[5] In line with my own expectations, much of the literature on shopping examines encounters between buyers and sellers. Noteworthy examples include the work by Everts and Jackson (2009) on the corner grocery shop, Gregson and Crewe's (1997) research on the car boot sale, and Cook's (2008) collection *The Lived Experiences of Public Consumption*, which takes the reader to markets in different parts of the world. These projects share with vom Lehn (2014) an interest in the interactional dynamics between customers and small commercial players, rather than an interest in, and analysis of, 'the big fish'. In addition, and whilst I share with vom Lehn an interest in 'the organisation of practice' (2014: 1450), my own research soon made me acknowledge the importance of the more-than-human elements of this organisation. As explained by Sayer, markets do not only bring together human beings:

A market … includes not only commodity exchanges … and the associated transfers of money and property rights, but the practices and setting

---

[5]Webster's new collegiate dictionary, for instance, translates encounter as 'to come upon face to face' … to come upon unexpectedly' … 'a chance meeting' … a direct often momentary meeting' (1979: 372).

which enable such exchanges to be made in a regular and organised fashion. (2000: 2)

I concur that market practices are situated, meaning that 'they' are performed in and through material settings and other tactile things (Pink 2012; Shove et al. 2012; Sparrman et al. 2012). My analysis of interactional organisation therefore had to attend to the more-than-human elements of interaction and this moved closer to a post-social approach (Knorr Cetina 1997; Knorr-Cetina and Bruegger 2002), especially in relation to the insistence that objects and other technical devices can operate as actants in the relationality of everyday life (Pyyhtinen 2016). Product packaging can be seen in this way, whilst, as I discuss in the next chapter, exhibitor stands do a lot of the work of organising the practice of exhibition. The interactional practices in the markets I included in my research can thus be seen as situated enactments, not only of selling the products and services of child caring, but also of the practice of child caring. This does not take away from the fact that these situated and textual qualities are mostly products and outcomes of the work of marketers. It does give rise to the question how 'the durable' elements of these sales encounters can be made sense of and how, if at all, these relate to the practice of child caring?

Following inspiration from discussions from feminist theory, ANT and practice theory and methodology (Law 2004; Nimmo 2011; Schäfer 2017; Taylor 2013), I have pursued what may be termed a *horizontal* methodology as a strategy for understanding market interactional organisation. This means that I will treat the different empirical materials in my research in the same way. From the very outset of the research, my priority was to understand how the business of child caring is organised, and how, in turn, it organises the interactions between those we look upon as sellers and buyers. I wanted to interrogate what this reveals about cultural understandings of young children, leading to understandings *that* they should be cared for and *how* they should be cared for. In other words, I was interested in whether and how 'the young child' is performed as 'in need' of 'care', in the face-to-face interactions I observed in retailing encounters, in the conversations I had with new parents, sales staff, and early childhood professionals, in the product packaging and brochures I brought home with me, in the child care tools that are brought to market and sold as aids for prospective and new parents, as they commence the task of caring for their young offspring, and in the cacophony of sales narratives that may be found in this environment, and that shifted during the research from paper based materials to website based content. But the analysis I present does not only flow in one direction. My concern is not only with the practices that point to the structuration of the teleoaffective qualities of child caring and the discourse of childhood, but also how the structure or discourse of childhood implicates practices of selling and buying.

Talking with Prospective and New Parents

Twenty semi-structured interviews were conducted with visitors of The Baby Show in London and Birmingham in 2006. To interview visitors, I attended The Show as an exhibitor, and so it was that on two occasions, I decorated a tiny exhibition space with hand-drawn pictures made by my daughters, and brought along colouring pencils and paper just in case I recruited an interviewee with a young child.[6] The interviews lasted between 35 minutes and 1.5 hours, and I asked questions about the experiences of pregnancy, relations with family and friends, the work of preparing for the baby, the needs of a baby, shopping, and experiences of attending The Show.

Twelve interviews were conducted with couples, and 8 with mothers. Of the twelve interviews with couples, 10 were, or were about to become, first time parents. Two couples had children from previous relationships, though for Hannah, who attended the Show with her husband Peter, this was her first pregnancy. Amongst the mothers, only Christel was pregnant with her second child, and her daughter Ruby,

---

[6]Clarion Events operates with a strict conception of the people that visit the shows it organises, and makes a distinction between exhibitors and visitors. Researchers with an interest in engaging with visitors are thus seen as exhibitors, and required to purchase exhibition space. Ethical approval for the overall research was sought from Durham University, including interviews with prospective and new parents. Interviewees were fully informed about the research, and were given a £15 Mothercare voucher as a thank you for giving their time to participate.

who was 18 months at the time of the interview, was sleeping in her buggy while we spoke. The only interviewee who was not pregnant was Jasmin, and she had given birth to daughter Iris 5 weeks before attending The Show. Of interest was that amongst the pregnant mothers who agreed to the interview, four were visiting with their own mothers. Couples and pregnant mums-to-be, visiting with their own mothers, were common visitor combinations at The Show. The sample of interviewees who participated in the study reflected the diversity of visitors who are attracted to spending time at this bespoke consumer exhibition in other ways. I spoke, for instance, with two teenage mums-to-be, and with pregnant women in their 20s and 30s. Most of my interviewees were white British, but I also spoke with two Asian families, and amongst 5 of my interviewee families, there was a mix of ethnic backgrounds. Interviewees lived within a broad geographical radius around London and Birmingham. One couple, from West Yorkshire, had possibly travelled the furthest for their day out at the Birmingham show. Finally, interviewees were from working class (5), technical & white-colour (6), and professional (9) backgrounds. Some of these visitors had received free entrance tickets to attend The Show through their antenatal activities. All interviewees have been given pseudonyms, and when citing from our discussions, I offer brief summaries of socio-demographic information.

Conclusion

In this chapter, I outlined the practice approach that was adapted and adopted to use as a frame for the analysis of two practices: that of child caring and the organised interactions of markets in which the value of the young child and pecuniary value are co-realised. Focussing first on the practice of child caring, I argued for a broadening out of the concerns that have thus far guided applications of theories of practice in consumption research in two ways. First, by being aware of and moving beyond the performativity of child caring as an entity, to accept that this practice can be carried by different entities and in a range of situated contexts. I argued that this means that child caring can be, and is, carried by commercial practitioners as well as other actants. Second, I pointed to the peculiarities of this practice, and engaged with the question how prospective and new parents carried this practice, given they are 'new to the job'. Drawing on Theodor Schatzki's argument that practices are organised through a teleoaffective structure, and principles and instructions, I argued that it is especially in the conceptual understanding of the practice of child caring that the young child is imagined in the business of child caring. Teleoaffective structuration of child caring happens in and through the repeated performances of different actants in the organised and situated context of markets. I finished with a discussion of the methodology. I argued for the inclusion of non-human actants on the basis that the markets I encountered in my work offer an interesting mix of human and non-human elements, and I offered a discussion of the ethnographic and textual research that supports the analysis offered in the book.

Bibliography

Arvidsson, A. 2005. Brands: A critical perspective. *Journal of Consumer Culture* 5 (2): 235–258.

Apple, R.D. 1987. *Mothers and medicine: A social history of infant feeding, 1890–1950*. Madison: University of Wisconsin Press.

Apple, R.D. 1995. Constructing mothers: Scientific motherhood in the nineteenth and twentieth centuries. *Social History of Medicine* 8 (2): 161–178.

Apple, R.D. 2006. *Perfect motherhood: Science and childrearing in America*. New Brunswick, NJ: Rutgers University Press.

Bloch, M. 1991. Language, anthropology and cognitive science. *Man (New Series)* 26 (2): 183–198.

Burningham, K., S. Venn, I. Christie, T. Jackson, and B. Gatersleben. 2014. New motherhood: A moment of change in everyday shopping practices? *Young Consumers* 15 (3): 211–226.

Cook, D.T. 2004. *The commodification of childhood: The children's clothing industry and the rise of the child consumer*. Durham, NC: Duke University Press.

Cook, D.T. (ed.). 2008. *Lived experiences of public consumption: Encounters with value in marketplaces on five continents*. Basingstoke: Palgrave Macmillan.

Edwards, O.W., and V.E. Mumford. 2005. Children raised by grandparents: Implications for social policy. *International Journal of Sociology and Social Policy* 25 (8): 18–30.

Ellis, C., and A.P. Bochner. 2000. Autoethnography, personal narrative, reflexivity: Researcher as subject. In *The handbook of qualitative research*, 2nd ed, ed. N. Denzin and Y. Lincoln, 763–788. Thousand Oaks, CA: Sage.

Everts, J. 2010. Consuming and living the corner shop: Belonging, remembering, socialising. *Social and Cultural Geography* 11 (8): 847–863.

Everts, J., and P. Jackson. 2009. Modernisation and the practices of contemporary food shopping. *Environment and Planning D: Society and Space* 27 (5): 917–935.

Falk, P., and C. Campbell (eds.). 1997. *The shopping experience*. London: Sage.

Ferguson, H. 2008. *Protecting children in time: Child abuse, child protection and the consequences of modernity*. Basingstoke: Palgrave Macmillan.

Fuentes, M., and H. Brembeck. 2017. Best for baby? Framing weaning practice and motherhood in web-mediated marketing. *Consumption Markets & Culture* 20 (2): 153–175.

Goffman, E. 1961/2013. *Encounters: Two studies in the sociology of interaction*. Eastford, CT: Martino Fine Books.

Gram-Hanssen, Kirsten. 2011. Understanding change and continuity in residential energy consumption. *Journal of Consumer Culture* 11 (1): 61–78.

Gregson, N., and L. Crewe. 1997. The bargain, the knowledge, and the spectacle: Making sense of consumption in the space of the car-boot sale. *Environment and Planning D* 15: 87–112.

Gronow, J., and A. Warde (eds.). 2001. *Ordinary consumption*. Routledge: London.

Halkier, B. 2001. Consuming ambivalences. Consumer handling og environmentally related risks in food. *Journal of Consumer Culture* 1: 205–224.

Halkier, B. 2010. *Consumption challenged: Food in mediated everyday lives*. Farnham: Ashgate.

Halkier, B. 2013. Contesting food—Contesting motherhood? In *Motherhoods, markets and consumption: The making of mothers in contemporary western cultures*, ed. S. O'Donohoe, M. Hogg, P. Maclaran, L. Martens, and L. Stevens, 87–102. London: Routledge.

Halkier, B., T. Katz-Gero, and L. Martens. 2011. Special Issue on "Applications of practice theory in consumption research". *Journal of Consumer Culture* 11 (1): 3–13.

Hays, S. 1996. *The cultural contradictions of motherhood*. New Haven, CT: Yale University Press.

Humphery, K. 1998. *Shelf life: Supermarkets and the changing cultures of consumption*. Cambridge: Cambridge University Press.

Ilmonen, K. 2001. Sociology, consumption and routine. In *Ordinary Consumption*, ed. J. Gronow and A. Warde, 9–23. London: Routledge.

Ingold, T. 2000. The perception of the environment: Essays on livelihood, dwelling and skill. London/New York: Routledge.

Jackson, P., M. Rowlands, and D. Miller. 2005. *Shopping, place and identity*. London: Routledge.

Jenks, C. 2005. *Childhood*. London: Routledge.

Keller, M., and B. Halkier. 2014. Positioning consumption: A practice theoretical approach to contested consumption and media discourse. *Marketing Theory* 14 (1): 35–51.

Knoblauch, Hubert. 2005. Focused Ethnography [30 paragraphs]. *Forum Qualitative Sozialforschung* [Forum: Qualitative Social Research] 6 (3): Art. 44. http://nbn-resolving.de/urn:nbn:de:0114-fqs0503440.

Knorr Cetina, K. 1997. Sociality with objects: Social relations in postsocial knowledge societies. *Theory, Culture & Society* 14 (4): 1–30.

Knorr Cetina, K., and U. Bruegger. 2002. Traders' engagement with markets: A postsocial relationship. *Theory, Culture & Society* 19 (5–6): 161–185.

Kopytoff, I. 1986. The cultural biography of things: Commoditisation as process. In *The social life of things: Commodities in cultural perspective*, ed. A. Appadurai. Cambridge: Cambridge University Press.

Law, J. 2004. *After method. Mess in social science research*. London/New York: Routledge.

Lawler, S. 2000. *Mothering the self: Mothers, daughters, subjectivities*. London: Routledge.

Lee, N. 2005. *Childhood and human value: Development, separation and separability*. Maidenhead: The Open University Press.

Magaudda, P. 2011. When materiality 'bites back': Digital music consumption practices in the age of dematerialization. *Journal of Consumer Culture* 11 (1): 15–36.

Martens, L. 2010. The cute, the spectacle and the practical: Narratives of new parents and babies at the baby show. In *Childhood and consumer culture*, ed. D. Buckingham and V. Tingstad. London: Palgrave Macmillan.

Martens, L. 2012. Practice 'In Talk' and Talk 'As Practice': Dish washing and the reach of language. *Sociological Research Online* 17 (3): 22.

Martens, L., and S. Scott. 2017. Understanding everyday kitchen life: Looking at performance, into performances and for practices. In *Methodological reflections on practice oriented theories*, ed. M. Jonas, B. Littig, and A. Wroblewski, 177–191. Charn, Switzerland: Springer.

Miller, D. 1998. *A theory of shopping*. Cambridge: Polity Press.

Miller, T. 2005. *Making sense of motherhood*. Cambridge: Cambridge University Press.

Molander, S. 2011. Food, love and meta-practices: A study of everyday dinner consumption among single mothers. *Research in Consumer Behavior* 13: 77–92.

Nava, Mica. 2000. Modernity tamed? Women shoppers and the rationalisation of consumption in the interwar period. In *All the world and her husband: women in twentieth-century consumer culture*, ed. M. Andrews and M.M. Talbot. London: Cassell.

Nimmo, R. 2011. Actor-network theory and methodology: Social research in a more-than-human world. *Methodological Innovations Online* 6 (3): 108–119.

Pink, S. 2012. *Situating everyday life: Practices and places*. London: Sage.

Pink, S., and J. Morgan. 2013. Short-term ethnography: Intense routes to knowing. *Symbolic Interaction* 36 (3): 351–361.

Pink, S., K.L. Mackley, R. Morosanu, V. Mitchell, and T. Bhamra. 2017. *Making homes: Ethnography and design*. London: Bloomsbury.

Prout, A. 2005. *The future of childhood*. London: Routledge.

Postill, J. 2010. Introduction: Theorising media and practices. In *Theorising media and practice*, ed. B. Brauchler and J. Postill, 1–32. New York: Berghahn Books.

Pugh, A.J. 2009. *Longing and belonging: Parents, children, and consumer culture*. California: University of California Press.

Pyyhtinen, A. 2016. *More-than-human sociology*. London: Palgrave Macmillan.

Røpke, I. 2009. Theories of practice—New inspiration for ecological economic studies on consumption. *Ecological Economics* 68: 2490–2497.

Sayer, A. 2000. Markets, embeddedness and trust: Problems of polysemy and idealism. Published by the Department of Sociology, Lancaster University, UK, at http://www.comp.lancs.ac.uk/sociology/papers/Sayer-Markets-Embeddednes-and-Trust.pdf.

Sayer, A. 2003. (De)Commodification, consumer culture, and moral economy. *Environment and Planning D: Society and Space* 21: 341–357.

Sayer, A. 2004. Approaching moral economy. In *The moralization of the markets*, ed. N. Stehr, C. Henning, and B. Weiler. New Brunswick/London: Transaction Publishers.

Schäfer, H. 2017. Relationality and heterogeneity: Transitive methodology in practice theory and actor-network theory. In *Methodological reflections on practice oriented theories*, ed. M. Jonas, B. Littig, and A. Wroblewski, 35–46. Charn, Switzerland: Springer International Publishing.

Schatzki, T. 1996. Social practices: A Wittgensteinian approach to human activity and the social. Cambridge: Cambridge University Press.

Schatzki, T. 2002. *The site of the social. A philosophical account of the constitution of social life and change*. Pennsylvania: Pennsylvania State University Press.

Schatzki, T., K. Knorr-Cetina, and E. von Savigny (eds.). 2001. *The practice turn in contemporary theory*. London: Routledge.

Shove, E., M. Watson, M. Hand, and J. Ingram. 2007. *The design of everyday life*. Oxford: Berg.

Shove, E., M. Pantzar, and M. Watson. 2012. *The dynamics of social practice: Everyday life and how it changes*. London: Sage.

Southerton, D. 2013. Habits, routines and temporalities of consumption: From individual behaviours to the reproduction of everyday practices. *Time & Society* 22 (3): 335–355.

Sparrman, A., and B. Sandin. 2012. Situated child consumption: Introduction. In *Situating child consumption: Rethinking values and notions of children, childhood and consumption*, ed. A. Sparrman, B. Sandin, and J. Sjöberg. Lund: Nordic Academic Press.

Sullivan, O., and J. Gershuny. 2004. Inconspicuous consumption: Work-rich, time-poor in the liberal market economy. *Journal of Consumer Culture* 4 (1): 79–100.

Taylor, A. 2013. *Reconfiguring the natures of childhood*. London: Routledge.

Taylor, J.S., L. Layne, and D.F. Wozniak. 2004. *Consuming motherhood*. New Brunswick: Rutgers University Press.

Thomson, R., M.J. Kehily, L. Hadfield, and S. Sharpe. 2011. *Making modern mothers*. Bristol: Policy Press.

Truninger, M. 2011. Cooking with bimby in a moment of recruitment: Exploring conventions and practice perspectives. *Journal of Consumer Culture* 11 (1): 37–59.

Vihalemm, T., M. Keller, and M. Kiisel. 2015. *From intervention to social change: A guide to reshaping everyday practices*. Farnham: Ashgate.

vom Lehn, D. 2014. Timing is money: Managing the floor in sales interaction at street-market stalls. *Journal of Marketing Management* 30 (13–14): 1448–1466.

Warde, A. 1997. *Consumption, food and taste*. Thousand Oaks: Sage.

Warde, A. 2005. Consumption and theories of practice. *Journal of consumer culture* 5 (2): 131–153.

Warde, Alan. 2014. After taste: Culture, consumption and theories of practice. *Journal of Consumer Culture* 14 (3): 279–303.

Warde, A. and Southerton, D. (eds.). 2012. *The habits of consumption*, vol 12. Helsinki: Helsinki Collegium in the Humanities and Social Sciences.

Webster's New Collegiate Dictionary. 1979. Springfield: G & C Merriam Company.

Williams, R.H. 1991. *Dream worlds: Mass consumption in late nineteenth-century France*. California: University of California Press.

Woolgar, S. 2012. Ontological child consumption. In *Situating child consumption: Rethinking values and notions of children, childhood and consumption*, ed. A. Sparrman, B. Sandin, and J. Sjöberg, 33–52. Lund: Nordic Academic Press.

Zelizer, V.A.R. 1985. *Pricing the priceless child: The changing social value of children*. New York: Basic Books.

4

The Business of Child Caring

Introduction

This chapter introduces the business of child caring, using the consumer exhibition as the starting point for an analysis of how this business is organised. The reader joins me on a day out at The Baby Show, to become familiar with some of the main components that make up this consumer exhibition. Along the way, I include visitors' reflections on their shopping practices, experiences of their day out at The Show and their reasons for visiting. Drawing on product leaflets and website content, I move on to discuss 'the product content' of the practice of child caring. I identify six pathways (or projects) of child caring and argue that each of these pathways is supported by the same teleoaffective structure, which brings together four main qualities of the young child: those of loveable, vulnerable, pure and the 'need' for nurturing. In the final part of this chapter, I provide an analysis of the spatial and material organisation of exhibitions, and consider how these organise the interactions between exhibitors and visitors. It is argued that the larger companies organise their exhibitions in ways where face-to-face interaction is minimal. In the conclusion, I consider whether the main

© The Author(s) 2018
L. Martens, *Childhood and Markets*, Studies in Childhood and Youth,
https://doi.org/10.1057/978-1-137-31503-8_4

organisational components of the consumer exhibition are shared across different market environments.

Visiting The Baby Show

My first visits to The Baby Show in 2005 and 2006 engendered a strong sense of the novelty of this kind of commercial environment. I noted during my first visit how interesting it was that such an event attracts so many people, who, in exchange for an entrance ticket, were introduced to a range of products, brands, services, consumer advice and information on early parenting, freebees, as well as a variety of types of entertainment and relaxation.[1] Prior to visiting The Show, visitors can research the event online, as The Show's website contains information on the exhibitors and the celebrity-experts who are scheduled to talk. Visitors are advised to plan ahead to get the most out of their day. The website and The Show's guide, which is handed out to visitors 'on entry', provide important forums for communication between Clarion Events; the company that organises the national shows, and The Show's visitors and exhibitors.

When the doors opens for visitors at 9:30 in the morning, and all exhibition stands are in pristine order and fully staffed, a sense of quiet invites the visitor in. The Show opens out in a vista of early family interest without giving a clear sense of where to go first. Here is an invitation to meander, taking one of the avenues that leads out from the entrance, and to stop at stands to browse and talk simply as they appear in view and catch the wanderer's attention (Fig. 4.1). As indicated in this ethnographic fieldnote extract, the fact that this is a show for people with an interest in pregnancy and early childhood is written into the very fabric of the display, and as the visitor progresses, she/he starts to accumulate a sense of the variety and complexity of The Show's offerings:

---

[1] On my first visit to The Baby Show in Glasgow in 2005, I paid £9 in entrance fees. In 2014, the price at the door of the NEC in Birmingham was £20. In my discussions with visitors, I know that free entrance tickets are offered to prospective parents through antenatal classes and midwives to draw people in. Each Show has its own price structure, with the London Shows being a little more expensive than the regional ones, and a price reduction for those who purchase tickets in advance online.

Calm and relaxed as you enter; soft pastel blue carpet underfoot; pink stands. Although quite busy with lots of pushchairs everywhere, there is a sense of calm. From the main entrance there is no clear path to follow: go where you feel, explore. Distinct areas at the ends e.g. Fairy non-bio stand, Huggies play bus, areas sponsored by large, successful companies. Ask a Midwife. Many different stands: busiest 'Magic Custard' bronze casts of babies' hands and feet; Huggies free booty bag with nappies and baby wipes; Babylicious frozen baby food, free samples.

At the Fischer Price exhibition, which in most shows that I visited, was located close to the entrance, I look at a range of colourful baby bouncing chairs that are decorated in bright colours, with animal and flower patterns and small dangling toys for baby hands to feel and handle. The stand's logo proclaims that the company's 'baby gear' is about 'play – laugh – grow' and 'the joy of learning'. I have a discussion with the exhibition staff, including the UK sales manager, about the safety regulations that guide their toy/furnishings, and we talk about how the company sends new products out to families to try and report back on. I move onto another stand, much smaller than the previous one, and occupied by a new company called Open Play. It sells playground installations built in Italy and enjoying the European Safety Standard for Children's Play Equipment EN1176. One of the things this means, I am told, is that the equipment can be placed on grass and that it is low enough for the child not to hurt itself badly when falling off. Both companies appear to be focused on the importance of play and development in early childhood, yet, at the same time, both are also concerned that child play should be safe.

The Show clearly makes a distinction between big and small commercial players. Banners hang from the ceiling to announce, from a distance, where to find the big brands,[2] and this same pattern is repeated in The Show Guide, where commonly known brands get special mention in the floor plan, and in the introduction of the visitor to the various 'services facilities' that are on offer that day. The big brands are sponsoring rest areas, relaxation services, with reclining chairs and massage on offer,

---

[2]Regularly present at The Show have been Volvo, Fisher Price, Mothercare, Huggies, Pampers, Phillips Avent, Tommee Tippee, Persil/Comfort and Fairy non-bio.

Fig. 4.1 Walking through The Baby Show at Birmingham's National Exhibition Centre

information services staffed by registered midwives, health visitors and child nurses, play areas for small children, child crèches, baby and infant feeding areas and nappy changing areas. Apart from the big brands and retailers, which occupy the larger exhibition areas and can clearly afford the price ticket of 'leisurely space', exhibitor stands of varying sizes are populated by a multitude of much smaller entrepreneurs and retailers. And not all stands are populated by commercial enterprises. Charities and other not-for-profit organisations also make an appearance, and in past years, this has included the NHS and the National Childbirth Trust. For Lesley (Couple, 33 weeks, first time parents, early 30s, white, professional),[3] who was pregnant and visiting The Show with her partner, this diversity was

---

[3]Lesley visited The Baby Show with her partner Dan. When presenting quotations from interview transcripts, I have placed in brackets first information on whether the interview was with a couple or with a mother or mothers. This is followed by information on how many weeks into the pregnancy my interviewees were, whether the pregnancy was first time or not, the age of the interviewees, ethnicity and their class status based on their employment.

appreciated: 'I think they have got a good mix of different types of big companies, small companies, niche market, mass market. It is a really good mix, I think.'

Moving on, I learn that vitamin supplements are recommended for the pregnant woman and for the infant child. Supplements, like Pregnacare and Abidec, are listed under the heading of 'healthcare' in The Show Guide,[4] and along with 50 other companies that are listed here and are exhibiting at The Show, the visitor is taken into a scientific world, where everyday life is sketched as accentuated by a range of health risks, for which the products on sale offer a 'carefully worded' solution. In starting a conversation with staff on the Pregnacare stand, I am a little surprised to find that I am talking with an independent registered midwife, whom the company has appointed to talk with visitors. The midwife claims her independence from the company, saying that her discussion with parents will reflect her medical knowledge. Crucial for her, she says, is folic acid, as deficiency in this has definitely been proven to be related to higher rates of brain and spine abnormalities in the developing foetus body, and is related, for instance, with conditions such as spina bifida. She does make the point that folic acid supplements are needed in the first 12 weeks of pregnancy, as this is when crucial developments in the foetal spine and brain occur. Exhibitors at The Show offer goods and services targeted at pregnancy, birth and women's health, with companies also offering clothing to accommodate the growing bump and changing breasts; creams and lotions to help prevent stretch marks on expanding body parts; antenatal classes that come in the form of luxury week-end breaks for the expectant couple, or that offer techniques to facilitate a 'calm, controlled, comfortable and safer' birth[5]; and different aids for the birth experience itself, with birthing pools, birthing balls and tens machines commonly exhibited at the show.

One thing that soon becomes apparent is how everyone and everything appears to home in on the bodies of babies and infants, and

---

[4]The Earls Court Show Guide, 2009.
[5]Entry for HypnoBirthing on page 35 of The Earls Court Show Guide, 2009.

to a certain extend also those of carers. Groups of products are destined to ensure normal body growth, and offer solutions for abnormalities, such as 'flat head' syndrome; a consequence of babies spending too long sleeping on one side of their bodies, or, more common nowadays, following advice to counter 'sudden infant death' syndrome, on their backs. When visiting the Plum Baby stand, I learn that babies have more taste buds on their tongues than older people, making their sense of taste more, rather than less, acute. The company thus argues that weaning foods should be extra tasteful, offering an implicit critique that 'standard' offerings are bland. The importance of early sensory experiences is a sales feature of other products, too, and products alternately sell auditory, olfactory and visual experiences to sooth or stimulate the young child. Thus, Johnson's Baby recommends baby massage with the use of specially designed oils, and its range of products, especially its baby shampoo, has become well known for its distinctive smell. Perfect baby bodies are rife in the images encountered at The Show, and baby body parts—especially faces, hands and feet—offer themselves for safekeeping through casts and photographs. New parents are invited into practices of bodily closeness and adornment, whether through baby carriers and advice on the importance of skin-to-skin contact, or through the purchase of colourful cloth nappies with fun designs.

Not to forget, The Show also highlights the importance of information and education, which is reflected in services and products, and which discuss the issues that arise during pregnancy and the eventualities of birth and life with a young child. New at the Earl's Court Show in 2009 is an Internet-based company called Greatvine.com, which provides a service connecting those seeking advice with relevant experts. At this same show, the 'show stage' offerings have for the first time been split up into 'entertainment' and 'advice'. The main podium, called the 'Comfort Pure Stage' in the guide, is the forum for discussions with celebrities and celebrity experts, along with various interactive entertainments for young children and prospective parents. A range of child-care experts are lined up for the 'Expert Advice and Information Theatre', to talk about topics as diverse as nutrition during pregnancy, breastfeeding, baby sleep and soothing, through to potty training and child development.

With so much going on, time soon moves on, and by noon, I sit in the Pampers Central Café in the middle of the exhibition space:

Empty chairs are starting to get scarce, even though it is only midday on a Friday, and I am sitting at a table with two other visitors. There is a vendor who sells coffee, tea and pastries and people are cuing up to be served. Food is in fact everywhere at The Show. Mums and dads and other relatives sit and feed infants, with breastfeeding and bottle-feeding both in evidence. Young kids are eating varying degrees of solid foods, brought along by their parents, or served as freebees in the exhibition stands of companies like Heinz and Plum Baby. The Rachel's Organic stand is clearly popular, with people cuing up the try out their various yoghurts. Food courts surround this NEC exhibition area to feed hungry people! Also on site today are a 'Pick & Mix' and an ice cream vendor – health and indulgence clearly live side by side. The ice cream vendor does not appear to be busy and the sweet vendor has a notice up to say that the sweets are not suitable for children under the age of 3.

Early afternoons, The Show is definitely much busier and the crowd can become so dense that it is hard to walk through the corridors at anything but a snail's pace, making one pregnant couple I interviewed question how so many people with their prams and babies would be able to exit the building in an emergency? As the day moves on, the complexities of the visual, auditory and embodied experiences induced whilst walking through The Show also increase. The memory of what has gone before recedes into the background, as the invitation to move on is ever present, driven by an emerging curiosity in what the next stand that is coming into view is offering, or the music that is beckoning through the suggestion that 'something fun' is happening at the back of the exhibition hall.

By 2 p.m., I arrive at The Baby Show stage, where a crowd of people, young and old, along with their prams and buggies, and their babies and toddlers, are seated around an oval shaped stage, waiting for the start of an interactive sing and dance show with the Teletubbies. Noise levels are definitely up from when I entered The Show in the morning, and it becomes louder still when the music that is part of the show starts. Ahead of the show, presenter Lucy Piper walks around on the stage, telling the audience what is in store for the afternoon's entertainment, whilst handing out freebees. Over the years, there has been an expansion in what may be seen as dimensions of added spectacle. Mothers with toddlers have been drawn in by the feature of celebrities on The Show Stage, whilst The Baby Show (and also some local newspapers) have offered immensely popular—judging by the length of the queue of patiently waiting parents—free photo shoots of babies and toddlers, to be entered into competitions, for instance, to be the next 'face' of The Baby Show.[6]

For this variety of reasons, at least a proportion of visitors experience The Show as entertaining and exciting. This was expressed, for instance, in my discussion with Charlotte and Ben (Couple, 6 months old daughter, first time parents, 20s, white, working class), who were visiting the Birmingham show with their toddler daughter, blissfully asleep in her pram during our conversation. The couple, who were at The Show for a family day out ('…weekends is precious times spent as a family, so…'), had been informed about the event by a friend, who had said 'it was really good 'n that'. Charlotte's excitement was sparked right at the start, when they were handed a set of free tickets from some other visitors:

> *Charlotte*: We was lucky today actually, yeah, we were going to get cheap tickets off Ebay, but erm… then we didn't bother and we said we would pay on the door, and we got some free ones off some people on the shuttle, who were given them free from the hospital. So I said I would give them the money for them but they said: 'Oh no, it's all right'. So we were really lucky as we got in here for free.
> *Lydia*: Is it … £13 each?
> *Charlotte*: Yeah, that is £26 that we saved, so …

---

[6]From 2007, The Show has featured a photographic image of one infant on its promotional materials, and this image has been sourced from the photographs taken at The Show.

Charlotte's excitement, associated with saving money, and being handed free samples, continued as she explained about what they had been doing at The Show since arrival:

> *Charlotte*: Babylicious, that… I have been trying to get her food like that for ages! That is proper food! Just bargains really, freebees, get all excited, they just keep giving you things and you are like: 'Thank you!'

In asking the question why they had come to The Baby Show, the distinctive mix that was on offer was expressed in a brief summing up by pregnant Veronica and her mother Sally (Mothers, 26 weeks, first time parent, late teens, white (baby mixed ethnic), working class):

> *Lydia*: Why have you come to The Baby Show today?
> *Sally*: To see what is available… Veronica: To get little bits 'n bobs really. Sally: Got bits 'n bobs, and we have seen lots of other very different things and useful things. Veronica: Ideas, information, general stuff, and just have a day out with my mum.

The Show was clearly recognised as a place where expectant and new parents, grandparents and other interested adults, could shop around, gaining information about products, handling the merchandise, and seeking out good bargains. During my conversation with Terry and Sarah (Couple, 23 weeks, first time parents, 30s, white, professional) it became clear that, like some of the other new and expectant parents I interviewed, shopping was part of the long-term task of finding out about, and preparing for life with a baby child (Kehily 2014). By the time they visited The Show, Sarah and Terry had already done a lot of product research by reading magazines and visiting online forums. They indicated how, unlike the research that could be done through these forums, The Show allowed them the opportunity to handle the products they were interested in:

> *Sarah*: I think I first spotted it (an advertisement in a magazine for The Baby Show) and said to you (partner Terry): 'This is on.' … and I said: 'Well, I would quite like to go and have a proper look at things', rather than leafing through the magazines, and have a touch and a feel of things, like the travel systems, and how heavy are they, and things like that.

Travel systems[7] are amongst the most expensive purchases that prospective parents can make and these were a recurring theme during my conversations with visitors. When it comes to making decisions on how the baby or toddler will be carried, there is a lot of choice out there, and there are a range of practical issues that parents consider. Because of their public visibility, travel systems are also one of those items where the brand tag appeared to be important (VOICE 2010a, b). Here, Sarah and Terry think a series of these concerns through in relation to their decision to purchase a top of the range branded pram at The Show:

> *Sarah*: … We went to stands that sell the travel system that we are looking at, as we are looking at one that doesn't seem to be that available everywhere, the Bugaboo. It is very lightweight and it seems like it is going to last all the way through from the age of 0 to about the age of 3, or whenever it is you stop using it. So we decided it was better to spend the money on something that would last all that time, rather than potentially find ourselves buying and replacing the prams every year, as you end up spending more that way.
>
> *Terry*: And it is good as erm…, it has got good second-hand value on Ebay. It is one of the most expensive ones you can buy but you can sell it back on again for £200–£300 on Ebay erm…, as they are so well built that people still buy them. So when you take that into account it is actually not that expensive.
>
> *Lydia*: Is it top of the range?
>
> *Sarah*: Yes. It was £500 with the car seat.
>
> *Terry*: But it is guaranteed for 2 years, and it is lightweight, and it folds really small as well. So looking at the practical side, it is really worth spending some money as you are going to get some benefit from that.

Whilst Sarah and Terry had learned a lot about the 'big purchases' before coming to The Show, and Peter and Hannah (Couple, 24 weeks pregnant, H first time pregnant, 30s–40s, white, self-employed) were at The Show to talk with vendors about the more complex child caring

---

[7]Travel systems are a product group that includes car seats, prams, buggies and other baby carriers.

technologies, like the breast pump (see below), whilst other parents signalled that they had learned about the products they were interested in by speaking with other visitors. Here are Veronica and her mother Sally again, talking about their conversation with a visitor about the practicalities of the travel system they were themselves interested in:

> Veronica: We spoke to quite a lot of parents here. Someone who has the same pushchair as I am getting, I have asked questions about that and I have not had no come down, everyone seems pleasant. Sally: She wanted a bit of, well you know, asked them if they liked the pushchair and they said that it was superb. Veronica: The only thing is that the basket thing underneath… Sally: It is getting into it, that is all, but she said that it is lovely. Veronica: She said like the baby is 4 months old and she… Sally: Said he loves being in it. Veronica: And he lies in it flat and it is either supporting his neck up to see and look around instead of being flat on his back 24/7, which is a nice thing, so.

In these various conversations, prospective and new parents spoke about their shopping practices as a 'serious job' that required product research and a disposition for making wise purchase decisions, where product awareness, price consciousness and the pursuit of bargains were all seen as important.[8] The Baby Show facilitated this by offering visitors a broad range of informational resources and presenting everything on offer—as Jasmine (Mother, 5 week old daughter, first time parent, 30s, mixed ethnic, professional) and Terry (Couple, 23 weeks, first time parents, 30s, white, professional) thought—'conveniently under one roof'.

This quest for becoming a responsible parent-consumer was also obstructed by the inevitable impatience that was demonstrated by sales agents keen to make money, when visitors and the contents of their purse were competed over by a broad range of different exhibitors. The experience of the 'sales frenzy' was evident in the reflections of some visitors. Ceri (Couple, 31 weeks pregnant, first time parents,

---

[8]This journey of becoming a responsible parent-consumer is discussed further in Chapter 8.

teens & 20s, mixed ethnic, working class), who was visiting The Show with her boyfriend after receiving free tickets through her antenatal class, commented that she wanted to hide her belly because exhibitors were 'just jumping on me', whilst Hannah (Couple, 24 weeks pregnant, H first time pregnant, 30s & 40s, white, self-employed) commented on how, sporting a pregnant bump, was a sure way of receiving a lot of attention from exhibitors, whilst apparently ignoring prospective fathers. In this way, my interviewees were giving voice to their experience of 'getting played (Cook 2008: 4). Some prospective parents, who were in the early stages of pregnancy, felt that developing awareness about the products, rather than making purchases, was their priority. Yet, exhibitors were not discriminatory in any way, treating all visitors as potential buyers. Here, Ashia and Bishr (Couple, 17 weeks pregnant, first time parents, 30s, Asian, professional) talk about their experiences at The Show:

> *Lydia*: Are the stallholders paying attention to you?
> *Ashia*: Yes, they kind of grab you as you walk by, hand out leaflets and try to draw you in. For us it is just a day out, and it is a small step that we are taking at the moment, and as we get more advanced we will take more on board.
> *Bishr*: It is an awareness day today rather than a shopping day.

It is late afternoon when I am waiting for the train back home. It has been a long and tiring, but also a productive day! Mothers with buggies surround me on the platform. Some of them have come with their partners; some with their friends and other mothers; some have even come on their own, with their babies, for a day out. Whether walking around The Show or waiting on the platform for the train, the dominant scene is one of buggies, laden with branded shopping bags, with the most prized possession—the tiny baby sucking on a soother or the curious toddler warmed by a colourful fleece hat—tucked inside the buggy's cocoon and often barely visible. The overloaded buggy is no coincidence, for The Baby Show is a big event, and visitors are presented with fliers, freebees and appealing merchandise, with every step of the way.

Products, Practice Pathways and the Teleoaffective Structure of Child Caring

I have come away from The Baby Show with one solid paper bag from Organix, a brand company that sells organic food for babies and toddlers. I selected this bag to carry the numerous pickings collected at this show, because it seemed the most sturdy and spacious, and, along with some other visitors, I have purposefully discarded the other bags along the way. The collection of brochures, booklets and freebees in my Organix bag give an impression of the immense assortment of goods and services that come at a price, and that tap into the life experiences of those who are connected in one way or other with pregnancy, birth, babyhood, early childhood and parenthood. In this section, I consider what this range of leaflets and brochures conveys about the practice of child caring.

As pointed out in Chapter 3, child caring consists of a bundle of practices, which I have called practice pathways, around which different product groups have historically evolved. People will always have used sets of objects to aid them in their parenting practices: tools have a ubiquitous presence in human existence (Ingold 2000). Created and collected objects also have a place in the human lives through their role in symbolic and ritual practices (Lury 1996; McCracken 1988). Archaeologists and historians have explored the cultural significance of children in earlier times and societies, using remnants of past material culture in their work (Baxter 2005; Calvert 1992). Following Mennell (1996), we might expect the products used in child caring to have become more varied in the contemporary period. When coming to parenthood as a novice, with a lack of hands-on knowledge of young children and their care, the contemporary product world for babies, infants and early childcare certainly appears to be multifaceted and complex. Taking the consumer exhibition as representative of this product world, with everything displayed 'under one roof', visitors are certainly aware of this complexity. Carol (Mothers, 15 weeks, first time parents, 20s, white, working class), who was visiting The Baby Show in Birmingham with her mother, said: '… there is so much choice here. It is horrendous. There is a lot of choice.'

I will use this complexity to think through what products, and the ways in which these are organised into categories and groups, reveals about the practice of child caring. My argument is that categories of products map onto projects or pathways in child caring, and these in turn reveal something about the teleoaffective qualities of child caring. This discussion leads into the next part f the book, where I look at how different teleoaffective dimensions of child caring are performed in interactional market environments.

The categorisation of products into groups, along with a visual display of product groups, is a common signposting convention used in retailing environments, and shows prospective customers where specific products may be found. Note, for instance, the signposts for food groups hanging above shopping aisles in major supermarkets. A similar practice is evident in the organisation of products on the websites of major retailers. Table 4.1 provides a listing of the product categories found in the guide of The Baby Show for the exhibitions at the Birmingham NEC between 2006 and 2014. Looking across the years, the product categories do not vary a great deal, and they range from furnishings for the nursery, to healthcare products and gifts. Based on an analysis of website product categorisations of major retailers in this product field, along with an analysis of leaflets and brochures handed to me during my visits to consumer exhibitions between 2005 and 2014, Table 4.2 lists a series of product categories linked to pathways in the practice of child caring. This table excludes product groups that are associated with the priorities of family life, and that service parents as adults, rather than children. For instance, the listings in Table 4.1 for buggies and pushchairs, car seats, changing bags, childcare nurseries, all of which are concerned with families, mobility, and the everyday priorities of family life, are not represented in Table 4.2.

Product categories have been organised in accordance with six pathways in child caring: dressing, cleaning, feeding, keeping healthy and safe, soothing and stimulating. Scanning through the product categories, it is clear that some straddle across some of the pathways in child caring. This is, for instance, so for nappies and bibs, which may be regarded as items of clothing, but at the same time connect with cleaning (nappies, bibs) and feeding (bibs). Equally, baby carriers may be acknowledged as associated with family priorities and mobility, whilst

Table 4.1   Product categories listed in The Baby Show product locator in the show guide, Birmingham NEC, 2006–2014

Birmingham 2014	Birmingham 2010	Birmingham 2008	Birmingham 2006
Accessories	Accessories	Accessories	Accessories
Beauty and skin	Announcements	Announcements	Announcements
care	Beauty	Beauty	Beauty
Buggies, push-	Buggies,	Charity	Charity
chairs & prams	Pushchairs &	Childcare/nurseries	Childcare/
Business	prams	Education/books	nurseries
opportunity	Charity	Entertainment	Education/books
Car seats	Childcare/nurseries	Fashion baby/	Entertainment
Carriers & slings	Education/books	toddler	Fashion baby/
Changing bags	Entertainment	Fashion—mater-	toddler
Charity	Fashion baby/	nity	Fashion—mater-
Childcare nurseries	toddler	Finance	nity
Classes	Fashion—mater-	Food	Finance
Education books	nity	Furnishings—nurs-	Food
Entertainment	Finance	ery	Furnishings—nurs-
Fashion—baby/	Food	Furniture	ery
toddler	Furnishings	Gifts	Furniture
Fashion—mater-	(nursery)	Healthcare	Gifts
nity	Furniture	Holidays	Healthcare
Food & feeding	Gifts	Hygiene/nappies	Holidays
Furnishings—nurs-	Healthcare	Organic	Hygiene/nappies
ery	Holidays	Parenting advice	Organic
Furniture	Hygiene/nappies	Photography	Parenting advice
Gifts	Organic	Pregnancy advice	Photography
Healthcare	Parenting advice	Pushchairs and	Pregnancy advice
Hygiene and	Photography	prams	Pushchairs and
nappies	Pregnancy advice	Safety	prams
Organic	Safety	Toys	Safety
Parenting advice	Toys	Transportation	Toys
Photography	Transportation		Transportation
Pregnancy advice			
Safety			
Services			
Sleep			
Toys			

simultaneously serving as tools for infant soothing and sleep. Infant feeding may be regarded as a pathway in its own right, or as associated with keeping healthy, and stimulation—after all, as companies like Cow & Gate argue, food delivers the energy for being active.

Table 4.2 Pathways in child caring, product categories and the teleoaffective qualities of child caring

Pathways in child caring	Product categories	Teleoaffective qualities of child caring
Dressing	• Everyday clothing • Decorative clothing • Nappies & bibs • Sleeping bags, wraps and pajamas • Swimming nappies, rain and outdoor wear • UPV protective swim wear	Protecting, and entanglements with loving (gifts, interembodiment), purifying (cleanliness and aesthetics), and nurturing (the sleeping and the active child)
Cleaning	• Bathing & changing • Baby toiletries • Beauty and skin care • Nappies, bibs and wipes • Sterilising aids (esp. for feeding tools)	Purifying (cleanliness and aesthetics)—and entanglements with loving (interembodiment of bathing), nurturing (bathing and massage as soothing) and protecting (sterilizing to rid tools from germs)
Feeding	• Infant formula & follow-on milk (substitutes for breast milk and cow's milk) • Infant & toddler weaning foods • Feeding equipment (bottles, teats, breastpumps, sterilising equipment, early drinking cups and cutlery)	Nurturing—and entanglements with loving, purifying and protecting
Keeping healthy and safe	• Medicines • Teething tools • Supplements (vitamins) • Safety products (e.g. stair gates, monitors, car seats)	Protecting—and entanglements with loving and nurturing (active, growing child)
Nurturing through soothing	• Bathing and massage • Child carriers & wraps • Soft toys/cloths • Soothers/pacifiers • Teething tools	Nurturing the sleepy/tired child, and entanglements with loving, protection and purification

(continued)

Table 4.2 (continued)

Pathways in child caring	Product categories	Teleoaffective qualities of child caring
Nurturing through stimulating	• Toys • Experiential activities	Nurturing the active child—and entanglements with loving (gifts), purification and protection

The third column in Table 4.2 sketches the connection between pathways and the teleoaffective structure of child caring. Four main teleoaffective qualities of child caring: those of loving, protecting, purifying and nurturing, were identified in my analysis (see also Martens 2010, 2014). Looking at each pathway in child caring in relation to the various product categories, it is apparent that the teleoaffective qualities of child caring do not map onto pathways in a straightforward manner. Pathways of child caring are commonly guided by multiple teleoaffective qualities. The practice of dressing children, for instance, cuts across all four teleoaffective dimensions, such that everyday clothing may be seen as addressing the utilitarian need for embodied protection, whilst decorative clothing may serve as an expression of love or as adornment, decorative clothing may simultaneously address the practice of childhood purification. As discussed above, nappies and bibs, but also outdoor clothing, are also associated with purification, whilst baby sleeping bags, nightclothes and outdoor clothing enact the sleepy and the active child, and are associated with the priority of nurturing. Equally, whilst feeding may in the first instance be seen as a form of nurturing the active infant body, or vice versa, a way of filling the stomach ahead of sleep, as demonstrated in the sociology of food and eating, this practice is also importantly connected with the teleoaffective prioritisation of love (see e.g. O'Donohoe et al. 2013), but also, as demonstrated in subsequent chapters, with protecting and purifying. In relation to the latter, for instance, the identification in Table 4.1 of 'organic' as a product category in its own right demonstrates the contemporary 'salience' of associating young children with pure products, whether these are organic foods, beauty products, woollen clothing, or wooden toys.

In the next chapters, I will argue that pecuniary value is aligned with these qualities of the young child through repeated performances. In the work of bounding these teleoaffective qualities, and in their entanglement, varied ways of knowing the infant child are made possible. In turn, this creates possibilities for commercial organisations to carve themselves a space in relation to their competitors, whilst simultaneously catering for varied consumer preferences. The first three of these teleoaffective priorities: those of loving, protecting and purifying, will be discussed in Chapters 5, 6 and 7 respectively. The teleoaffective priority of nurturing is also interesting, especially as it relates to child development; a theme that continues to receive a lot of attention in theoretical debates on children and childhood (Jenks 2005; Lee 2005; Prout 2005), following into the areas of education, consumption and consumer culture, and, in relation to young children, the question of education in family life (Pugh 2009; Vincent and Ball 2007; Vincent and Maxwell 2016). In the following chapters, the theme of nurturing is only discussed where this is entangled with the other teleoaffective qualities.

Practicing Exhibition

Consumer and trade exhibitions bring together exhibitors and visitors, and it must be assumed that the interactional opportunities these events offer is one of the reasons why exhibitors and visitors pay to attend. Here, I provide an analysis of the spatial organisation of exhibitor stands and relate this to the kinds of inter-personal interactions these afford. One thing that is clear is that exhibitor priorities were varied. As I soon discovered during my discussions with stallholders, a proportion of exhibitors share with market stallholders the need to sell goods. However, not all exhibitors appeared to be interested in direct sales, and in fact, not even all stands offered products for sale. In the following, I develop a three-fold typology of interaction scenarios that illustrates this diversity of purpose. The first scenario, where the focus is on the sale of products, services and activities, is elucidated through an analysis of time spent in a corridor with small stallholders.

Spending Time with Small Entrepreneurs

Exhibitor stands all have a specific size and location in the larger exhibition environment. As The Baby Show offers visitors such a wide collection of exhibitors and activities, one puzzle exhibitors need to address is how to catch and hold the attention of visitors, at least for a while. The stand and how it is organised clearly plays an important role, and includes considerations of size, location and internal aesthetic organisation. The small exhibitors were 'small' in part because they had small exhibition spaces, and in comparison with larger exhibitors, these 'small fry' had less freedom to organise their exhibitions in ways that offered the best opportunities for them to mingle with visitors. Like other terrestrial market environments, individual exhibitor stands are usually organised alongside each other in passageways, through which the population of visitors move. Increasing chance encounters with visitors could be achieved when stands held a corner position; were located on either side of passageways (see the discussion on the Phillips Avent stand below); were positioned at the ends of passageways; or defied location in or around passageways altogether.

During my visit to The Scottish Baby Show in 2010, I spent some time in one of the smaller corridors, which was the location of the stands of seven small exhibitors. On one side were Snugbaby Slings, Trewscots, and Dream Scene Gifts; on the other side Nurture Kids, the Scottish Cot Death Trust, Julie's Baby Gifts, and Making Waves Scotland. Snugbaby Slings was demonstrating and selling its cotton tie-slings for carrying babies and toddlers, Making Waves Scotland was a company that organised baby-swimming activities, and the other companies sold gifts for babies, young children, and those involved in their care. For instance, Trewscots sold tartan clothing for babies and toddlers, whilst Dream Scene Gifts sold personalised wooden items such as picture frames, coat hangers and nameplates for rooms and doors. The stands of these small companies varied a little, being approximately 1.5 meters in depth, and between 3 and 4 meters in width. Four of these exhibitors held corner positions, which meant that they were seen more easily as visitors made their way to this corridor. Here, exhibitors had to move out of their stands in order to 'catch' visitors.

Amongst the smaller stallholders, I heard regular 'calculation stories', in which the costs of the exhibition space, the time spent hosting,
and the costs of the visitor entry fee, were all included in a reflection
on whether the event offered good opportunities for making money.
For those who were at The Show to make a profit from direct sales,
life could be tough. One of the vendors in this corridor commented
that coming to this show meant that she really only covered her costs.
For this reason, she only came to the Glasgow show. With the main
exhibitor on the Dream Scene Gifts stand, who had personalised gifts
to order, I discussed what made people stop and purchase something.
For this stand, the best customers were mothers who were visiting with
other mothers, as they encouraged each other into a purchase. She said
she 'lost' business with couples, when women would see something
of interest on their stand, but finding that their husbands had already
moved onto the next stand, so that discussion was not possible. She also
spoke about the tactic of talking with children in prams, as this then
ensured contact with the parent. As I stood there, two couples and a
mother with a child bought nameplates, a picture frame, and a heart.

Demonstrating Complex Care Technologies

At the Dream Scene Gifts stand, there was little need for product information, but, as discussed earlier, finding out about products was one
of the reasons my interviewees gave for visiting. Some of the tools and
technologies of early childhood are complex in their design and use in
child caring practices. In relation to this, three product groups: infant
feeding technologies, cloth nappies, and travel systems, were mentioned
as reasons by my interviewees for visiting The Show. Exhibitors in
these three product groups organised their interactive exhibition practices to include product demonstrations. Expectant couple Peter and
Hannah (Couple, 24 weeks pregnant, H first time pregnant, 30s–40s,
white, self-employed) commented on how demonstrations were useful
for learning about products, their qualities, and how products fit into
everyday life:

Lydia: so you have come partly to learn about what is on offer in terms of products?

Peter: We have spoken to quite a few people about breastfeeding, haven't we? We have had a demonstration on a breast pump, so we can express and leave the baby at home with Hannah's mum.

Hannah: Like with prams, for instance, they are not all for new-borns … so you are learning which position is better for them and… what will last.

Peter: … and what the law says. There's a new law about car seats.

The brand-company Phillips Avent is a merger of the domestic technologies giant Phillips and the British infant feeding tool and food container brand Avent. This happened at a time (2006) when Avent was market leader in the UK, and as new baby feeding technologies, such as the breast pump, were becoming more popular, increasing the rationale for the merger. Figure 4.2 shows the exhibition area of Phillips Avent at the Birmingham NEC in 2009, demarcated from the larger exhibition and the corridors through the cream-coloured floor space, with demonstration hubs in the middle of this space, and four exhibition 'towers' in strategic locations. At this show, the brand's exhibition was spread out over two areas, with one of the broad passageways splitting the exhibition up into two sections. The exhibition tower seen on the far right of Fig. 4.2 points to the location of the second part of the stand, with the demonstration area pictured in the main frame. The area on the far right held the company's stocks, and here visitors could make purchases to take home with them, benefitting from The Show's special offers. Visitors may be seen walking in between the two areas, and the photograph shows how a number are crowding around the demonstration desk at the front. Seats are located around the desks for visitors to sit on, and each desk has a little banner poking up with the words: 'HOW DO I …'?

One of the interesting qualities of this exhibition stand is how open it is. There are no walls to be seen, and the exhibition towers with the brand logo Phillips Avent at the top ensure that the stand can be seen from some distance away. This is an example of how brand companies, who have the capacity to invest in their attendance at The Show, can

Fig. 4.2 Demonstrations at the Phillips Avent stand at Birmingham NEC Baby Show (2009)

purchase their visibility, which, as demonstrated here, is enhanced by stand design. With stand arrangements along both sides of a visitor corridor, and alongside two corridors, the brand company enhances visitor attention: whilst walking through any of these corridors there is no competitor stand in the near vicinity. The exhibition towers illustrate how this brand company sells a suite of tools and technologies, with the breast pump, the feeding tool steriliser, and the bottle warmer, as the three main electrical 'appliances'. The dominant use of white in the colour scheme and the photographic images of baby and carer intimacy in the exhibition towers, speak of the binary qualities of scientific reputability and intergenerational intimacy.

I join the stand on a Saturday afternoon, when the demonstrator is in the middle of his presentation. He is surrounded by a clutch of prospective parents who are listening in. Standing there, we hear about 'what the products can do' and 'what you can do with the products'. We also listen into stories about everyday life with a small baby, and the potential challenges of reaching a consensus with a partner about 'how to do things' when bottle feeding a baby. We also hear about the diverse 'doing scenarios' that highlight the uses and usefulness of the different tools, and we learn important scientific 'rules' about infant feeding, for instance, that feeding tools need to be kept germ free. The demonstrator we listen to presents himself in an informal way, as 'a dad' who does not 'know it all', though is nevertheless cheekily clever. He discusses the brand's three different tool sterilisers, making a number of observations in quick succession:

> Their traditional steriliser is organised so that 6 bottles may be sterilised at one time, along with their tops and items from the breast pump. It works in 8 minutes and then stays sterile for 6 hours (Did I get that right!? ... searching on the website, the answer is 'yes'). However, once it is opened, the contents are no longer sterile. Given that their bottle system, including the lid, makes for a sterile environment for 24 hours (Have I got that right!?), he suggests that parents make up the number of bottles they need during a 24 hours day, to store them in the fridge, and to use them as and when they are needed, along with the digital bottle warmer. Their alternative digital steamer works in 6 minutes, but may be programmed to re-sterilise over a 24-hour period. At £45, it is £15 more expensive than the £30 traditional steriliser. The final and cheaper product is a steriliser for the microwave, which works in 4 minutes and once done, will remain sterile for 24 hours (not, I presume, once the lid has been taken off). He outlines its advantages by stating that it can be stored in the microwave, so does not take up kitchen surface space and is tidied away when not in use.

These fieldnotes suggest how easily consumers are invited to get to grips with a range of product and pricing complexities before deciding whether and what to purchase. Knowledge about germs and tool contamination is embedded in this discussion, and diverse 'hours of sterility' demarcates the different products, with the suggestion that longer sterility time means a better quality product is purchased, and obviously for more money. References are also made to the challenges of the temporal organisation of everyday life: here with specific reference to the practicalities of infant feeding. Finally, the microwave steriliser is recommended for its space saving qualities, which is a practical concern that will appeal to people with small kitchens or those who appreciate a minimalist style. He continues his story, moving from the sterilisers to the bottle and baby food heater, and then the breast pumps. Along the way, his tells jokes to keep the attention of his audience. For instance, when he advices one prospective dad not to try the electric breast pump on himself, which is followed by a quip in which he tells the audience how ineffectual he was trying out the handheld breast pump on his wife, thus emphasising the better use value of the more expensive electric pump.

Show-Casing the Brand

In relation to the larger brands, two peculiarities kept me thinking for a while. One was that there were some recurring brands, like Volvo—which was a sponsor of The Show for some years—and some cleaning product brands—like Fairy and Comfort—for which the presence in this world of new families and early childhood did not seem all that clear. A second peculiarity was that these brands seemed to be at The Show primarily for the purpose of 'brand display'. Comfort and Fairy frequently occupied extra large exhibition areas, where nothing much was apparently happening apart from exhibition staff handing out balloons and branded bags with information brochures and product samples. Brand placement, it seemed to me, was a process of becoming recognised by potentially new customers, perhaps with the prospective of this brand awareness being carried over into other retailing contexts and environments at a later date. It was very clear that these larger brand-companies had larger marketing budgets, with which they purchased the large exhibition areas, advertising space on The Baby Show website and in the guide, ceiling banners that were visible throughout the show, and handed-out vast quantities of logoed bags and balloons to large numbers of visitors. But in terms of exhibitor–visitor interaction, the exhibition practices here seemed far removed from the kind of interpersonal interactions that are discussed in most ethnographic studies on shopping (e.g. Cook 2008; Everts and Jackson 2009; vom Lehn 2014), that characterise what is typical for small businesses. Instead, in these exhibitions, communication happened in faceless and mediated ways. I will return to this point in Chapter 9. As discussed above, recent years have seen these brands co-opted into sponsorship of a broad range of visitor services.

The 'brand placement' scenario was elaborated in some interesting ways by, what may be seen as smaller brand-companies that had a clearer 'home' in this particular commercial world. These demonstrated slightly different purposes for being at these shows. One was building a customer contacts database. Commercial players operating in this particular market face challenges related to the character of the client group. Pregnant women, prospective parents, and families with small infants, are not only dispersed amongst the general population, but, as discussed in Chapter 3, also move in and out of this life course stage at significant speed. Time is therefore of the essence for marketers, who have to continuously get acquainted with a renewed client group as people move from pregnancy into the early stages of parenthood, whilst new families become established families with growing children. For vitamin supplement products like Sanatogen Mother-To-Be and Pregnacare, who trade on the need for folic acid in the early weeks of pregnancy, the window of opportunity is very small indeed! Some exhibitors therefore invited visitors to leave their contact details by entering prize draws. In completing one for Philips Avent at the East Midlands Baby and Toddler Show in 2009, the form offered me various tick-boxes giving me choices about how I wished to be contacted by the company in the future. In recent years, brand companies have shifted the work of building a contact database to their online interactional environments, for instance, through invitations for new families to sign up for baby clubs.

Conclusion

The purpose of this chapter was to start to develop insight into the organisation of the business of child caring. I concentrated on the consumer exhibition to approach the matter of how this business is organised because, as I argued in Chapter 3, it presents a distinct and under-researched commercial environment in its own right, in which people, products and the socio-technical qualities of terrestrial exchange encounters comingle. I also argued that it represented the broader business of child caring, providing access to other encounter platforms, including terrestrial and online retailing, brands and advertising, lifestyle magazines, the home party, and the broad range of services, and products and their packaging.

The consumer exhibition provides insight into common organisational qualities of the business of child caring, some of which may be seen as distinct to this specific terrain. First, evident in the organisation of The Baby Show and other encounter platforms is the attention to, and organisation of products, services and information, in accordance with the various stages of this life course. This is not only a matter of age-grading young children (Cook 2004), but also the staging of distinct experiential phases in the process of becoming parents, including the experiences of pregnancy, birth, the early weeks, and so on. Accounting of these experiential phases is very common, and on websites can take on the form of extensive informational content about what prospective parents may expect as they move further into the process of parental becoming over time. It is clear that pecuniary value practices are aligned with these experiential phases, and indeed, as is the case for children (Cook 2000; Cook and Kaiser 2004), these 'phases' are actively construed in the process. Second, information and education—the subject matter of Chapter 8—is another ubiquitous element of the organisation of the business of child caring that may be found in the consumer exhibition, and in other assorted sources of information, ranging from parenting magazines, through to product information brochures, with websites serving as a prominent contemporary mediated technology for the transmission of content. A third shared organisational element of the business of child caring is the techno-medical-science presence. The manifestation of techno-medical-science in the business of child caring relates to the information that is provided, and includes the role of experts and expert entrepreneurs. Techno-medical-science density serves other purposes, which will be foci for further discussion in Chapters 6, 8 and 9. Finally, The Baby Show provides access to the quality of entertainment and spectacle, which is shared with other commercial environments, including the parenting magazine. As witnessed by the generation of commentaries on the phantasmagorical qualities of commercial culture, this is of course also a generic feature of the organisation of exchange encounters.

In addition to the identification of these organisational dimensions, this chapter made a start with an analysis of the content of the business of child caring. Drawing on Warde's (2014) argument that the existence of a practice as a social entity may be recognised in the material culture that points to it, and that is associated with the practical performances of the practice, I cross-referenced an analysis of the product brochures I collected at the visited exhibitions with product categories on the websites of major retailers, to draw up a definitive set of practice pathways of child caring. These were dressing, cleaning, feeding, keeping healthy and safe, and nurturing (soothing & stimulating). I argued that the product categories that mapped onto these pathways pointed to four teleoaffective qualities of child caring; those of loving, protecting, purifying and nurturing, and that the entanglement of these qualities was the most common way of presentation within the pathways.

In the next part of this book—Chapters 5, 6 and 7—I argue that the teleoaffective structure of child caring, or, the definition/knowing of the entity 'the young child', is an actively performed element in the interactional practices in this market. At the heart of this lies a ceaseless effort to confirm the importance of the young child. Attributing the qualities of vulnerability and purity onto the loveable young child, attending to the various possible nuances of those qualities, whilst cross-referencing with the organisational features discussed above, is the prime method in which, in the business of child caring, the value of the young child is aligned with pecuniary value. In the final chapters (8 and 9), I return to the organisational qualities of this field of commercial practice, and consider how these form moral responses to the teleoaffective structure of child caring. In this discussion, it becomes possible to see how the young child is not only performed in this field of practice, but how these become 'structural' outcomes that frame the possibilities of action by the carriers of the practice of child caring.

Bibliography

Baxter, J.E. 2005. *The archaeology of childhood: Children, gender, and material culture.* Lanham, MD: Rowman and Littlefield.

Calvert, K.L.F. 1992. *Children in the house: The material culture of early childhood, 1600–1900*, 142. Boston: Northeastern University Press.

Cook, D.T. 2000. The rise of 'the toddler' as subject and as merchandising category in the 1930s. In *New forms of consumption. Consumers, culture, and commodification*, ed. M. Gottdiener, 111–130. Lanham, MD: Rowman and Littlefield.

Cook, D.T. 2004. *The commodification of childhood: The children's clothing industry and the rise of the child consumer.* Durham, NC: Duke University Press.

Cook, D.T. (ed.). 2008. *Lived experiences of public consumption: Encounters with value in marketplaces on five continents.* Basingstoke: Palgrave Macmillan.

Cook, D.T., and S. Kaiser. 2004. Betwixt and be tween: Age ambiguity and the sexualization of the female consuming subject. *Journal of Consumer Culture* 4 (2): 203–227.

Everts, J., and P. Jackson. 2009. Modernisation and the practices of contemporary food shopping. *Environment and Planning D: Society and Space* 27 (5): 917–935.

Ingold, T. 2000. *The perception of the environment: Essays on livelihood, dwelling and skill.* London: Routledge.

Jenks, C. 2005. *Childhood.* London: Routledge.

Kehily, M.J. 2014. For the love of small things: Consumerism and the making of maternal identities. *Young Consumers* 15 (3): 227–238.

Lee, N. 2005. *Childhood and human value: Development, separation and separability.* Maidenhead: The Open University Press.

Lury, C. 1996. *Consumer culture.* Cambridge: Polity Press.

Martens, L. 2010. The cute, the spectacle and the practical: Narratives of new parents and babies at the baby show. In *Childhood and consumer culture*, ed. D. Buckingham and V. Tingstad. London: Palgrave Macmillan.

Martens, L. 2014. Selling infant safety: Entanglements of childhood preciousness, vulnerability and unpredictability. Special issue entitled, *"New Parents and Young Children in Consumer Culture" of Young Consumers* 15 (3): 239–250.

McCracken, G. 1988. *Culture and consumption: New approaches to the symbolic character of consumer goods and activities.* Bloomington and Indianopolis: Indiana University Press.

Mennell, S. 1996. *All manners of food: Eating and taste in England and France from the Middle Ages to the present.* Chicago: University of Illinois Press.

O'Donohoe, S., M. Hogg, P. Maclaran, L. Martens, and L. Stevens (eds.). 2013. *Motherhoods, markets and consumption: The making of mothers in contemporary western cultures.* London: Routledge.

Pugh, A.J. 2009. *Longing and belonging: Parents, children, and consumer culture.* Berkeley, CA: University of California Press.

Prout, A. 2005. *The future of childhood.* London: Routledge.

Vincent, C., and S.J. Ball. 2007. 'Making up' the middle-class child: Families, activities and class dispositions. *Sociology* 41 (6): 1061–1077.

Vincent, C., and C. Maxwell. 2016. Parenting priorities and pressures: Furthering understanding of 'concerted cultivation'. *Discourse: Studies in the Cultural Politics of Education* 37 (2): 269–281.

VOICE Group. 2010a. Buying into motherhood? Problematic consumption and ambivalence in transitional phases. *Consumption, Markets and Culture* 13 (4): 373–397.

VOICE Group. 2010b. Motherhood, marketization, and consumer vulnerability. *Journal of Macromarketing* 30 (4): 384–397.

vom Lehn, D. 2014. Timing is money: Managing the floor in sales interaction at street-market stalls. *Journal of Marketing Management* 30 (13–14): 1448–1466.

Warde, A. 2014. After taste: Culture, consumption and theories of practice. *Journal of Consumer Culture* 14 (3): 279–303.

5

Loving: Emotional Movements

Introduction

This chapter presents an analysis of the aesthetic organisation of the commercial spaces and objects of early childhood. The discussion is based on my ethnographic research at consumer and trade exhibitions; examinations of exhibitor displays, brand-company webpages, and products; and my conversations with new and prospective parents. The aim is to demonstrate the role aesthetic practices and conventions play in the enactment of the particular understanding of 'the young child' as loveable. Love in family life, and the primacy of the love for young children, often sits in an implicit way in scholarly discussions of child caring. In Furedi's (2001) *Paranoid Parenting*, for instance, the reader learns a lot about what makes contemporary child caring an anxiety provoking experience, but this discussion proceeds from an implicit understanding that 'children are worth it', that they are 'loved' and 'cared about', and that they therefore are deserving of care and attention (see also Lawler 2000). In *The Normal Chaos of Love*, Beck and Beck-Gernsheim (1995) argue that it is from this foundation of emotionality and affect that all other parenting concerns derive their meaning.

© The Author(s) 2018
L. Martens, *Childhood and Markets*, Studies in Childhood and Youth,
https://doi.org/10.1057/978-1-137-31503-8_5

For these reasons, I start the discussion of the teleoaffective structuration of child caring with an exploration of how young children are performed as precious and lovable entities in the stuff of early childhood, and in the sales practices and materialities I explored.

Harris (2001: xi) warns that everyday life is characterised by a lack of awareness of the mundane aesthetics that characterise it. Yet, early childhood is associated with a distinct set of aesthetic conventions, and I argue below that these are promulgated in the organisation of sales practices. Understanding of the ways in which early childhood is aesthetically comprehended, in the display practices, visual representations and objects that I encountered during my research, in quite distinct and customary ways, matured over repeated encounters. The discussion starts with the aesthetic elements of commercial culture, and focuses on the use of colour schemes and the mobilisation of 'the cute' in playthings and display practices. This is followed with a discussion on how carefully fabricated images and objects provide insight into the ways in which the emotional qualities of early childhood are not just conveyed in visual ways, but can serve to induce multi-sensory emotional responses through intimations of touch, intimacy and closeness that connect with memories and the imagination (Pink 2009). I finish with a discussion of the material practices of love making in family life, which shows that the aesthetisation of early childhood is not limited to commercial practices.

Knowing 'The Young Child' and Mobilising Adult Emotions

In her critical appreciation of the practices of dining out, Joanne Finkelstein (1989) talks at some length about how the ambience created in eating establishments is a salient tactic through which restaurateurs orchestrate the experiences of diners. Commercial space obtains a specific ambience through the manner in which it is aesthetically and sensually ordered and organised, and the mood of such settings adds to (or detracts from) the desirability of the commodities and services on offer (see also Gregson and Crewe 1997). As the most complex commercial environment in this research, The Baby Show managed to harness the mood of early childhood through the use of pastel colour schemes in the carpeting of the floor space, which alternated between pastel pink and blue in consecutive shows. Another example is the design of The Baby Show Stage, the back-stage border of which was coloured with the use of soft pinks and reds at the 2006 show in Birmingham, whilst the stage was surrounded by soft cushions, for kids to lounge, sit and play on.[1] At the same time, it could be argued that The Show's reality as a spectacle contrasted with certain expectations of an appropriate baby-hood ambience. As expressed by one of The Show's experts, speaking on the topic of calming of babies in preparation for sleep, The Show contained too much stimulation to make it an appropriate event for very young children. Crowd noise and density, the continuous noise emanating from The Baby Show Stage, and the bright lights, all created distance from the expectation of quietness, peace and calm as appropriate qualities of early childhood.

A fuller understanding of what constitutes an appropriate infantile ambience, and the aesthetic practices feeding into this, may be gleaned by observing the multitude of aesthetic accomplishments achieved in the individual exhibitor stands at The Show. Not surprising is the fact that colour schemes, including pastel blues, pinks, lilacs and so-called neutral colours[2] were very much in abundance in exhibitor stands, and across other encounter platforms. Whether we browse the website of a brand company like Johnson's Baby, or contemplate the colours dominating the Baby Sense[3] stand at the Earls Court exhibition in October 2009, they tell a similar visual tale—that peaceful babyhood symbolically equates with pastel colours and colour schemes. Pastel colours

---

[1]These simultaneously ensured that if toddlers clambered onto the stage, they would not hurt themselves when falling off.

[2]Neutral colours (including pastel yellows and creams) are colours which do not gender categorise the baby, but which are nevertheless suitable for 'the young child'.

[3]Baby Sense is a South African company, which exhibited at The Show during some of the years included in my research. It sells a variety of baby soothing products. The company's website, first accessed in 2009, and again in 2017, is http://www.babysense.co.za/.

suggest calm and tranquillity, and used in the surroundings of babies, whether in furnishings, everyday objects or baby clothing, emphasises that quality in early childhood. Muted and pale colours were used profusely, though not solely, in a range of baby clothing, blankets and wraps, whilst numerous cuddly looking bunnies, bears, mice, ducks and other animals were presented in subdued pastel, rather than primary colours, used either as decorative materials or as objects for sale at The Show.

This is not to say that primary colours were absent. Indeed, the opposite is true. Yet, in contrast to pastel shades, primary colours were used to accentuate the active, growing and awake infant. Thus, activity blankets; the toddler's first cutlery, cups and plates; toddler toys; and toddler gear and furnishings, generally came in primary colours. Pastel colour schemes do not seem appropriate as an expression of the bouncy toddler, though the gender demarcations evident for babies, the pink and blue pastels used in various baby products, find their continuation in more vibrant pinks and lilacs for toddler girls with primary colour reds, blues, greens and yellows, dominating articles for toddler boys. These more vibrant colours are readily recognisable when visiting the children's clothing departments of specialist retailers. When glancing into and across the retailing space of the out-of-town store of Mothercare, first in the direction of the baby clothing section in the middle, and then to the left and the right, where clothing for older children is displayed, by gender, one can see the accentuation of subdued and soft colours in the baby clothing range contrasted with the primary and vibrant colours found in the clothing for toddlers and older young children.

Moving Objects: Cute, Memories and Emotions

Meet Sophie the Giraffe.[4] Made of rubber, she is at once soft and cute. Cream coloured with orange-brown spots predictably decorating her body, she also has, unpredictably, rosy cheeks and round black eyes that

---

[4]Sophie the Giraffe, along with some other soft toys for young children, is produced by the French company Vulli. In 2017, Sophie had her own website. See http://www.sophielagirafe.fr/en/.

look out at the observer with a sense of innocence and a small measure of surprise. Nothing in her expression marks her out as threatening—though some might disagree! What are your thoughts? Sophie is innocence incorporated. She stands upright on four solid feet, is about 5 inches tall, with a tail that is draped delicately over her hind leg. When squeezed she makes that funny squeaky noise. Ultimately, Sophie is recognisable in the rubber & squeaky toy of babyhoods of days-gone-by which, unlike her, have not withstood the test of time.

Looking at Sophie from within her presentational box, or from her website, something about her biography is revealed. "Born in Paris in 1961," the packaging proudly proclaims! Since her birth in 1961, Sophie has become a commonplace object in baby-containing households in France and a small thing endowed with 'big love'. In France, nine out of 10 children are said to have, or have had, a Sophie in their lives, and she is now passed on from generation to generation, all sucking her feet as babies, and perhaps including her in animal play at a later stage. Still produced in France, nothing much has changed about her since 1961, either regarding her appearance—which many will recognise as embodying a measure of Retro Chique—or about the materials that go into her production. In fact, the non-toxic rubber and vegetable dyes used in her production are said to attract the type of adult clientele that seeks the natural. Whilst Sophie has remained a French secret for most of her life, as my research progressed, moves were underfoot towards her internationalisation, and anno 2017, it is clear that she very much appeals to new parents and other interested adults outside France[5]; those who, unlike their French counterparts, do not have Sophie etched emotionally into their own childhood memories. As such, Sophie combines a set of child and adult 'interests', serving as a tactile object through which the young child can explore the world through the different senses; a teether to gnaw on when the gums

---

[5]I first came across Sophie when speaking with her then UK distributors at the Baby Product Association trade exhibition. Since then, Sophie has become popular in the UK; something that has been stimulated by discussions of parenting internet sites. To the careful observer, she may be seen sharing the living room couch with Labour leader Ed Miliband, when he fronted The Guardian newspaper's weekend magazine in March 2011.

are sore whilst teething; an animal toy that may finds its way into the menagerie when the child gets older; and an object of adult interest because of its retro credentials that spark childhood memories beyond those experienced across family generations in France.

Sophie is a typical example of the aesthetic of cute embodied by images and objects that often represent 'an animal'. In Sophie, we recognise without fail a 'real' giraffe. Along with her patterned body and the long neck that connects her body with her head, she sports those two soft horns that are situated between the ears that crown a giraffe's head. But Sophie is also very much a misrepresentation, or, as Harris (2001: 3) would have it, her features suggest 'the grotesque, the malformed'—something some people experience with a sense of alarm. Through her big round black eyes, the rosy colouring on her almost human cheeks, and legs that, whilst allowing her to stand upright, adopt the cute in their proportions, she is ultimately an imagined creature; the culmination of a designer's understanding of the ideals of childhood, encapsulating within it a set of desirable infantile qualities alongside an adult appreciation of the diminutive.

She is part of an extensive assortment of cute animal-shaped toys, figurines and visual representations that decorate and crowd everyday life. We come across them when visiting Toys-R-Us, the local card and gift shop, when peeping into the pram of a new-born baby, seen displayed on the mantelpiece of the lady who is selling her home or sitting next to a sad looking young child on the billboard advertisement of a national charity. Animals of all sorts, shapes and designs, with bodily proportions and features that often emphasize the diminutive in grotesque ways, serve not only as children's toys, but also as decoration on the products and tools used in childcare, as central characters on well-wishing cards, calendars, posters and diaries, and as china and retro figurines in the homes of people who display them as ornaments. Traditionally, only certain animals would do, the teddy bear along with the bunny rabbit perhaps enjoying longevity beyond others (Hinde and Barden 1985; Morris et al. 1995; Varga 2009a, b). Today, it would seem that with the right kind of bodily 'improvements' any animal or young child can be turned into 'cute' to serve as companions for sprucing up the emotional lives of adults (Cross 2004a, b).

"Oh, How Cute!" Affect Inducing Display Practices

Returning to The Baby Show, one common element of aesthetic practice is the decoration of exhibitor stands and baby gear, such as baby
beds, car seats and prams, with cute objects and imagery. At The Show,
nursery furniture—such as infant beds—and storage containers in
exhibition stands, were typically 'draped' with, and thus beautified by,
soft cuddly animals. Whilst early childhood ambience, recognizable in
commercial environments like Mothercare, internet websites and baby
consumer exhibitions, says something about what it is that makes these
spaces about the infant, and thus, what a young child is, in this instance
we see how various *goods*, and more generally, the larger utilitarian tools
of child caring in family life, are signposted as 'about' young children in
an otherwise dominant adult aesthetic. Subject to distinct fashions, car
seats, travel systems and prams stand out for their lack of a clear visual
connection with infants in their visual appearance. In a sense, these are
products *for* adults, reflecting and adopting an adult aesthetic through
the use of colour schemes incorporating combinations of darker and
often dull colours. Black, navy blues, greys, browns, and cream colours
without doubt generate a better aesthetic fit with the interior decor of
the car, than with the small creature that is encapsulated within it. But
there is also a vibrant market supplying stimulation toys, to be fitted to
a variety of child carriers and furniture, to keep the child busy and animated when 'stuck' in the car seat or waiting for dinnertime. These typically come in the form of funny and cute looking animals made with
special fabrics that allow the active child to engage in multi-sensory
experiences. Their addition to the car seat or the pram makes such products more clearly recognizable as child centred. An interesting contrast
to the subdued colour schemes of these 'publicly' visible child caring
tools are the flamboyant baby bouncers and other indoor seats sold by
Fisher Price for use in the home. It may be that the baby bouncer that
is positioned amongst the living room's other furniture says something
about the acceptability of a more dominant child aesthetic in the private
sphere of the home, where the emotionality of newfound parenthood
and the sacred quality of the young child may be allowed to blossom.

The aesthetic of cute was also used as an affect inducing display practice at The Show. This became clear to me when I had my own exhibition stand at the Birmingham Baby Show in 2006. My tiny 1.5 square meter stand bordered on the much larger exhibition space of the UK online pregnancy and infant fashion company Blooming Marvellous. The side of the Blooming Marvellous stand that bordered ours displayed a series of bodysuits, hanging on clothes hangers and down from the stand's ceiling board alongside one another (see Fig. 5.1). Each bodysuit featured a catchy slogan. Enclosed in a red heart shape adorning one suit was the slogan: "made with 100% love". Other baby grows sported catchphrases like "don't wake me, I'll wake you!" and "I love my daddy", which could be found on other baby articles at The Show. During our days exhibiting, we would see visitors apparently approaching our stand with gleeful expressions on their faces, pulling their companion along whilst verbally uttering the expression: "Oh, how cute!" right in front of our stand, only to then move that little bit further along to examine the bodysuits on display at the next stand. I was left with the realisation that it was not my children's artwork, that I had brought along to decorate the white walls of our stand, that made these visitors so delighted.

The word 'cute' seemed to operate as a self explanatory and brief verbal expression of affect, made by visitors who, in their journey through The Show, could at times be overheard exclaiming: "Oh, how cute!" when something was recognised as such in their field of vision, confirming a shared sense of emotional experience with each other. As well as such verbal exclamations, visitors joined each other in lingering over products, to touch and feel them. One example was a baby bed, where the bed linen that was decorated with a soft furry Tiny Tatty Teddie was, according to the exhibitor, subject to much joint fingering. Yet, 'cute' is not so much part of the discursive elaboration and understanding of childhood. Here is an uncommon verbalisation of 'cute' in my conversation with Sarah and Terry (23 weeks, first time parents, 30s, white, professional) who speak about the place of 'cute', alternately conceptualised by them as 'sweet' and 'nice', in their selection decision for a baby rocker.

Lydia: Are you into cute? Sarah: Yeah, definitely. Lydia: What sort of things? Sarah: I bought today… as we got a rocker and I definitely went for one

Fig. 5.1 Baby bodysuits hanging, in washing line fashion, on the side of an open exhibition area at The Baby Show

that, well, as well as it being able to rock and being nicely padded and everything, I did go for the cutest one as well. There is an element of that. It is funny, as the practical side of me says 'It doesn't have to be cute, they don't really care if it is that cute or not' but then of course there is that need. I do definitely feel the need at the moment for things to be quite sweet and quite cute, so yeah… Lydia: What about you? Terry: Less so I think, I am more practical. But if it is not much more money, then yeah, you have got to get something that looks that little bit nicer. Lydia: What is it about cute? This place is full of cute! Sarah: Don't know. Lydia: It is like you go round and you have to smile and… Terry: Babies, they do things to people!

Other interviewees had really nothing to say about 'what cute is' and discussion about cute was never volunteered.

In this examination of the aesthetic organisation of display at The Baby Show, it is apparent that differences in personhood are narrated visually in the use of colours and objects. Thus, through the use of pastel colours, the youngest of children are associated with quietude and calm, with the more active, awake and learning child symbolised in vibrant and primary colour schemes. Colour schemes extend the differentiation of children on the basis of age to differentiation on the basis of gender. Young children are further set apart from adults through the careful demarcation of a child-like aesthetic encapsulated in the larger objects used for the purposes of everyday life in families with small children. Smallness in goods, symbolised for instance in the cute and cuddly toy, and the very process of valorising the small, speaks of the young child as loveable (see also Kehily 2014). In Chapter 7, I will go on to argue that products, like the baby grows discussed earlier, are also a resource for carers to create adorable infants, thus purifying 'the young child' in accordance with ideas as to what they should be like.

Moving Images: Performing 'Natural' Embodied Intimacy

A vibrant industry that satisfies the demand for pictorial representations of infants operates with a set of standards of what counts as beautiful in young children. Rotund and corpulent looking babies are no doubt still held to be beautiful in many cultures, perhaps representing, as done in societies and at times when food scarcity ruled the day, the desire for abundance that also implicated what was deemed beautiful in the female body. Plump looking baby angels are common historical figures found in paintings and statuettes, often accompanied by equally corpulent female figures (Holland 2004). Even in the post-war years, chubby babies were regarded as the epitome of the healthy child and a sign of good mothering practices; something that was accentuated by the growth in popularity of infant bottle-feeding alongside the realisation that new-borns put on weight more quickly if fed on formula milk (van den Cruyce et al. 2009). Even though the weighty baby body has been subject of much recent criticism, especially from the medical-science lobby, my discussion with health visitors at The Baby Show suggested that chubbiness remained an indicator of the body beautiful in babies in affluent societies.

Young children may be seen to work as fashion models at the consumer exhibitions I visited, and their carers are invited to have their babies and toddlers photographed to become 'the next face' in promotional materials, on the front pages of magazines and in regional newspapers. These practices, and the baby models who may be seen in photographic materials used to decorate exhibitor displays, product packaging, product brochures and in company sales magazines and websites, all indicate that there is a burgeoning entrepreneurial culture 'out there' that seeks, creates and displays 'cute young children' photographically, catering for the dotting and desiring adult gaze (see also Cook 2009). In contrast to the sheer abundance of such visual representations, real 'flesh and blood' babies were not 'used' in exhibitor displays[6] or, to move one step further, offered 'for sale' there.[7] Baby dolls were used only sparingly, for instance, by exhibitors who were demonstrating the use of their products in care practices, such as the cloth nappy. Only one exhibitor was found who used a reborn baby doll[8] in their exhibition display.

The websites discussed below have been selected for demonstrating embodied intimacy with a peaceful and quiet infant, constructing a form of affective interembodiment in a perfect sanitised space. I discuss two examples. In the first, I provide an analysis of a range of brand-company websites that sell orality tools.[9] In the second, I discuss

---

[6]It was, however, not uncommon for smaller commercial players (family businesses) to bring their young children and babies with them to The Baby Show, and on one of my excursions, a toddler could be seen to help demonstrate the uses of the baby sling, by sitting, facing outwards, wrapped up against the body of his father.

[7]The question whether infants can be 'for sale', can take on monetary value in their own right, is reflected in the culturally contentious examples of adoption, surrogate mothering, and IVF conception. These practices were not present in the commercial environments researched here, confirming the heightening of cultural contradictions around such practices when associated with pecuniary value. See Traver (2013) for a discussion on adoption; Thompson (2005) on IVF, and Taylor et al. (2004) for other examples.

[8]Reborn baby dolls are dolls that are made to look and feel like real babies, by crafts persons who call themselves artists.

[9]These are tools that go into the mouths of infants, and can include as diverse a range of products as feeding bottles, soothers or pacifiers, teething tools, early toothbrushes, early cutlery and drinking cups.

the website of Johnson's Baby, a brand-company well known for its baby cleanliness and soothing products. The visual displays on these sites call to mind olfactory and other sensory memories of familial intimacy and love. [10]

The natural perfection of the baby body and the embodied closeness of infant and carer open the web-based encounters Phillips Avent and NUK International have designed for visitors of their sites. On the Phillips Avent site, the reader is welcomed by a short moving image, which keeps repeating itself. In the clip, we first witness a blue-eyed, smiley and contented baby with a round face. The baby is very much 'awake' and old enough to communicate with a carer, who is not visible in the clip, in an embodied way in which the expressive eyes and the mouth movements are highlights. We see the mouth moving in a brief expression of happy excitement, backed up by the baby's sparkling eyes, before its facial expression returns to a more quiet and open one that seems to suggest expectation. The focus then moves to the baby's hands, and we see the fingers moving delicately, before the camera homes in on the moving feet, captured in the still in Fig. 5.2, which are folded onto one another, suggestive of relaxation. The focus then returns to the baby's facial image, and the sequence is repeated.

---

[10]The websites analysed here were those of Johnson's Baby and the major brand-companies that supply feeding and orality tools: Phillips Avent, Tommee Tippee, NUK, MAM, and Dr. Browns. For Johnson's Baby, the UK sites for 2009 and 2011 were analysed. The sites of the orality tool companies analysed all date from April and May 2013. Tommee Tippee is an American owned company, which has a major production site in the UK. Philips Avent is the merged outcome of the British infant feeding tools brand company Avent, and the Dutch domestic technologies giant Philips. The merger took place in 2006, which signals the shift to a 'mixed feeding' narrative (see Chapter 7). MAM is of Austrian origin. NUK originates in Germany. These brand companies all trade globally. The website content of these international commercial organisations change regularly, and many maintain different sites for specific countries. In 2013, for instance, NUK had a 'generic' international English language site, and also sites for a range of different countries. For some countries, the organization of the site differed considerably from that of the international site, for others, some or all of the materials used on the international site were used. For NUK and MAM, I analysed the international English language sites. For the other companies, I analysed their UK sites. As website content changes over time, the procedure I used was to copy the website content of each brand-company by making screen prints of each page of information, and by storing any additional materials, including any information brochures that were available from the sites. This allowed for the archival of textual and visual materials to return to later.

This type of embodied perfection is replicated on other feeding tool websites. Images of babies and small infants, by themselves, are common on all the sites. So too are babies in an embodied embrace with a carer. The gender of the carer differs between sites, with NUK's International site showing babies in interembodiment only with mothers, whilst the Tommee Tippee site includes pictures of fathers and their babies, pointing to the active work these companies do to 'distinguish' themselves from the competition. As well as featuring fathers, along with a website colouration that contains a lot of black, on this site the dominant infant has dark curly hair and intense brown eyes, looking alertly into the camera, and offers a diversion from the 'white' infants mostly pictured. Again, setting itself apart from Phillips Avent and NUK, the MAM website visualizes the older 'toddler' infant, usually featured with one of the brand-company's tools, and the repeated slogan 'because you are unique'.

One of the curiosities here is the apparent cultural acceptability of picturing babies in and through their nudity. Varying degrees of nudity appear to be very much allowable and serve to enact the perfection of infant skin and the rounded beauty of miniature body parts. As illustrated by the folded feet in Fig. 5.2, body parts, especially faces, hands and feet, are frequently framed, though reproductive organs are excluded. When it remains culturally problematic to picture human nudity, the visual convention that normalizes baby nudity is one way in which 'normal cultural rules' become redundant in infant humans, confirming their 'otherness' through the division between nature and culture (Lupton 2013).

Johnson's Baby exhibited at the Earl's Court Baby Show in 2009, when I took away a bag with two brochures, a coupon card and a card to enter a price draw. The exhibition stand stood out for its massive visual displays of mothers with their babies, asleep, and engaged in bathing and soothing rituals, which could be seen from some distance away. After The Show, I visited the brand-company's website in 2009, and again in 2011. In the photographic imagery displayed on the site in 2009, mothers and babies were clearly models, staged and captured just at the right moment to accentuate an image of perfect bliss. The imagery in 2011 had a clearer touch of 'the real' about it,

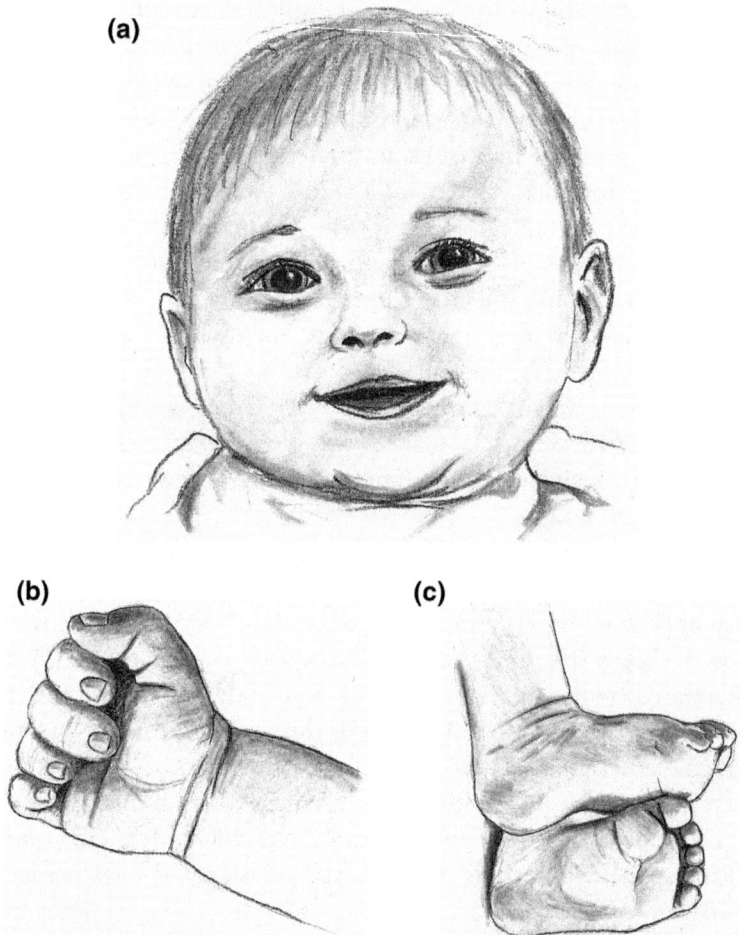

Fig. 5.2 Smiling face, hands and feet as commonly visualised baby body parts in sales literature

with attention going into collapsing the distance between the imagery and the viewer's personal experiences. Of interest is how these images convey a sense of the perfect mother-child relationship, not simply visually, as they implicate the potential multi-sensory bodily pleasures of an embodied intimacy with a young child, suggested through the practices of bathing, massage and bed time routines. Here are images, which suggest that bodily touch and closeness are possible and desirable, and ultimately pleasurable and satisfying. For some observing the intimacy that unfolds, additional sensory experiences may come into play. For instance, in mothers' memories of the smell of their baby's head, and, perhaps needless to say, in the smell of Johnson's baby shampoo itself, which is etched into the memories of generations of people, whose mothers used this lasting brand of baby shampoo in their own cleansing practices over time. In this way, the sanitised and staged images and videos, presented on these websites, operate in ways similar to that of film, engendering a haptic conversion, whereby the image invokes a sense of love and intimacy that moves from the visual to that of embodied multi-sensory closeness in memory (Marks 2000).

Harris (2001: 9) argues that 'we' are not content with babies 'in their natural state'. The photographic imagery found in brand-product websites, product brochures and packaging, and parenting magazines, are visual orchestrations that highlight the positive emotional qualities of caring for an infant child. These sanitised representations do not present other realities: for instance, of leaky infant and material bodies, or of the fretful child (Brownlie and Leith 2011; Lupton 2013), though at The Baby Show, these realities were present in the form of products and potions that helped counter the undesirable elements of care for the young child.

Practices of 'Personal Life' Love Making

Couple Sally and Dave (32 weeks pregnant, both have sons from previous relationships, aged 28 and 37, white, working class) were visiting The Baby Show partly because they had received free tickets. During their discussion, both spoke at some length about their extended family and their relationships with siblings and parents. There was also discussion about the couple's two sons, who were both from previous relationships, with Sally being a single teenage parent during her son's early years. Her son was now 10 years of age and living with them. Dave's son visited regularly, and the couple were really pleased that their two sons got on so well. The question whether anything at The Show had caught their eye sparked an extended discussion on the way the couple performed familial love and engaged in memorialisation practices around childhood and family that involved specific forms of consumption. In the following conversation excerpt, Sally makes it clear that she wished to make the arrival of the new baby a shared and positive experience that included their two sons, and one of the ways of doing this was through gifts and keepsakes. In this particular example, the couple talk about being drawn to the opportunity to create casts of their children's hands.

Lydia: Has anything caught your eye?
Sally: Only…
Dave: The hand print …
Sally: Yeah, the hand print thing, is it Little Images or something like that? And they have got a stand and you can have their handprint done in a cast. I said I would like to have that done for the three children. They have actually got one there where the oldest one is at the bottom and the middle and the baby is at the top. So we like that and she said it was £160. But I said I would pay that. I wouldn't have a problem with paying that as I think it is a really nice keepsake, and it is including the boys in as well, for when we have the baby. That is our main thing, isn't it? You know what I mean. I have already said about buying the children presents after the baby, as it has been only them for such a long time, to have one (a baby) with that kind of age gap, I don't want them to feel pushed out, or ignored or anything. So it is just a case of trying to include them and I think having the cast done with 3 of their hands is a way of including them in the process of us having a baby.

Over the years, various companies have exhibited at The Show offering this kind of service, with the Magic Custard Company, mentioned early in Chapter 4, offering bronze casts of hands and feet, and other companies offering the miniaturisation of casts into silver hangers that are turned into jewellery. This particular example reiterates the cultural appeal of specific small body parts of infants discussed earlier. Sally and Dave's conversation points to the shared quality of these aesthetic practices. But family keepsakes can take on a variety of forms. Thus, Dave acknowledged still having the clip that was put on his son's umbilical cord after birth, whilst Sally spoke at some length about keeping her son's teeth and the first baby clothing—'every tooth he has lost, I have kept it, which is a bit weird, but I can't throw them out for some reason'. The couple were also keen on displaying family photographs in their home:

Sally: Photos are my big thing, aren't they? Everywhere you go in our house there are photographs. Of families!

Dave: Portraits that we had done when we were away.

Sally: We had them done in Turkey, didn't we, somebody actually drew the boys and they are up. Any family pictures, they are in the hall, coming down the stairs they are everywhere. We are going to have to start making room for the new pictures!

Anthropological and sociological studies on subject-object relations offer insight into the ways in which human lives, material objects, and emotions are entangled (e.g. Mauss 2000; Miller 1998). They show that the symbolic meaning of objects is malleable, subject to change in the practices and rituals of everyday life. Natalie Djohari (2016) offers an interesting analysis of the biography and emotional value of the baby wrap in the lives of parents as their young child grows up. She first discusses how new wraps become personalised in and through use, with the parents in her study discussing how the material of the wrap changes through use, becoming more flexible and adopting the physical smells of embodied intimacy. The second part of the discussion is about divestment practices of wraps, when children have become too old for them to be used. Djohari carefully analyses the rituals through which the wraps are passed on between parents, in an economy of exchange in which the biographies of the wraps in the intimate lives of owners contribute towards their second hand pecuniary value. As for the equally interesting study by Linda Layne (1999, 2000), on the memorializing rituals of parents who have experienced the loss of their yet to be born or new-born child, Djohari illustrates how love and loss are entangled with the emotional experiences of adults who care for, and care about, the young child. The commercial world in this study offered for sale a range of products that are commonly used in familial 'personalising' and 'memorializing' rituals, rituals in which love, and also loss, writ large. Specific objects—the wraps discussed by Djohari (2016), a large fluffy teddy bear, or a 'reborn' baby doll—may all come to embody the heartfelt emotions around the love, loss or absence of a small child.

Conclusion

What better way is there for making the young child important than by accentuating its emotionally intense loving qualities? Loving is a foundational component of the teleoaffective structure of child caring, linking the loveable child—as the 'end'—with the various pathways of child caring, and imbuing this practice with its affective salience. Love is a strong motivating factor for actions of all sorts, not just those relating to children: analyses of advertising demonstrate that love sells well and in diverse ways (see e.g. The Persuaders 2004). The business of child caring may be seen as part of this broader commercial environment, where intonations of love for, and affection towards, young children is converted into pecuniary value creation opportunities that communicate directly with the projects of child caring (see Table 4.2). Examples include items of clothing and accessories—for instance, a fashionable pink soother from MAM, or a funny soother with animal faces from Philips Avent—which proclaim that this is a child that is both cute and adorable, and specific types of commodities—such as photographs and body casts—lend themselves as long term memorabilia for the sedimentation of loving relations in personal life (Smart 2007). As illustrated in the imagery used in the commercial literature of Johnson Baby, and the example of Sophie the Giraffe, objects and imagery can work as strong multi-sensory emotional connectors to embodied memories, and of smell and touch, which in turn demonstrate how products can be made desirable. At the same time, the image industry holds stable the signification of the young child as lovable and adoring in the face of complexity. The images that populate the commercial environments I researched during the course of my research do not often represent crying babies or babies with leaky bodies (Lupton 2000; Murcott 1993), even though the possibility of these realities exists in the very products that are sold.

The aesthetic practices identified in this analysis: the use of colours; the definition and use of cute; and the representation of baby beauty through visual imagery, are repetitious. With each performative act, whether this is a visual display as part of an exhibition area or a representation that sits on product packaging, the cultural conventions of *what a young child is like* are reproduced and normalised. These aesthetic conventions do not only work to create a lovable child. The young child is, at the same time, Othered in and through these practices. For instance, the associations of colours with categories of 'human being' render children different from adults on the grounds of age and maturity, whilst simultaneously distinguishing between children on the basis of age and gender. The sleepy child that is implied in the pastel colours of babyhood is further removed from adulthood than the bouncy toddler, whose vibrancy is signified in the primary colour schemes used in products. At the same time, and as we shall also see in the next chapter, through the repeated visualisation of babies and bodies, young children are associated with nature, and culturally distanced from the worlds of culture and adults. Finally, in relation to cute, Harris argues:

> The process of conveying cuteness to the viewer disempowers its objects … making them appear more ignorant and vulnerable than they really are. … cuteness is ultimately dehumanizing, paralysing its victims into comatose or semi-conscious things. In fact, the "thingness" of cute things is fixed firmly in our minds …. (2000: 6–7)

Whilst my intention was to demonstrate how the teleoaffective quality of love is performed in and through the aesthetic conventions of this commercial world, this analysis also suggests entanglement with the broader generational-cultural practices of childhood discussed in Chapter 2. Uneven relations of power between young children and adults make it possible for childhood to become a locus for the inarticulate longings and emotional neediness of adulthood (Honeyman 2005; Scanlon 1995; Taylor 2013). The market of the cute illustrates this best, as it moves, more clearly than the other examples discussed in this chapter, beyond the familial context of child-parent-carer relations. Moving beyond wondrous innocence as an emotional relationship between child and carer, it illustrates the broader cultural need for innocence, expressed through all 'things minute'.

Bibliography

Beck, U., and E. Beck-Gernsheim. 1995. *The normal chaos of love*, 1–44. Cambridge: Polity Press.

Brownlie, J., and V. Leith. 2011. Social bundles: Thinking through the infant body. *Childhood* 18 (2): 196–210.

Cook. 2009. The ingratiating child: Conundrums and questions in the commercial depiction of childhood. Unpublished paper for The Ethics of Representing Childhood: Popular Culture, Performance, and Pedagogy, 1–19, March 5–7, Arizona State University.

Cross, G. 2004a. Wondrous innocence print Advertising and the origins of permissive child rearing in the US. *Journal of Consumer Culture* 4 (2): 183–201.

Cross, G. 2004b. *The cute and the cool: Wondrous innocence and modern American children's culture*. New York: Oxford University Press.

Djohari, N. 2016. Trading in unicorns: The role of exchange etiquette in managing the online second-hand sale of sentimental babywearing wraps. *Journal of Material Culture* 21 (3): 297–316.

Finkelstein, J. 1989. *Dining out: A sociology of modern manners*. New York: New York University Press.

Frontline: The Persuaders. (2004). Documentary about the American advertising industry. Web link: http://www.pbs.org/wgbh/pages/frontline/shows/persuaders/view/.

Furedi, F. 2001. *Paranoid parenting*. Chicago: Chicago Review Press.

Gregson, N., and L. Crewe. 1997. The bargain, the knowledge, and the spectacle: Making sense of consumption in the space of the car-boot sale. *Environment and Planning D: Society and Space* 15 (1): 87–112.

Harris, D. 2001. *Cute, quaint, hungry and romantic: The aesthetics of consumerism*. Cambridge, MA: DaCapo Press.

Hinde, R.A., and L.A. Barden. 1985. The evolution of the teddy bear. *Animal Behaviour* 33 (4): 1371–1373.

Holland, P. 2004. *Picturing childhood: The myth of the child in popular imagery*. London: IB Tauris.

Honeyman. 2005. *Elusive childhood: Impossible representations in modern fiction.* Columbus, OH: Ohio State University Press.

Kehily, M.J. 2014. For the love of small things: Consumerism and the making of maternal identities. *Young Consumers* 15 (3): 227–238.

Lawler, S. 2000. *Mothering the self: Mothers, daughters, subjectivities.* London: Routledge.

Layne, L. 1999. The child as gift: New directions in the study of Euro–American gift exchange. In *Transformative motherhood: On giving and getting in a consumer culture*, ed. L. Layne, 1–27. New York: New York University Press.

Layne, L. 2000. He was a real baby, with baby things: A material culture analysis of personhood, parenthood and pregnancy loss. *Journal of Material Culture* 5 (3): 321–345.

Lupton, D. 2000. 'A love/hate relationship': The ideals and experiences of first-time mothers. *Journal of Sociology* 36 (1): 50–63.

Lupton, D. 2013. Infant embodiment and interembodiment: A review of sociocultural perspectives. *Childhood* 20 (1): 37–50.

Marks, L.U. 2000. *The skin of the film: Intercultural cinema, embodiment, and the senses.* Durham, NC: Duke University Press.

Mauss, M. 2000. *The gift: The form and reason for exchange in archaic societies.* New York: WW Norton.

Miller, D. 1998. *A theory of shopping.* Cambridge: Polity Press.

Morris, P.H., V. Reddy, and R.C. Bunting. 1995. The survival of the cutest: Who's responsible for the evolution of the teddy bear? *Animal Behaviour* 50 (6): 1697–1700.

Murcott, A. 1993. Purity and pollution: Body management and the social place of infancy. In *Body matters: Essays on the sociology of the body*, ed. S. Scott and D. Morgan, 122–134. London: Falmer.

Pink, S. 2009. *Doing sensory ethnography.* London: Sage.

Scanlon, J. 1995. *Inarticulate longings: The ladies' home journal, gender, and the promises of consumer culture.* New York: Routledge.

Smart, C. 2007. *Personal life.* Cambridge: Polity Press.

Taylor, A. 2013. *Reconfiguring the natures of childhood.* London: Routledge.

Taylor, J.S., L. Layne, and D.F. Wozniak. 2004. *Consuming motherhood.* New Brunswick: Rutgers University Press.

Thompson, C. 2005. *Making parents: The ontological choreography of reproductive technologies.* Cambridge, MA: MIT press.

Traver, A. 2013. On markets and motherhoods: The case of American mothers of children adopted from China. In *Motherhoods, markets and consumption: The making of mothers in contemporary Western cultures*, ed. S. O'Donohoe, M. Hogg, P. Maclaran, L. Martens, and L. Stevens, 210–221. London: Routledge.

van den Cruyce, N., J. Bauwens, and K. Segers. 2009. Reflections of a child: Depicting healthy childhood in the 1940s and 1960s. *Revue belge de philologie et d'histoire* 87 (3–4): 759–774.

Varga, D. 2009a. Teddy's bear and the sociocultural transfiguration of savage beasts into innocent children, 1890–1920. *Journal of American Culture* 32 (2): 98–113.

Varga, D. 2009b. Babes in the woods: Wilderness aesthetics in children's stories and toys, 1830–1915. *Society & Animals* 17 (3): 187–205.

6

Protecting: Assembling Infant Embodied Vulnerability

Introduction

> Obviously a small baby is so … dependent on you. It's not like an older child who can look after themselves, up to a point. They are not getting into the dangers. With a baby it is so different. They are so dependent on you that you've got to keep them safe. (Hannah, Couple, 24 weeks pregnant, H first time pregnant, 30s–40s, white, self-employed)

This chapter discusses how the young child is enacted as vulnerable, in commercial sales practices and products, and in parental narratives, leading to *protecting* as one of the main teleoaffective qualities of the practice of child caring. Child vulnerability is foundational to many fields of contemporary practice, including education, health care, social work, and scientific research (Ferguson 2008; Parton 1991), and the consequences of this 'defining condition of childhood' (Furedi 2008: 41) has stimulated much scholarly debate, considering the implications alternately for children (e.g. Backett-Milburn and Harden 2004; Jenks 2005; Valentine and McKendrick 1997) and for parents (Furedi 2008; Nelson 2010; Ogle et al. 2011). Recent years have also seen a growing

© The Author(s) 2018
L. Martens, *Childhood and Markets*, Studies in Childhood and Youth,
https://doi.org/10.1057/978-1-137-31503-8_6

interest in child protection and safety as a theme in explorations of consumption and consumer culture (e.g. Afflerback et al. 2013; Coutant et al. 2011; Keenan and Stapleton 2013; MacKendrick 2014; Martens 2014; Nelson 2008). I here offer an analysis of the ways in which pecuniary value is realised through the entanglement of knowing the infant child as lovable and vulnerable. Whilst my focus is on infant vulnerability, I argue that vulnerability only leads to protecting because the child is seen as worthy of such care. Reflecting the emphasis on embodiment in the aesthetics of early childhood, in these commercial practices, infant vulnerability is generally understood as embodied vulnerability.

Infant commodity culture is crowded with products that are designed to 'safeguard', 'guide', 'monitor' and 'promote the health of' the young child, and alternatively, to bring 'peace of mind' to child carers. My analysis starts with a consideration of three ways in which safety connects with products. I then move on to consider renditions of the young child as *vulnerable, enigmatic* and *unpredictable*. Performances of the youngest of children as *vulnerable* and *enigmatic* opens up opportunities for pecuniary value creation, when product innovation is linked to problem multiplication, and in which techno-medical-science ways of knowing the infant child abound. In this category combination, 'the child' is not in any way held responsible (and thus rendered innocent). Performances of the young child as *unpredictable*, as opposed to *enigmatic*, point to shifting understandings of vulnerability in relation to age, development and agency. In the final part of the chapter, I draw on my interviews with prospective and new parents to discuss how protecting children gains affective salience through the co-occurrence of the young child qualities of *vulnerable, lovable* and *pure*. I here also compare commercial and parental enactments of the young child.

Infant Safety and Products

Looking through the product categories associated with different pathways in child caring (see Table 3.2), it is possible to identify products with a safety theme in all of the pathways, not solely the pathway I have termed 'keeping healthy and safe'. In the literature on clothing and fashion, the role of clothing is described as about embodied protection (Edwards 1997). However, the category for 'activity wear' that includes clothing for outdoor activities has a very clear connection with protection, for instance, from cold weather, from rain and from UPV sunrays. In the product group for baby bathing and massage, the baby bath that may be purchased is intended to make bathing easier by preventing the submersion of the baby's head in water. And companies that sell massage oils speak at length about the use of the right oils and the possibilities that oil impurities that penetrate the baby's skin can cause health problems. Skin health and safety is a more general theme in relation to infant cleanliness and the products that are promoted for practices in this child caring pathway.

It is possible to identify three ways in which child safety is present in products. Firstly, as a product in its own right, which I have called the *child safety product*. Secondly, in the form of *child safety advice*, which can be freely given, for instance, when included in website content, or which comes in the form of a product like the Which? Guide[1] and parenting magazines. Finally, as a quality of any product or service on offer in this world that incorporates what I have called *child safety consciousness* (Martens 2014).

The Mothercare's website categorises child safety products to include various infant feeding tool sterilizers, car seats, child monitors and child restrainers that include fire guards, play pens, stair gates, harnesses, etc.). There is also a selection of products designed specifically to tackle dangers in the home. The most common of these are latches for kitchen cupboards, fridges, freezers and toilets; window catches; cushioned covers for pointy table corners; and guards for cookers and other domestic equipment. Products that are aimed at making the lives of children safer are certainly a growing market. This much was evidenced from my visits to The Baby Show, where, across the years I visited, I encountered the latest baby monitor inventions—each sporting the latest in-build technologies for keeping track, for instance, of a baby's breathing.

---

[1] The Which? Guide is a publication—now present as an online resource—from the UK's charity the Consumer's Association.

The second safety category that is concerned with children's safety consists exclusively of instructional material in the form of parenting magazines, guidance books on childcare, and product manuals, leaflets and websites. I call these *child safety advice* products, though, as argued in Chapter 8, much advisory material can now be accessed free of charge. An example is Mothercare's website, where child safety advice and safety products can be found throughout. On the 2005 site of this retailer, the categories of child safety products (gates and play-pens, guards, monitors and safety essentials) were visually located in the centre of the page, whilst on the right-hand side of the page, the reader could access safety guides on baby monitors, baby bedding, and general home safety. The website also provided tabs along the top to access products and advice relating to different ages and stages of childhood. Searching through the content of these different pages suggests safety concerns are specific for the age of young children. The expectant parent 'preparing for a baby' or dealing with an exploring two-year-old toddler, is encouraged to engage with this 'knowledge' of the shifting safety hazards that are identified as crucial in early childhood, and that rely, as is developed below, on a conceptualisation of the young child as vulnerable in embodied ways. On today's site, the childcare and safety advice materials that the retailer makes available are also related to the life course stage and the child's age.[2]

Child safety consciousness is a general concern in the business of child caring. Awareness of child safety is demonstrated when products and services are questioned on the grounds of whether these are sufficiently safe to use, whether by those doing the caring or by the young child. Child safety consciousness brings together commercial organisations, regulatory organisations, medical-science practitioners and parents in the responsibility of child safeguarding. It is institutionalised through official British and international safety standards, appearing often as labels and symbols on goods and in advice on how to use products

---

[2]https://www.mothercare.com/advice-buying-guides-and-services/advice/babys-here/caring-for-your-baby/baby-proofing-your-home/advice-ms-baby-caring-sub17.html, accessed on 12 January 2018.

safely. A broad range of domestic products carry warning labels that advice, for instance, about fire hazards or on keeping products out of children's reach. The toy for older children is one example of this, as are domestic cleaning products that deemed harmful to young children. The latter have in-built features that prevent easy child access (Martens and Scott 2006). It would be wrong to see these products as safety products, but all have aspects of child safety incorporated into their design. Later in the chapter I look at how parent interviewees expressed awareness of product safety standards and looked out for such standards when shopping for products. I will return to child safety consciousness in Chapter 9, where I discuss how the qualities of young children implicate commercial practices in moral ways.

These categories of safety may be discussed individually. However, they also overlap and at times clash with one another. The child stair gate and the car seat are examples of child safety products that may be questioned on the grounds of their child safety consciousness. One of the ways this happens is when safety standards change, as discussed in Martens (2014), where, with the move to new safety standards, products manufactured under earlier standards are rendered out of date, and by implication, unsafe. Equally, new parents in this study identified car seats as unsuitable second hand products, as there was no certainty about the history of the product, and in particular, whether it had been involved in an accident, which rendered the product no longer suitable for use. Christel, mother of an 18 months old daughter, enacted awareness of these concerns by talking about getting her car seat second hand from a friend:

> We have got a second hand car seat as well. That was from my friend Tanja, she gave us the car seat. The first one we had was with the pram and this is the second one she is in. As long as I know the history, so I know, but they advise not, in case you don't know the history. But I mean, I knew the history of it so it was fine.

Whilst safety standards may be welcomed, it is also easy to see that shifts in safety standards contributes to the obsolescence of products, and for some parents will clash with the need to live in a cost-effective way.

I move on now to discuss how the very young child is understood as at the same time vulnerable and enigmatic in embodied ways. Through the concomitant understanding of the young child as loveable, the quality of vulnerability in the young child creates the teleoaffective priority or aim of protecting. Rendering the young child enigmatic (or 'hard to know') not only creates flexibility in knowing the young child, but also opens up new avenues for the creation of pecuniary value. In order to know the enigmatic young child, moreover, recourse is made to medical-science knowledge. Not surprisingly, it is especially in relation to products that are sold in order to help protect the child that we find medical-science narrative density.

Knowing the Enigmatic Embodied Infant Child

Whilst the business of child caring will proclaim that it operates in the best interests of the child, it is also always a profit-making venture. To operate effectively in a competitive environment means that commercial organisations have to establish a position for 'their' product amongst other products in the market. This usually means making it clear how a product does and/or means something different from others. New products can be successful as long as believable stories of their worth and usefulness can be established in addition to those that already exist. In the analysis I identified two nuances in the strategies pursued to create pecuniary value around vulnerability. First, in enacting infant vulnerability, there was a pervasive presence of techno-medical-science busyness. I will seek to offer an explanation for this later. Second, pecuniary value creation strategies also vary in accordance with 'child age', shifting from the enigmatic to the unpredictable child. In what follows, I will look at each of these in turn.

Assembling Infant Vulnerability

Infant feeding tools, which do not belong to the category of safety products, nevertheless illustrate how child safety is a major theme through which brand-companies communicate the utility of their product, and make claims about their specific niche market position. In analysing the website content of infant feeding tool brand-companies Dr. Brown's, Mam, NUK, Phillips-Avent, and Tommee Tippee, I looked for the ways in which the 'young child' was known on these sites.[3] These websites provided insight into a history of problems with infant feeding, where bottles and industrially produced milk substances are used, as this history was narrated to expound the virtues of contemporary products. By highlighting these historical problems, the narratives simultaneously promulgated the knowledge of the young child as having a fragile and delicate body. Three historical 'problems' were the subject of risk discussion: germs, air bubbles and Bisphenol A (BPA). The last of these is the most recent, and will be discussed in more detail in Chapter 9.

Amongst the pollutants that have become part of commercial narratives of infant feeding, the oldest is the threat posed by germs. Germ dangers have historically hampered the adoption of infant bottle-feeding, and this problem was equally pertinent to artificial infant foods as it was to feeding tools: both could harbour harmful germs. It is not surprising that bottle-feeding infants could become popular only when formula milk and bottle cleaning and preparation was developed in such a way that the multiplication of germs was inhibited (Atkins 2016; Nimmo 2010). Through the creation of products that help child carers

---

[3]The websites analysed here were those of Phillips Avent, Tommee Tippee, NUK, MAM, and Dr. Brown's. All date from April and May 2013. Tommee Tippee is an American owned company, which has a major production site in the UK. Philips Avent is the merged outcome of the British infant feeding tools brand company Avent, and the Dutch domestic technologies giant Philips. The merger took place in 2006, which signals the shift to a 'mixed feeding' narrative (see Chapter 7). MAM is of Austrian origin. NUK originates in Germany. These brand companies all trade globally. The website content of these international commercial organisations change regularly, and many maintain different sites for specific countries. In 2013, for instance, NUK had a 'generic' international English language site, and also sites for a range of different countries. For some countries, the organization of the site differed considerably from that of the international site, for others, some or all of the materials used on the international site were used. For NUK and MAM, I analysed the international English language sites. I analysed the UK sites of the other companies. As website content changes over time, the procedure I used was to copy the website content of each brand-company by making screen prints of each page of information, and by storing any additional materials, including any information brochures that were available from the sites. This allowed for the archival of textual and visual materials to return to later.

perform 'sterilisation,' for instance, by using refrigeration and by cleaning baby feeding equipment, germs have become part of the assemblage
of infant feeding that has witnessed a shift away from breastfeeding
towards bottle-feeding. Germ knowledge is embedded in the enactment
of the infant body as fragile. The general recommendation circulating
in advice on early child care is that feeding tools should be sterile in
the early months of an infant's life, and narratives like this render infant
bodies more vulnerable than those of older children and adults.

Air bubbles in milk have been turned into another historical problem, associated especially with bottle-feeding and connected to the
embodied problem of baby colic, and the lesser embodied evils of
burping, sickness and wind. Baby colic, and its relation to the feeding
of infants, has been on the list of salient early childhood challenges for
some time. Even so, baby colic remains elusive in the sense that science
is 'at odds' as to the exact causes of this prolonged fretfulness of a cohort
of young babies in their first months of life. Marketers of feeding bottles
acknowledge this 'uncertainty' to an extent, but nevertheless define baby
colic as a problem that they address in product design, leading to a set
of techno-scientific design features, including so-called 'colic valves,' for
dealing with air, air pressure, and milk flow in bottles. Dr. Brown's is a
feeding tool brand-company that has staked its niche market position
on this very problematic, and has produced a bottle with an intriguing
tubular device. As described in a short video on the 2013 website, the
bottle is said to deal with air and vacuum in the bottle in an effective
way, and the website further points to the ways in which the bottle's
specific design helps to maintain the essential vitamins in formula milk.

The narratives on baby feeding tool websites pay witness to a history of concerns that have arisen as a consequence of the assembling of
infant feeding into a practice that involves man-made foods, feeding
tools and other technologies. Three issues; those of germs, baby colic
and BPA, provide evidence of the complex front-stage 'medical-science
knowledges' that infuse the sales narratives on these websites. These pay
witness to an interesting cultural inversion. It is through the discovery
of solutions to the diverse problematic features of 'existing/older' products that contemporary designs gain their 'functionality': the problem
of the tool has become a problem of infantile vulnerability, for which

the new tools are argued to operate as solutions. In the instance of baby feeding, this effectively hides the causality of the tool as a problem. Finally, one of the interesting facets of problems like germs, small air bubbles, and chemical components, like BPA, is how these pollutants are so small, as to render them invisible to the human eye. Small children and small polluting agents clearly 'suit' each other. These are 'problems' created by science in the double sense of the word: first, by literally creating new problematic 'agencies' through product inventions and design, and second, by working on the meaning of these agencies, transforming these to suit the purposes of pecuniary value creation, and by doing so, to fix a uniform understanding of the child as vulnerable.

Embodied Malleability and Abnormality

A different facet of the vulnerable baby body emerges through the harnessing of techno-medical-science knowledge that renders this body malleable and subject to malformation as a consequence of caring practices and routine tool use. Examples of this were found on orality tool websites, where infant soothers/pacifiers were assessed in relation to the shaping of the baby's mouth through routine use. Concern with 'normal' body development in infants stretches back in time, having for instance appeared historically in arguments against finger sucking.[4]

During my fieldwork of consumer exhibitions, this medical-science narrative stood out in the exhibitions of two companies, where infant embodied malleability and abnormality was the main narrative undergirding the rationale for the products these companies sold. Technology in Motion, exhibiting at The Scottish Baby Show in Glasgow (2010) and the SleepCurve mattress, exhibiting at different Baby Shows (e.g. in 2008 and 2009), both addressed the problem of infant flat head syndrome, for which the medical term is Plagiocephaly. The website

---

[4]A thank you to my colleague Dr. Emma Head, with whom I had an interesting conversation on finger sucking and its historical association with the malformation of children's mouths and teeth.

of Technology in Motion first sums up the embodied malleability of young children:

> Babies can be at risk of flat head syndrome because their skull remains soft and pliable in the earliest stages of their life. This pliability is because the several plates of bone, which fuse the skull together, are initially loose, gradually joining as your baby gets older.[5]

Both companies point to scientific findings that flat head syndrome has been on the increase since the introduction, in 1996, of the medically endorsed recommendation to place young children on their backs during sleep. In turn, this recommendation was a result of efforts to reduce the incidence of another elusive problem in infancy; that of baby cot death (also known as sudden infant death syndrome, or SIDS), and which Veronica's mother Sue identified as one of the uncertainties in caring for babies that most worried her when her children were young (see below). The SleepCurve mattress, designed by Philip Owen, a Paediatric Osteopath, exhibited at The Baby Show, is argued to inhibit the development of flat head syndrome, whilst simultaneously improving breathing in sleeping infants. It thus offers a solution for the enigmatic problems of SIDS and flat head syndrome. At The Baby Show, the Osteopath spoke to the audience alongside a video. Here, the speech that goes with the product demonstration video on the website has been transcribed:

> I would like to explain the whole concept of the SleepCurve mattress to you. I designed this mattress with the comfort and wellbeing of babies in mind. It's difficult to achieve this on a flat surface, as there is no space for the bulge on the back of the head. The chin goes into the chest, or the head rotates to the side. Lying a baby on a SleepCurve mattress allows the baby's head to be supported. This is the optimum position of the spine, and spine and head are both supported naturally, allowing the baby's airways to be fully open. The curve provides a space for the bulge on the

---

[5]The Technology in Motion website was consulted on 11 May 2016, at https://www.technology-inmotion.com/flat-head-syndrome/what-is-flat-head-syndrome/.

back of the head, whilst also relieving the pressure on the baby's soft skull bones. The SleepCurve mattress is the only baby mattress to have been clinically proven to aid the self-correction of flat head syndrome. The mattress is shaped to fit the natural curves of the baby, not only in this direction, but also at the back of the head, so the head is properly cradled and supported. These heat channels that have been introduced into the mattress surface allow the baby to be kept cool, comfortable and supported.[6]

As was the case for feeding tools in the previous example, here too we can glean the narration of a history in which the change in a practice has an unanticipated and undesired effect on the body of the infant child, resulting in product innovation. In these examples of embodied vulnerability, described in a diverse range of product narratives, the young child is lacking in any kind of wilful agency, but subject to a range of actants, of medically endorsed knowledge (how to put a baby to sleep to lower the risk of SIDS), translated into specific child caring routines (the practice of routinely putting babies to sleep on their backs), with the use of specific child caring tools (a flat mattress, in a bed).

Knowing the Unpredictable Embodied Child

Diversification in pecuniary value creation practices also makes use of gradation on the basis of age (Cook 2004). In relation to protecting, this may be recognised in two types of enactment: the one just discussed, which sees the young child as enigmatic and as lacking agency, and the understanding of the young child as unpredictable, in which the young child is attributed greater agency, for instance, through a focus on young children in this early life course stage 'becoming mobile.' The example I discuss below concerns the sales narratives of vitamins.

---

[6]The product demonstration video on the SleepCurve website was consulted on 11 May 2016, and found at http://www.sleepcurve.com/why-buy-a-sleepcurve-mattress/.

Vitamin brands had a general presence at the consumer exhibitions I visited, with products targeting pregnant women and young children, and focusing on folic acid, omega-3 and multivitamins. In view of the historical popularisation of vitamins (Falk 1994; Apple 1996), oral supplements are interesting for the medical-science density in marketing content. During my fieldwork, one vitamin sales strategy was similar to those discussed earlier, and operated by criticising older and competitor products as a way of highlighting the good qualities of the products that were on sale. Here, the topic was the fish oil that was sourced for the production of omega-3 supplements, and specifically, whether these were sufficiently pure, and came in a form that was easily absorbed by the body. In relation to oil purity, it was pointed out that the traditional cod liver oil was sourced from fish livers; now categorised as storage containers for the world's industrial pollutants. The company representative I spoke with was keen to point out that the company sourced its oils from the whole fish, and also subjected the oil to a filtering process to ensure its purity.

The question of vitamin absorption highlights a multiplicity of agencies, including that of the young child's unpredictable body and the agency of vitamins. I discuss the content of a series of slides that were playing on a video screen at the exhibition stand of one of the vitamin brands I visited. The slides contained moving 'amoeba' shapes, featuring pictures of young children inside them, ranging from small babies to older children. The ways the different slides 'build up' the story for why vitamins are an essential part of the diet of young children is particularly interesting, and a number started with the question: 'Did you know?'

Slide 1:   'Did you know? Green vegetables are rich in vitamin C and other protective vitamins and minerals, as well as fibre'

Slide 2:   'Did you know? Calcium – is important for the development of healthy bones and teeth, and can be found in milk, cheese, yoghurt, soya beans and green leafy vegetables (such a broccoli, cabbage)'

The following three slides then proceed to point to a series of reasons for why children are not getting the vitamins they need, and relies on information taken from the British Nutrition Foundation:

Slide 3:   'Did you know? Some children eat less than half the recommended five portions of fruit and vegetables a day – and in any average week one in five 4 – 18 year olds eat no fruit at all.'

Slide 4:   'What's so important about vitamins? Children need specific vitamins to stay healthy, but it can be tough getting them to eat properly'

Slide 5:   'On top of that, vitamins can be used up or lost quickly. So it's vital that kids get their vitamins every single day'

These slides make reference to the unpredictable child, with a causality that resides in the idea of the child as fussy eater, or maybe with small appetites reflecting their small bodies, or perhaps with bodies that use up vitamins more quickly. There again, being sketched as potentially unpredictable by 'disappearing quickly', vitamins are also attributed agency. None of these difficulties are further elaborated, leaving a lot to guesswork, though possibly with the overall effect of creating a believable rationale for vitamin supplementation in young children. The unpredictable vulnerable child is also present in safety narratives relating to child safety products. Examples are discussed in Martens (2014), and also recognised in parent commentaries, to which I now turn.

Love Hurts: Teleoaffective Entanglement and the Heart-Wrenching Qualities of Child Caring

The quality of child safety consciousness is a form of product/tool and child caring moralisation that is grounded in understandings of the child as vulnerable, and with the youngest of children, this is in the first instance an embodied, rather than a psychological, form of vulnerability

(Lawler 2000). The narrative practices found in commercial literatures, but also in talk by prospective parents, may thus be seen to accentuate the quality of embodied vulnerability in the very youngest of children. The examples in this chapter also demonstrate how the different facets of the teleoaffective structure of child caring are entangled, strengthening the structure and also the intensity of the priorities embedded in it. It is possibly for this reason that Schatzki talks about child caring as heavy in its affectivity:

> Practices vary greatly in both the complexity of their teleological structuring and in the depths of their affective ordering. Western cooking practices, for instance, are typically heavy in teleology and light in affective structure, whereas Western rearing practices display considerably more of the affective. (2002: 80)

Loving and protecting are entangled in a way whereby the priority of protecting is given meaning through the priority of loving. The feeling of responsibility towards the safety of a person assumes that this person is deemed worthy of care and carefulness, and, in the example of the young child, is loved. The cultural fact that young children are lovable sits as an unspoken truth-value in the safety narratives I have examined so far: I argued the same in Chapter 5. The products that serve as aids in countering infant flat head syndrome, for instance, are marketed as interventions that will stimulate mothers to bond with their babies by countering 'embodied abnormalities'.

Whilst 'loving' worked as a certainty that needed no verbal elaboration, the idea that young children need safeguarding carried a similar quality of obviousness. Thus, following Hannah's (Couple, 24 weeks pregnant, H first time pregnant, 30s–40s, white, self-employed) description of the dependent nature of the young child (see chapter opening quote), her partner Peter said his concern with child safety was 'just common sense'. Peter followed this brief statement up by repeatedly stressing the importance of safety for them ('safety is a priority'; 'so, safety is a big thing'), listing the various ways in which the couple practiced safety with their children. For the expected baby, they were also already thinking through various safety issues, including their intension to keep the family pets away from the baby room. In relation to products, they were very keen on finding bargains, but they would not consider prioritising this over safety ('we won't cut corners'; 'Hannah is always looking out for British standards').

During the parental interviews, the strongest sense of affect—of the heart-wrenching experiences of caring for loved young children—came from those who had experience of caring for and about them. Those who were pregnant were enacting protection for the baby that was growing in the belly, but the emotional consequence of this growing baby-in-the-belly was downplayed. Marcia (Mothers, 20 weeks, first time pregnancy, 30s, white, technical-professional), for instance, volunteered early in our discussion how, as a consequence of being pregnant, she was paying considerable attention to her health:

Marcia: I never saw myself as someone who is particularly healthy, but I am the healthiest I have ever been at the moment.

Lydia: Is that right, because of the pregnancy?

Marcia: Yes. I eat proper food and I stopped drinking, (I am now drinking) lots of water, eating a lot more fruit and veg, as well.

Lydia: Because you are pregnant?

Marcia: Yes. Yes. I have always had a sort of thing about organic fruit and veg, but it is a lot more expensive, isn't it. But now I am not drinking, I am not going out half as much, so I have got a lot more money, so I can afford the organic stuff! That is one way of looking at it anyway.

At the same time, she was talking about the growing child inside her as 'it', not yet wishing to see this child as a human being, and sharing with other prospective parents a degree of hesitancy about putting too much love into the expected child at this stage. A similar hesitancy in expressions of 'love' was given by Veronica (Mothers, 26 weeks, first time pregnancy, late teens, white but baby mixed ethnic, working class), who spoke about her experiences of working in a children's nursery and not wishing to get too close to the little children she cared for. In both instances, the hesitancy is associated with the risk of losing the child, and touches on the discussion in Chapter 5 and the research by Layne (2000) on parents who experience stillbirth or infant death.

Charlotte and Ben (Couple, first time parents, 20s, white, working class), whose baby daughter was 6 months at the time of the interview, also expressed the intensity of their love for their daughter, for instance, through anxieties associated with making mistakes. Here, Charlotte narrates the heart-wrenching experience of her daughter falling out of her pram, after she had forgotten to fasten the straps of her buggy:

> Charlotte: I think it is hard, I think you have just to... things happen, you just have to let them go over your head, as you would just end up... Cos like, I took her out, took the dog for a long walk, and it was really hot, and I took her coat off and I forgot to strap her back in. So, when I went back home and put her in the kitchen, and the lady next door had asked me to take a parcel in, and the parcel man came. So, when I said: 'Oh, I have got a key to let you in' and as I walked, I checked and she was still asleep, and all I did was walk past my window. And 2 seconds later she was on the floor, she had rolled, got out of her pushchair, you see. So I started panicking, so I took her down to the hospital and that, and they checked her all over, and she was fine like. It made me feel really guilty, really bad. But then, accidents happen, you know what I mean?

Interestingly, it was Veronica's mother Sue who 'admired' contemporary safety products that, in her words, gave a mother 'peace of mind' in an emotional response to caring for a loved one who is vulnerable to the fatal and enigmatic problem of sudden infant death syndrome:

> Sally: I think what is out there for new mums is fantastic to when I was a mum... You know like, they didn't do baby shows when I was pregnant. You didn't see what was available and things, so it has been great today cause there's been lots of things that you think: 'Yeah, that will really give peace of mind,' and I would have loved, like there is a little technique that you put on the baby's nappy and if the baby stops breathing for so many seconds it would give it a little shock and it would restart. If it didn't then it would give a longer bleep. So it would bleep either way but it would certainly make you aware that the baby had stopped breathing. When I had my first (baby child) I was always worried about cot death.
>
> Lydia: Cot death, it has gone down quite significantly, hasn't it?

Sally: Yeah, but it is all the things that are there and something like that to give people some peace of mind because it does, you know. I don't think in the first few months of a baby that a mum rests properly in any case, as it is: 'Oh, the baby has slept too long, it should have been awake by now', whereas something like that, you would check it to see if it is okay, and it would be: 'Oh, she is okay,' so there are a lot of good things to make being a mum in the beginning much easier, I think, you know, if they can afford to pay some of the prices for the things.

The strong sense of love for a small creature one is feeling responsible for, and who is deemed vulnerable in different ways, made mothers, like Sue, look favourably on the kind of tools commerce provides to give parents peace of mind, though a clear limitation with the little technology she discussed, which was called Respisence, was the price tag. Veronica and Sally had thus taken the leaflet to think about whether they could afford to purchase this product. But not all parents thought about safety products and child safety in the same way. Charlotte and Ben, along with other new parents in the study, were conscious of the need for young children to learn about the risks in life, rather than to be overly protective (Ben: 'I don't think you can wrap them up in cotton wool and not let them do anything'). Another parent, Christel, who was pregnant with her second child, argued against the necessity to baby proof the house by challenging the uniform understanding of the vulnerable young child that, as we saw earlier, is promulgated in commercial narrations. She here comments on her ways of doing safety with her 18 months old daughter, in which she talks about her daughter as going through an individual growth path, suggesting that children are all different:

Lydia: What about safety, is that something that is important for you?
Christel: Yeah, it is important. We haven't really baby proofed our house, a lot of people say you should baby proof your house, but I think, we looked at it as though… When she is growing up in the house then she didn't touch…. As we did Tinytalk as well, we did things like—things are hot and we do the actions and so she knew about the fire, not to touch the fire. So, when I say hot now, she backs off a bit. So no, we haven't really baby proofed the house. We have got

a stair gate at the top of the stairs. Not at the bottom of the stairs. I am trying to encourage her to walk down the stairs, but she is not really interested in stairs.

Lydia: Does she go on the stairs?

Christel: She goes up the stairs yes, but with us behind her. But she won't go up on her own. She was not a very active baby, she started crawling quite late when she was about 11 months, and she didn't start walking until she was 15 months. So, she is a very much a sit-down baby, and look and read. She wasn't... I think maybe in a house where you had a really active baby, but she wasn't really active, so....

The aim of this section was to illustrate the potency of teleoaffective entanglement, through the example of the heart-wrenching feelings and experiences accounted by new and prospective parents in relation to the lovable and vulnerable qualities of the infant child. Listening to the voices of parents is interesting for another reason: this is that the nuances of knowing the child are different. Characteristic of commercial narratives is the propensity to hold the quality of the vulnerable child stable, when using other qualities—such as 'the child as enigmatic' and 'the child as unpredictable'—and strategies like the utilisation of techno-medical-science knowledge, to create a diverse range of reasons that rationalise a range of products. Parents are very much aware of the teleoaffective entanglement of loving and protecting, but are also negotiating other priorities, such as the need for the child to learn about risks and dangers, and for the body to become resilient, for instance, to germs. But parents are not drawing on techno-medical-science knowledge in the same way as happens in commercial narrating. I will return to this in Chapter 8, when I discuss parental dispositions to learning and researching the craft of child caring.

Conclusion: Vulnerability as a Dynamically Durable Teleo-Affectivity

This chapter has shown how the teleoaffective priority of protecting, in the practice of child caring, is performed by commercial and parental actants. The analysis shows how protecting the young child is a generative pecuniary value creation strategy that can support a range of products on the basis of a range of ways of knowing this child as vulnerable in embodied ways. In order for protecting to be rendered important, it is entangled with the prior understanding of the young child as lovable. Embodied vulnerability was a ubiquitous and unvarying understanding of the young child in this analysis, with alternative renditions, for instance, of resilience, conspicuous for their absence (Christensen 2000; Furedi 2008). The unvarying presence of embodied vulnerability points to one of the lessons learned from science and technology theories. This is that cultural categories are socially constituted, but nevertheless take on apparent fixity through repetitious performances. The young child's embodied vulnerability, in this context, becomes a durable outcome through the dynamic performance of the multiple actants that populate childhood, and the relations through which these are brought together (Prout 2005; Pyyhtinen 2016).

The ubiquitous quality of embodied vulnerability poses a commercial challenge: how can it support pecuniary value creation in a competitive market, with multiple existing commercial practitioners and others chomping at the bit? Child protection can be a goldmine, and ultimately amenable to the business of child caring, when scientific knowledge is drawn upon to actively 'discover', endlessly anew, new reasons for protecting young children. This analysis has shown that scientific knowledge practices are used prolifically to discover new things about infants that in turn justify product innovation, diversification and uptake. Yet, these new knowledges operate 'within the confines' of the teleoaffective entanglement of loving, protecting, purification and nurturing: sales narratives and products 'simply' offer different scenarios through which the embodied vulnerability of infants is confirmed. The examples of medical-science ways of knowing the young child I have presented here suggest that the embodied vulnerabilities of young children are multiple, but these are and remain vulnerabilities rather than other imaginable child qualities.

Techno-medical-science density, in this field of pecuniary value creation, warrants a few additional comments. The first is that techno-medical-science representations found in commercial sales practices are, of course, front stage narrations. This means that these have been carefully 'cleansed' and choreographed to bring across a specific message (Nimmo 2011). In my research, I only had sight of these front stage narrations. It is rather unlikely that the medical-science knowledge that goes into product design and production is the same as those that are part of carefully constructed sales narratives, and that may perhaps be best understood as forms of pseudo-science. One may surmise that the range of medical-science knowledge drawn upon in product design and manufacturing is much broader, more nuanced (or technical), and not suitable for 'public' consumption for various reasons. But there will need to be some coherence between production-science and sales-science, if only for the reasons that, in the end, the products that are sold have to 'work' in the way 'it says on the package'.

Second, the medical-science practices drawn upon in relation to infant vulnerability create additional layers of knowing the young child that confirm its 'youthfulness'. As discussed in Chapter 5, the focus on the bodies of infants in sales representations confirms youthfulness in the infant child, working actively through the nature-culture binary. So does the emphasis on the enigmatic child: the child that is mysterious, hard to know, and puzzling, is also a child that is challenged by the lack of language proficiency to communicate about itself (Cook 2004; Honeyman 2005). Something else has to speak on 'its behalf'. Techno-medical-science talk has, for various reasons, spoken a lot on behalf of the young child (Prout 2005). Especially interesting is how the enigmatic child merges with other enigmatic entities that are, for instance, imperceptible to the human eye and unknowable by way of normal human perception. The analysis presented in this chapter highlighted how a range of small entities—vitamins, germs, chemical components, and air bubbles—can become known only in and through medical-science knowledge. A further strategy that supports the range of products & services that can be found in this commercial environment is the practice of staging the changing age and development of the young child. This is one of the prime themes discussed by Cook (2004) in his historical analysis of the children's clothing industry. In relation to the teleo-affectivity of protecting, shifting emphasis from the enigmatic to the unpredictable child creates age-related development stages, especially where the latter refers to growing child mobility.

Understanding the density of techno-medical-science resources in sales practices and product safety consciousness suggest further nuances. As well as creating (within limits) new understandings of the child, science narratives are used to tell stories that are believable and trustworthy. This suggests that commercial organisations are moral entities, and that sales narrating is a moral practice. Using practice language, it points to the ways in which commercial organisations are subject to the normativities of the practice of child caring, and will also shape these in and through their performances. This point will be developed in subsequent chapters, and especially in Chapter 9. Finally, in the next chapter, where I concentrate on the teleo-affectivity of purifying, reliance on the modern confidence afforded by techno-medical-science turns into a less certain sales strategy, as it can easily be located in the realm of the profane through reference to 'artificiality' and 'pollution' (Beck 1992), and thus rendered oppositional to the natural and pure child. It will be argued that this cultural contradiction has given rise to new opportunities for pecuniary value creation, creating a more diversified market of products, where commercial organisations position their products in relation to these oppositions in different ways.

Bibliography

Afflerback, S., S.K. Carter, A.K. Anthony, and L. Grauerholz. 2013. Infant feeding consumerism in the age of intensive mothering and risk society. *Journal of Consumer Culture* 13 (3): 387–405.

Apple, R.D. 1996. *Vitamania: Vitamins in American culture*. Camden: Rutgers University Press.

Atkins, P. 2016. *Liquid materialities: A history of milk, science and the law*. London: Routledge.

Backett-Milburn, K., and J. Harden. 2004. How children and their families construct and negotiate risk, safety and danger. *Childhood-A Global Journal of Child Research* 11 (4): 429–447.

Beck, U. 1992. *Risk society: Towards a new modernity*. London: Sage.

Christensen, P.H. 2000. Childhood and the cultural constitution of vulnerable bodies. In *The body, childhood and society*, ed. A. Prout, 38–59. London: Macmillan.

Cook, D.T. 2004. *The commodification of childhood: The children's clothing industry and the rise of the child consumer*. Durham, NC: Duke University Press.

Coutant, A., V.I. de La Ville, M. Gram, and N. Boireau. 2011. Motherhood, advertising, and anxiety: A cross-cultural perspective on Danonino commercials. *Advertising & Society Review* 12 (2): 1–19.

Edwards, Tim. 1997. *Men in the mirror: Men's fashion, masculinity and consumer society*. London: Cassell.

Falk, P. 1994. *The consuming body*. London: Sage.

Ferguson, H. 2008. *Protecting children in time*. Basingstoke: Palgrave Macmillan.

Furedi, F. 2008. *Paranoid parenting: Why ignoring the experts may be best for your child*. London: Continuum.

Honeyman, S. 2005. *Elusive childhood: Impossible representations in modern fiction*. Columbus, OH: Ohio State University Press.

Jenks, C. 2005. *Childhood*. London: Routledge.

Keenan, J., and H. Stapleton. 2013. 'It won't do her any harm' they said, 'or they wouldn't put it on the market'. In *Motherhoods, markets and consumption: The making of mothers in contemporary Western cultures*, ed. S. O'Donohoe, M. Hogg, P. Maclaran, L. Martens, and L. Stevens, 71–87. London: Routledge.

Lawler, S. 2000. *Mothering the self: Mothers, daughters, subjectivities*. London: Routledge.

Layne, L. 2000. He was a real baby, with baby things: A material culture analysis of personhood, parenthood and pregnancy loss. *Journal of Material Culture* 5 (3): 321–345.

Mackendrick, N. 2014. More work for mother: Chemical body burdens as a maternal responsibility. *Gender & Society* 28 (5): 705–728.

Martens, L. 2014. Selling infant safety: Entanglements of childhood preciousness, vulnerability and unpredictability. Special issue entitled "New parents and young children in consumer culture". *Young Consumers* 15 (3): 239–250.

Martens, L., and S. Scott. 2006. Under the kitchen surface: Domestic products and conflicting constructions of home. *Home Cultures* 3 (1): 39–62.

Nelson, M.K. 2008. Watching children: Describing the use of baby monitors on the Epinions.com. *Journal of Family Issues* 29 (4): 516–538.

Nelson, M.K. 2010. *Parenting out of control: Anxious parents in uncertain times*. New York: New York University Press.

Nimmo, R. 2010. *Milk, modernity and the making of the human: Purifying the social*. London: Routledge.

Nimmo, R. 2011. Actor-network theory and methodology: Social research in a more-than-human world. *Methodological Innovations Online* 6 (3): 108–119.

Ogle, J.P., K.E. Tyner, and S. Schofield-Tomschin. 2011. Watching over baby: Expectant parenthood and the duty to be well. *Sociological Inquiry* 81 (3): 285–309.

Parton, N. 1991. *Governing the family: Child care, child protection and the state*. London: Macmillan.

Prout, A. 2005. *The future of childhood*. London: Routledge.

Pyyhtinen, A. 2016. *More-than-human sociology*. Basingstoke: Palgrave Macmillan.

Schatzki, T. 2002. *The site of the social: A philosophical account of the constitution of social life and change*. Pennsylvania: Pennsylvania State University Press.

Valentine G., and J. McKendrck. (1997). Children's outdoor play: Exploring parental concerns about children's safety and the changing nature of childhood. *Geoforum* 28 (2): 219–235.

7

Purifying: Embodied Cleanliness and Natural Products

Introduction

Drawing on an analysis of narratives from prospective and new parents, and an analysis of the symbolic work achieved in a set of sales narratives, this chapter examines *purifying* as one of the major components in the teleoaffective structure of child caring. The association of child caring pathways with product categories and the teleoaffective qualities of child caring, presented in Table 4.2, pays witness to the diverse ways in which *purifying* is present. It includes a pathway called cleaning, where the listed product categories are bathing and changing; toiletries; beauty and skin care; nappies, bibs and wipes; and sterilising aids. Some of these product categories cut across others. Nappies and bibs, for instance, are accessories in the wardrobes of early childhood, representing technologies for dealing with infant bodily excretions. As we saw in Chapter 6, cleanliness is a concern when feeding babies, whilst the purity of orally ingested substances, including vitamin supplements, was a mentioned concern when talking with representatives at the exhibitions of vitamin companies. Finally, product brochures remind shoppers that the tools that are sold, such as toys or feeding

© The Author(s) 2018
L. Martens, *Childhood and Markets*, Studies in Childhood and Youth,
https://doi.org/10.1057/978-1-137-31503-8_7

159

bottles, also need to be subjected to a regime of cleanliness. Walking through this product world, as I did during my ethnographic research at consumer and trade exhibitions, it is hard not to notice the range of products, tools and technologies that are concerned with purity, and the plentiful references to everything natural and organic. Unlike infant cleanliness practices and products, which are well-established in the practice of child caring, organic products are relatively new additions to the product portfolio that is on offer, becoming popular as confidence in the inventions of modernity started to wane in the 1970s and 1980s (Beck 1992; Martens and Scott 2006).

The argument developed in this chapter is that purification consists in a set of ritualised practices, performed on babies *and* products, *and* in material-embodied and symbolic ways, creating a range of material and symbolic orders that keep the pure child pure. As testified in a generation of scholarly arguments (Douglas 2003; Murcott 1993; Latour 1993), purification signals a reality characterised by material-discursive hybridity and messiness, and it is in essence the work of hiding this complexity (Law 2004; Nimmo 2010). Purifying is also the messiest of the three teleoaffective elements that bind understandings of the young child with the priorities of child caring, because it is a response to multiple forms of material and symbolic pollution: whether these are forms of human pollution (Others of any kind may become regarded as a threat, and we know that distinction is a ubiquitous cultural practice in relation to class), cultural pollution (e.g. in the form of inappropriate television content), or material-symbolic pollution (e.g. in the form of plastic toys or embodied secretions). In relation to the young child, Murcott points to a dual threat: of babies creating material dirt around the orifices that they cannot themselves manage, when cultural conceptions of the young child as pure and innocent make them simultaneously subjects of cultural pollution, stimulating mitigation rituals:

> As Douglas' work suggests, the idea of dirt is literally linked with the body, and especially its orifices. But it is not only to do with the margins of the body, but also the margins of society. Babies must be protected from dirt both from the world beyond them and from the dirt that as living beings their bodies both create and represent. (1993: 134)

Purifying in its diverse forms is thus closely associated with keeping stable the categories of culture, including the binary oppositions that haunt childhood, such as the profane and the sacred, and culture/artificial and nature/pure. Taylor (2011, 2013) argues that a common cultural strategy is to bring entities that carry similar symbolic associations together, and the example she discusses is that of the child and nature. Both carry similar cultural connotations: they are valued, vulnerable and in need of protection and purification. Purification signals a material ethics or morality:

> A material ethics is an ethics that considers the levels of embodiment of the concept into material reality, and vice versa: the way matter (as bodies, natures, forms of existence) is conceptualized in and modelled by discursive practices. (Iovino 2012: 64)

Thus, the idea that children are or should be pure leads to cleanliness rituals in which this morality is enacted. Vice versa, infant bodies and products may be shaped by cultural ideas of purity, such that the sale of organic foods came into its own especially when these became connected with the vulnerable child (James 1993). In relation to all of these dimensions of purification, attempts may be made to create pecuniary value.

The chapter is organised in two parts. I start by following the recently growing interest in re-usable nappies in an analysis that gives some insight into the hybrid realities of early parenting, in which practical, embodied, environmental and symbolic concerns are brought together. I mostly draw on my interviews with prospective and new parents to discuss plans and values towards child care and products, where the focus returns to the process of dealing with baby excrement, which, as argued by Murcott (1993), points to the concomitant realisation of infants as pure and polluting. In the second part of the chapter, the focus shifts to an example of the purifying work performed in sales practices that render products natural, thus enhancing their suitability as components in child caring practices. I here return to infant feeding tools and present an analysis of recently converging sales narratives in which the tools are 'naturalised' through design changes that are argued to make these closer to the embodied qualities of infants and the process of breastfeeding.

Cleansing the Child: Diverse Concerns, Diverse Nappies

Nappy[1] companies always had a presence at the consumer exhibitions I visited. Two of the main brands of disposable nappies: Pampers and Huggies,[2] exhibited at The Baby Show over the years, adopting the style of exhibition described in Chapter 4 as 'showcasing the brand'. Pampers frequently sponsored a baby changing 'service', where visitors could use free disposable nappies to 'change' their infants. Common reusable nappy companies exhibiting at The Show were Totsbots, Bambino Mio and Bumgenius, with The Cotton Nappy Company offering prospective parents free advice: 'Confused about which washable nappy to buy? Come and obtain free independent advice on which nappy to purchase for your little one.'[3] These companies typically adopted the 'demonstration' format for their exhibition, with one company setting their demonstration up as a competition, where prospective mums and dads could play against one another in an effort to change most nappies on a baby doll in one minute, with the winner receiving a sticker. As well as adding a dimension of fun, perhaps the point of this activity was to show that real nappies are not so scary as many prospective parents think. Amongst my interviewees there was a definite sense of the 'strangeness' and 'challenge' of early child caring practices, including nappy changing, with a degree of anxiety about doing some of the practical hands-on care for their babies the very first time. Here, Charlotte and Dave (Couple, 6 months old daughter, first time parents, 20s, white, working class) remember those early worries:

> Charlotte: It is just like, when you first change a nappy and things like that. Ben: And sterilizing bottles. Charlotte: You just pick it up. Ben: You leave the hospital and you have never done anything like that at all. I have

---

[1] Nappies are commonly known as diapers in the US.

[2] Pampers and Huggies are disposable nappy brands, produced respectively by Proctor & Gamble and Kimberly Clarke.

[3] The Baby Show guide, Birmingham NEC 2008, p. 24.

never really known, you know… you have to sterilize bottles, but you just pick up on things, you learn yourself a lot of things.

When visiting the Scottish show at the SECC in 2010, I came across The Real Nappy Campaign, which was part of the Waste Aware Scotland programme and ran by the charity Environmental Campaigns (Scotland). In their advice brochure, real nappies are summed up as follows:

> Most real nappy systems consist of a soft, absorbent nappy, which is covered by a leak-proof, breathable cover (also known as a wrap). A one way liner is placed inside the nappy to catch solids. A booster liner (booster pad) can also be used with most nappies to soak up more wetness.[4]

The (re)turn to nappies that are reused, and washed between uses, has seen a shift in product design that make them not unlike disposable nappies. Possibly most prominent is the pre-shaped quality of reusable nappies. Where the terry-towelling nappies some interviewees mentioned as common in the 1970s typically were square cotton sheets that needed to be folded to be fitted around the baby's bottom, the reusable nappies sold today are more commonly one-piece pant-like items, with poppers or other fastening technologies, rather than the safety pin of yesteryears, used to ensure that the nappies stay in place. In this way, they are marketed to incorporate some of the convenience of the disposable nappy. The Real Nappy Campaign's advisory brochure lists the different kinds of reusable nappies available on the market as shaped nappies, all-in-one nappies, and flat nappies, with covers and liners mentioned separately. And in the Bambino Mio information brochure one can read that, in addition to nappies, the company sells laundry bags and nappy bucket, baby wipes, nappy cleanser and washing powder, a nappy bag for storing nappies, muslin squares, a hand sanitiser, training pants, a potty, and nappy swim pants and swimsuit. Other companies sell skin creams to deal with baby bottom problems, such as rashes.

---

[4]The Real Nappy Campaign (2010), A Guide to Using Real Nappies, Waste Aware Scotland, p. 3.

With this variety of products for dealing with bodily excretions, it is relatively easy to understand that prospective parents felt the need to investigate the different options, and this was a frequently expressed reason for visiting The Show. In fact, half of my interviewees spoke about their interest in reusable nappies. Where this interest was not significant, talk about dealing with 'baby dirt' was limited to brief comments about the necessity of nappies in everyday life. In Western cultures, nappies are a ubiquitous technology for dealing with baby excrement. Yet, Dombroski's (2012) interesting cultural analysis of Chinese and Australian family practices for dealing with baby bodily eliminations, shows how 'the nappy' is not a universally used technology. Yet, in this study, prospective parents easily slotted nappies into the category of products that were seen as essential items, as expressed here by Ashia and Bishr (Couple, 17 weeks, first time parents, 30s, Asian, professional):

Lydia: What kind of goods do you think are necessary when you have a baby?

Bishr: There are so many things you can walk around the show and buy, but it is what is a necessity and what is a luxury? Our necessities are everybody's necessities, like—a pram and a cot, and nappies, and things like that.

Making a decision about what kind of nappies to use was a matter of cost, environmental concerns and aesthetics. Below, I address how nappies were tied up in prospective parental enactments of environmental concerns and in cultural views about second hand products (Waight 2013, 2014). I will then briefly consider the enactment of adorability in infants. Whilst purifying is one of the teleoaffective urgencies of the practice of child caring, these two sections show that they connect with substantially different material-symbolic concerns and performances, that in turn connect with different products, and thus, signal different opportunities for the making of pecuniary value.

Beyond the Pure Child?: The Pure Environment and Costs

Two couples in the study, Lesley and Dan (Couple, 33 weeks pregnant, first time parents, 30s, white, professional), and Cheryl and Liam (Couple, 31 weeks pregnant, first time parents, 30s, white, professional/technical), volunteered strongly held environmental values. Whilst other respondents mentioned environmental concerns, for instance, in expressing their interest in reusable nappies, these couples couched their discussion on nappies, and provisioning for their expected baby in general, within a broader narrative about what kinds of consumers they were, and what their aspirations were for the new families they were establishing. Both couples were university educated young professionals, but with different social backgrounds. Not all professional middle-class participants made a claim to the environmental concerns expressed by these two couples, and neither did the working-class participants, who enacted a different set of priorities (Martens 2012; Halkier and Jensen 2011).

Lesley and Dan saw their environmental values as part of a broader set of social values, and they were keen to bring up their child in a way where it was confronted with these values. The couple had already made a range of life style decisions that reflected this, such as moving away from London to make room for a family and to create financial flexibility so that they could live on one income, when Lesley would stay at home to mother. The couple now lived in a medium sized city, did not own a car, and used public transport to get to work. Both were lawyers, but they had made a decision early in their working lives to practice in jobs with a social dimension, thus rejecting lines of work where, as Dan explained, they could easily become rich. Both were also from working class backgrounds. Lesley summed up their values:

> … it comes from wanting basic values, of wanting a child who is polite, and friendly, and chilled out, and cares about environmental issues,… bringing a child up without creating too much havoc environmentally, … and understanding social principles about caring and sharing.

Cheryl and Liam, on the other hand, relied on two cars in order to get to work from their semi-rural home, with Liam doing a one-hour return journey each day. But their house was small and thus imposed structural limitations on the amount of stuff they could own. Like Lesley, Cheryl spoke passionately about her values towards the environment and categorised their spending habits as 'frugal':

> ...I feel very strongly about lots of things and lots of green and ethical things, like waste and the effect on the planet. I almost want to be an advocate for that, you know...

The potential environmental impact of the transition to becoming new families has recently become a subject of scholarly interest (see, for instance, Burningham and Venn 2017; Burningham et al. 2014; Waight 2013, 2014). Their visit to The Baby Show brought home to both couples the potential of this life course transition leading to greater product and purchase 'intensity', and the experience made them talk about how they were planning to navigate a pathway through this world that was more 'environmentally friendly'. Cheryl said with a degree of confidence that she did not think their transition into a new family would change their existing spending habits—'I mean, I don't think we will change that much. I hope we don't. I think we are strong enough not to'. The consumer exhibition was seen as embodying the excesses of this consumer world, but also demonstrated 'the alternatives', whilst offering an educational experience for teasing out the challenges of 'consuming less':

> Liam: We didn't come here saying that we will buy lunch and buy drinks, we will bring it all ourselves. That is our sort of mentality. That is why we are looking at reusable nappies. We don't want to keep buying nappies, and buying nappies, and throwing them in the bin. A lot of the stuff here is very much geared that way, although it is surprising to see how many things ... people are starting to look at being reusable.

Along with disposable nappies, the excesses and potential waste of consumer culture were symbolised by the various things that were handed out at The Show. Lesley, in particular, spoke about declining flyers, as these would only end up adding to the content of their home's recycle bin, making her feel guilty. Cheryl, on the other hand, was actually quite taken by the freebees handed out at The Show, though she acknowledged the contradictory nature of this:

> The freebies are a bit naughty as they are singly wrapped. There is that whole balance isn't there. I got free nappies, or free, you know, things, but at the same time, they are not that good for the environment so. There is hundreds of stuff, it really does concern me how many…

Their observations also demonstrated awareness of the contradictions of being professionals, with reasonably good incomes, and of being consumers, whilst simultaneously laying claims to being environmentally friendly. These came out strongly in the observations made by Lesley, who was vocal about the fact that what practicing environmental ethics meant for their consumption practices was not so clear-cut. She observed, for instance, that they could take it much further than they had ('it is not like we don't have a TV, and we live in a commune, and we have a compost unit. I would love to be like that, but we have got a power shower…'). She also had a healthy scepticism of the 'green consumerism' she saw represented so clearly at The Show. Being readers of the Ethical Consumer Magazine gave them insight into 'green consumer' brands, like The Body Shop and Ecover, making her wonder whether they were 'truly ethical behind the scenes?' Whilst Dan agreed that these matters made it all 'very difficult', they were clear that purchasing green products was still purchasing products, and thus constituted consumerism:

> … we are also not buying wholly into the whole… like the Green Babies place, we have bought some erm… non-petroleum jelly and some baby wash. We have not bought the whole range of everything, I just think you need a couple of basics, you don't need to buy the whole range - having the baby balm, the diaper cream, the shampoo, the lotion, all of that, as that is getting back into consuming.

Both couples also spoke about the need to learn about this product world, for instance, for working out what they did and did not really need. Liam spoke regularly about the things they would need, as opposed to the things that they would consider a luxury. The freebees received at The Show, and also the various disposable and unpractical items friends and family were giving them, would be received with grace and treated as luxury items. Here, Liam talks about The Show as providing an opportunity for learning to make these distinctions:

> ...you can discover something, as you can say that it came in really handy, that one thing that we got given, that came in really handy. Maybe we can find a place and use for that, or to really know that we don't need that. They say in all these magazines that you have to buy this particular amount of wipes, and if you can find out that you can use cotton wool, or a towel or something, then you don't have to keep using disposable things. So at the same time as being given disposable things, we can really cross them off our list and say that we really do or don't need them.

Cheryl and Liam frequently returned to the importance they attributed to being frugal, to spending their money wisely, for instance, on durable items, and on saving for the future. Financial and environmental concerns were also played off against each another by Lesley and Dan, evident, for instance, when Lesley clarified that they would be washing and tumble drying their own nappies, rather than using the more environmentally friendly, and also more expensive, nappy laundry company. Learning about what was really necessary in their forthcoming life with a small child, and the importance attributed to budgetary concerns, was not dissimilar to the critical discussion of Carol (Mothers, 15 weeks, first time parents, 20s, white, working class), who challenged the 'baby needs' narratives found in the commercial world in view of the budgetary realities of her life. Carol's case will be discussed in the next chapter as one of three ideal types of moral-selving found amongst new and prospective parents. The narratives of Lesley and Dan, and Cheryl and Liam, offer insight into how different teleoaffective priorities (of environmental and budgetary concerns) come into conflict in the reasoning of people about the choices they make (Halkier 2013; Halkier and Jensen 2011).

Part of what is interesting about the observations made by these two couples is the way in which their environmental life styles were not adopted as a consequence of transitioning into parenthood, but had been a way of life for them before they started on this trajectory. This stance was different from those of Marcia and Jasmin (two other professional middle class mothers in the study), who narrated their adoption of an organic life style as directly related to the transition into parenthood, based on their views of what was best for their babies. For the two environmentally aware couples discussed here, the question was much more one of whether and how to maintain their current environmentally conscious life styles in the face of their impending parenthood, and in which consumer culture was seen as stimulating consumerism. For these four participants, it could be argued that they viewed their life style as 'better' for their soon to be born child, even though this link was not made very explicit. By contrast, sales narratives did adopt a convention of featuring the pure child alongside a pure natural environment (Taylor 2011, 2013). Examples of this encountered in my research include the Ecover advertisement, discussed and reproduced in Martens and Scott (2006), and a webpage initiative of Fairy Liquid in 2009, which illustrated Fairy's baby hugging a green earth.[5] I will discuss this apparent parental reticence further in the conclusion.

Performing Infant Adornment

For Harris 'cuteness is not something we find in our children but something we *do* to them' (2000: 5–italics in the original). It is perhaps unnecessary to make recourse to the 'excreting bodies of real life babies' (Harris 2000: 11) to acknowledge that infants are not adorable *per sé*. However, as I argued in Chapter 5, the idea of infants as adorable and lovable small creatures is culturally very strong, and I here argue that certain aesthetic practices are the work of purifying in which this cultural idea is pushed

---

[5]Fairy Liquid is a well-known brand of washing up liquid, produced and marketed by the international company Proctor and Gamble.

in front of its opposite messy reality. The bodysuits at the Blooming Marvellous stand, discussed and illustrated in Chapter 5, suggest that slogan-rich baby grows, and some other articles—like nappies, and soothers, and even the baby carriers that were discussed in Chapter 5—are useful and used for the performance of infant adornment.

Thinking about the practice of infant adornment as 'dressing up', it is noteworthy that the product category of infant clothing and fashion accessories classified a set of exhibitors at The Baby Show. With names such as Babies in Sheep's Clothing, Huggies and Bumgenius, the play on the cute is apparent in the very names these companies adopt. This includes the diaper or nappy, an item of clothing found solely in the baby closet, and that plays an important role not just in the containment of material bodily excretions, but that has historically featured in visual imagery of the baby beautiful. In Chapter 5, I briefly spoke about the historical beauty of the chubby baby. This idea is visualised in representations that illustrate infants clothed solely in a nappy that accentuate the size of the baby bottom. Witness the 'immortalised' baby logo of Fairy Liquid, which has featured for so long on bottles containing this washing up product. Its 'hand-drawn' and caricatured image of a toddler in a nappy is representative of this common thread in pictorial representations. The bulky cloth nappy distorts the baby's bodily appearance, making it take on some of the grotesque that Harris (2000) pinpoints as characteristic of the aesthetic of cute, and that make children into disempowered objects of the adult gaze (see also Cook 2009). Whilst the disposable nappy has effectively done away with big baby bottoms, in the return of washable cloth nappies, their huggability appeal is a substantial part of the narratives that drive their sales. In conversation with the distributor and online retailer Hip, Hip Baby, at the Baby Product Association exhibition in 2009, I discovered that cloth nappies come with a broad a range of 'outer layer' aesthetic patterning, and the sales representative said that whilst cloth nappies clearly have a degree of durability, he accounted of parents returning for more nappies in order to dress their babies in different kinds of prints.

The diversification of nappies into disposable and reusable varieties, but also in terms of the 'purity' of the materials that have gone into their making (e.g. organic cotton, bamboo), and, as just discussed, aesthetic appeal, suggests varieties in parental concerns and tastes, and in the existence of niche markets. Of course, whilst nappies may reflect different kinds of concerns, these may also be brought together. For instance, reusable nappies can be made with organic materials and sport funny images, and disposable nappies can be made with organic and biodegradable materials. In addition, parents may well make use of a range of nappies, for instance, disposable nappies when travelling and reusable nappies when at home, and the nappy with the funny prints for when there is a family party. One of the interesting points of the analysis above, of parental conversations, is how a particular way of knowing the young child does not 'lead' in these discussions. Instead, 'the child that is yet to be born' is located in a broader narrative where references to costs, convenience and the environment suggest a range of broader concerns in family life. I will return to this in the next chapter.

Moralising Products: Natural Bodies and Natural Products

In thinking about products in relation to infant purity and purification, I may be concerned, as I was in the last two chapters, with the question how purity is performed as a quality in the teleoaffective order of child caring through the definition of what a young child is like. However, I may also and at the same time be concerned with the implications of this teleoaffective order, and its relationship with the rules and princi-ples that simultaneously 'determine' what is social in practices. One of the affordances of locating the practice of child caring at the centre of the analysis is that it helps to defy linear causal arguments. An exam-ple relevant here would be that markets are all-powerful in their defi-nition of young children, and thus create a world in which parenting becomes a highly complex and anxiety-provoking endeavour. A practice approach preferences complexity! Here, this means that knowing the child in specific ways is simultaneously performed and stabilised in a range of performances, and in turn, these stabilities inform those per-formances. Here, and in the next two chapters, my focus shifts to this second emphasis in the performance of practices, and thus from consideration of the stabilisation of understandings of the young child, to considerations of the implications these stable understandings have for the creation of moral entities—whether these are prospective and new parents, commercial organisations and their practices, or, as discussed below, the portfolio of products that are for sale.

By aligning products and what they do, with understandings of the young child, these are imbued with, and even designed in accordance with, a range of moralities (Verbeek 2006, 2011). I call this alignment, in which products are 'made' in the image of childhood, the moralisation of products. For products to be acceptable co-presences in child caring—in other words, to be 'fit for purpose'—entails attending to the symbolic meanings of childhood. Child safety consciousness, discussed in Chapter 6, as one way in which child safety is attended to, is also one example of the moralisation of products. In addition to product safety, products also need to be pure, and product purification is a practice that rids products from material-discursive pollutants (as happened in Chapter 6 in relation to perceived impurities in plastics and vitamins). The propensity to rid products of impurities is stronger, the closer these products get to young children. New parent participants, for instance, found the idea of using second hand reusable nappies problematic unless these had been used for an older sibling. Second hand clothing, on the other hand, appeared to be less problematic, because—as was a commonly expressed view—very young children grow out of their clothes so rapidly, these are near enough new anyway. New products generally held the upper hand in terms of qualifying for a purity 'label', though some prospective parents, including Cheryl and Liam, also spoke about personalising rituals in order to cleanse second hand goods. Similar factors may be seen to drive the popularisation of organic foods for infants and their carers (James 1993). At the visited consumer exhibitions, it was not surprising to find major infant food brands (Organix, Plum Baby, Ella's Kitchen, Rachel's Organic) trade on the organic qualities of their produce, even to an extent whereby, as opined by a representative from Ella's Kitchen, there now existed a general consensus that *all* infant foods now *are* organic. In addition to organic foods, skincare products and clothing (including, as was demonstrated earlier, nappies) could also carry 'organic' tags. Organic goods are clearly seen as more 'natural' than non-organic goods.

Below, I present an analysis of recent design 'innovation' of infant feeding tools, and the sales narratives that have accompanied this process, in which the main story line is 'naturalisation'. Infant feeding is a pathway of the practice of child caring around which moral concerns have, and continue to be, highly pronounced. Not surprising, therefore, is the considerable and continued scholarly debate, which shows that infant feeding is not merely a private concern, but a public issue, and a highly politicised one at that.[6] The redesign and marketing of baby feeding tools in the past 10 years may be seen as a response to the 'breast-is-best' campaign of the 1990s, which was formulated around the understanding that infant feeding was a matter of choosing between the alternative options of breastfeeding and bottle feeding, and that relied on specific ways of thinking about babies and their feeding practices and preferences (Lee 2011; Murphy 1999). The 'naturalisation' narrative that has accompanied the new generation of feeding tools works in two ways. On the one hand, it attempts to shift the moral worth of infant feeding tools, by subjecting these to symbolic purification in order to render them suitable tools in practices with pure and valued infants. On the other hand, it challenges the either/or understanding of infant feeding of the 1990s, and supports the sale of new technologies, such as the breast pump, to signal that babies can feed from bottles *and* breasts. In what follows, the moralisation of products

---

[6]For an overview of social science debate on infant feeding, see Lee (2011). In the UK, infant feeding was researched by Murphy and colleagues as part of the ESRC programme The Nation's Diet in the 1990s, and pointed to the politicisation of this practice as a consequence of the 'breast-is-best' advice, which came from the state-medical complex. Modern history discussions of infant feeding, and the relation to commercial foods can be found in the work of Rima Apple (1987), Stevens et al. (2009). Boyer (2010), Boyer and Boswell-Penc (2010) offer interesting critical feminist analyses on the breast pump and the commodification of breast milk, and Keenan and Stapleton (2013) offer an analysis of infant feeding and the challenges of consumption.

consists in bringing together a series of truth claims about 'natural' infants that focus on their bodies and their feeding preferences, with 'natural' products.

Naturalising Infant Feeding Tools[7]

A few years ago, I spoke with a sales representative at the Tommee Tippee stand at the Baby Show. They had just launched their 'Closer to Nature' range and were very enthusiastic about their new product and the way it 'spoke' to parents, with a special nod in the direction of fathers. The new Tommee Tippee bottle was stout in appearance (shorter and fatter than their past bottle) and where the teat was attached to the bottle, it had a rounded 'dome' shape, resembling, it was said, the shape of the mother's breast. The representative went on to demonstrate how their new teat was now bendable in all directions, purportedly mirroring more closely the flexibility of the mother's nipple, making it easier for the infant to 'latch on'.[8] The combination of bottle and teat may be regarded as a form of replicating the feeding 'functions' of the mother's breast, with the bottle serving as 'the container' resembling the breast and the teat resembling the functions of the nipple; the part of the mother's body that enters the baby's mouth and through which the feeding fluids enter the baby's mouth when stimulated by the infant's sucking motion. The rounded 'dome' shaped bottle by Tommee Tippee may be regarded as part of a 'new generation' of feeding tools that move away from the 'slim-line' bottle of the past, in preference for chunkier shapes, and accompanied by more explicit narrative attention to the teat and its design.

---

[7]I would like to wholeheartedly thank Dr. Emma Head for the various conversations we had on these web-based sales narratives, and for sharing her insights on so many occasions.

[8]Latching on is a medical term used for the process whereby the baby finds the mother's nipple, and takes this sufficiently firmly into the mouth to be able to suckle it.

When browsing the websites of other brand-companies[9] that sell feeding bottles, slogans like 'inspired by nature', 'simply intuitive' and 'closer to nature' appear to be commonplace.[10] Below, I examine how the sales content on these websites purify feeding bottles and teats through a 'naturalising narrative' in which the tools are argued to have been designed to more closely resemble the natural practice of breast-feeding. The narrative proceeds in two steps. First, an argument is made for the importance of gathering knowledge of relevant body parts (the breast, the nipple and the areola, and the baby's mouth, with its lips, gums, upper mouth palette and tongue) and the ways in which these interact during the practice of natural oral activities, such as sucking when feeding on the breast or as a means for soothing. How the mother's breast works, how the nipple functions, the employment of babies mouths, its muscles and the coordination of body parts, and how babies' digestion works, are all potential matters of interest. In addition to these embodied dimensions, which are couched in terms of the

---

[9]The websites analysed here were those of MAM, NUK, Phillips Avent and Tommee Tippee. All date from April and May 2013. Tommee Tippee is an American owned company, which has a major production site in the UK. Philips Avent is the merged outcome of the British infant feeding tools brand company Avent, and the Dutch domestic technologies giant Philips. The merger took place in 2006, which signals the shift to a 'mixed feeding' narrative. MAM is of Austrian origin and NUK originates in Germany. These brand companies all trade globally. The website content of these international commercial organisations change regularly, and many maintain different sites for specific countries. In 2013, for instance, NUK had a 'generic' international English language site, and also sites for a range of different countries. For some countries, the organization of the site differed considerably from that of the international site, for others, some or all of the materials used on the international site were used. For NUK and MAM, I analysed the international English language sites. I analysed the UK sites of the other companies. As website content changes over time, the procedure I used was to copy the website content of each brand-company by making screen prints of each page of information, and by storing any additional materials, including any information brochures that were available from the sites. This allowed for the archival of textual and visual materials to return to later.

[10]In a sketch of the history of the development of artificial infant foods, Mepham (1993) coins the phrase 'humanizing milk' and indicates that the 'priority' to design commercial products to 'mirror the real thing' is not a novel phenomenon. Like breast milk, so-called formula feeds are offered to infants in liquid form. These typically share with mothers' milk an 'off-white' milky appearance, and bottles containing formula feeds are prepared to resemble the temperature of the human body. However, it is the more lengthy historical and scientific practice of examining the chemical composition of breast milk, in an effort to use this knowledge to mirror its qualities in the development of formula milk that illustrates the scientific accomplishment of what is in essence a hybridised foodstuff. See also: Weaver (2003).

language of child development, there is interest in the infant's preferences and habit formation. The second step then involves telling the story of how these body parts, embodied functions and embodied experience are 'mirrored' in the design of tools.

The German brand-company NUK is interesting for the voluminous quality of its website content. Here, NUK sketches the history of its hallmark product: the well-known 'traditional' orthodontic and asymmetrical teat, first developed in 1949 by two German dental practitioners. In the first step of its naturalisation narrative, NUK assertively moves the body and breastfeeding into the fore-ground, creating these as the 'gold-standard' that calls their closest attention. The emphasis here is on the infant's embodied development:

> The mouth plays a key role in the healthy overall development of your child. Breathing, eating, sensory perception – all these things require perfect coordination between the jaw, tongue and lips. Breastfeeding is the perfect training for this from birth onwards. At its mother's breast, a baby learns to coordinate the movements, to strengthen its muscles and to prepare its mouth for the tasks to come - teething, chewing and, last but not least, speaking.[11]

Science and scientists are used as the best method for getting to know about the embodied qualities of feeding. Thus, whilst purification in relation to the young child means that 'artificial technologies' carry a strong negative cultural connotation, NUK nevertheless mobilises a strategy where science can discover 'nature', and thus celebrates the modern optimism and progress of science that has been such a common characteristic of modernity (Beck 1992; Beck et al. 1994). NUK asserts the importance of scientific knowledge by drawing on the preciousness of the infant child, and, as for the analysis in Chapter 6, the elusive embodied infant and the embodied practice for breastfeeding are explained in a step-wise narrative progression. It is because the child is so important, and breastfeeding a mysterious embodied practice, that

---

[11]http://en.nuk.de/#path=/nukshape/nuk_orthodontic&m=1, accessed on 30 April 2013. The next citation is also from this site.

science is necessary to ensure that the tools brought to market are subject to continuous reflective investigation, and may thus be claimed to be 'fit for purpose' in the best possible way.

The next step in the narrative is how the accrued knowledge of bodies, body parts, and how these interact in the practice of breastfeeding, is fed into tool design. NUK's focus is on tool shape. Setting the NUK design off against its competitors, its asymmetrical teat has always been different from other teats, and is so because it is shaped to reflect the shape of the mother's nipple when it is being sucked on in the infant's mouth. Here, textual explanation comes together with a neat schematic drawing offering three images of the breast nipple, the bottle teat and the teat of the soother when in the mouth of a baby. In each picture, the baby's incorporation of the nipple/teat into its mouth moulds these in the same way. In addition, the colour scheme of the mother's nipple and those of the tools is similar, creating the overall effect of similarity across these different 'materials'. NUK's schematic drawing is accompanied by the following explanatory text, in which the brand-company's early dental practitioners are said to have noticed:

> … first of all that the mother's nipple changes shape when the baby feeds and only then is optimal coordination in the mouth achieved. And this special asymmetrical shape is used as the model for all NUK teats to this very day. NUK has researched the shape right down to the smallest detail over many decades, developed it further and constantly adapted it in light of the latest medical findings.

In the past 10 years, Philips Avent and MAM have also heralded a 'new generation' of 'closer to nature' tools by essentially following the same two-step strategy, but with some noteworthy variations. Perhaps not surprisingly, given it also trades in breast pumps, Philips Avent emphasises how the use of its products makes it easy to switch between the breast and the bottle, pushing the baby and its feeding preferences into the foreground:

> The Natural bottle is our most innovative and advanced bottle, helping to make bottle feeding more natural for your baby and you. The bottle

is perfect for moms who plan on breastfeeding, as baby can now easily combine breast and bottle feeding. … The wide, breast-shaped nipple has been designed to help your baby latch on naturally.[12]

In the argument for making 'mixed feeding' easier for babies, and thus also for parents, different child 'development' narratives to the one presented by NUK are encountered. Whereas NUK talks about *optimal* feeding in relation to a series of embodied dexterities that young children need to develop in order to eat and talk, Philips Avent and MAM focus on the idea that babies quickly form habituated dependencies on specific practices of feeding and sucking, that was pivotal in the feeding advice of the 1990s, supporting the lay theory that parents had to choose right from the start whether to breastfeed or to bottle feed. What is interesting here is that babies are known in a specific way: of forming habits and preferences easily, but also their aversion to change. This forms the reason why the companies offer their redesigned 'more natural' products as providing the means for switching easily between the breast and the bottle.

By allowing infants to have embodied preferences, with a recommendation that these are to be accommodated, the reader catches first sight of a rendition of the child consumer. The sales narratives found on the MAM website are a good example of this, and moreover, one that switches from the shape of tools, to a more unusual discussion of the materials used in their production. MAM discusses the pros and cons of the two main materials it uses in teat production: latex and silicone. Both materials are given a critical appraisal on the website. Latex is a natural material that comes from the bark of trees. It has a long track record in use in infant feeding tools, is soft and has the colour of human skin, but is also less durable than silicone. Silicone, on the other hand, is a man-made product that is identified as harder and more 'modern' than latex. It is see-through and has a more clinical appearance. It is in relation to silicone that the company asserts the infant's embodied

---

[12]http://www.philips.co.uk/c/avent-baby-bottle-feeding/15069/cat/#stab=1&prd=tru,   accessed on 30 April 2013.

multi-sensory experience over and above that of the commonly held 'functional' benefits of this product material:

> Lots of parents choose silicone. There are good reasons for doing this. The clear material looks hygienic; it is odourless and tasteless; silicone does not age. There is just one disadvantage: Conventional silicone is slightly tougher than latex. It therefore feels artificial. But babies discover the world with their mouth. How things feel and taste is important to them. Babies love the smart Silk Teat® because it feels soft and familiar – like Mummy's skin. This makes the switch between breastfeeding and bottle particularly easy. And the little ones can relax right from day one.[13]

To the extent that these passages signpost the child consumer, the language that is used steers clear from the negative connotations of the child consumer. The babies in this story do not cry loudly to have their desires and needs heard and taken into account (Rosen 2015), nor do they have unreasonable needs. Instead, the explanation foregrounds the precious and lovable child, who rewards parents with 'a first beaming smile', making the accommodation of their interest into acquiring multi-sensory embodied experiences a no-brainer: why would one deny the tools that young children will love, as they resemble the feel of the mother's skin, allowing them to thoroughly 'relax' when they use these products?

Conclusion

Built around two parts, this chapter presented an analysis of purifying as a repetitive though diverse set of performances that structure the teleoaffective quality of the practice of child caring. In the first half, I reflected on the narrative performances of prospective parents in relation to the nappy, which parents in this study considered to be a ubiquitous purification tool. In the second part of the chapter, I offered

---

[13]http://www.mambaby.com/en/the-products/soothers/mam-silk-teat-26765-en.html,   accessed on 6 May 2013.

an analysis of 'naturalisation' narratives in the web page content of four international brand-companies that sell infant feeding tools. The specific focus in each part, and the conclusions that may be drawn, are distinct. In discussing prospective and new parents' conversations about nappies, it was clear that their consumer reasoning moved beyond understandings and concerns of the child, to incorporate the broader familial concerns of costs, convenience, and the environment. In comparison with the sales narratives that have been analysed thus far, relatively little was learned about the qualities of infants from the discussions with prospective parents. It is possible to pick up, in rather broad terms, that infants are lovable, vulnerable and pure. But this is never fleshed out in great detail. In comparing parental narrative enactments with those that may be found in commercial literature, the former appear reticent in comparison with the later. It may be that in other work on parents and parenting, parents conceptualise young children in more detailed and varied ways (e.g. Brownlie and Leith 2011; Lupton 2013; Murphy 2007). One explanation for this may be that my interviewees were mostly first time prospective parents. In comparison, Brownlie and Leith (2011) conducted research with parents who had gone through the experience of immunising their young offspring; something which clearly was a fundamentally paradoxical experience for many. What seems clear, though, is that despite drawing on the same set of teleoaffective qualities, the ways parents and companies talk about and know the young child varies in accordance with their specific priorities (see also Chapter 8).

In contrast, the second part of this chapter demonstrated how at least some sales narratives work to closely align the qualities of products with those of the young child. I called this section the moralisation of child caring products, and it reflects the duality of performing infant purity and the need to engage with the moral consequences of infant purity as a stabilised category of culture. When commercial organisations engage in the moralisation of their products, they give voice to being carriers of child caring (see also Chapter 9). In this particular example, child purity (or, the natural embodied child and the natural process of breastfeeding) was the starting point for an alignment in product design, which was shared across the major brand-companies who design, produce

and sell infant feeding tools. An explanation for this recent development needs to be sought in the broader political and cultural debate on
infant feeding. Thus, the 'naturalisation' of infant feeding tools may be
acknowledged as an attempt to shift the either/or discourse on infant
feeding that was dominant in the 1990s, and towards the view that
infants can be fed in more flexible ways. The 'naturalisation' strategy
pursued by feeding tool brand-companies is a 'new' pecuniary value creation strategy, supporting the drive towards mixed feeding as a new and
morally acceptable mode of feeding infants that also supports other new
tools, like the breast pump, which are now marketed by some of these
companies as part of a product package for feeding infants. The international site of NUK was an exception. Whilst working with the same
naturalisation narrative, this was rationalised by an argument that aligning tools with bodies and bodily moulding during feeding resulted in
optimised feeding and mouth development in the infant. Overall, naturalisation is an attempt to shift the worth and worthiness of products,
and the practices associated with it, from the profane to the sacred.

   Those familiar with critical analyses of 'nature' (e.g. Castree and
Braun 1998) will recognise, especially in the more elaborate NUK content, an appeal to the 'clean' or 'reputable' way of knowing nature in
and through reference to science knowledge. In NUK's accounting,
the starting point is the assumption that breastfeeding, and the human
body parts and functions that are combined in this practice, are how
Mother Nature intended infant feeding to happen. Breastfeeding is thus
taken as the gold standard that forms the subject matter for scientific
knowledge production. Yet, by knowing about 'the' shape of 'the' nipple in 'the' baby's mouth, both verbally and visually, the reader is confronted with a story of 'one shape fits all', which is contradicted in later
website content, for instance, when breastfeeding is sketched as posing
problems due to bodily malfunctions, such as inverted nipples. In reality, of course, bodies and body parts have varied physical forms, and
will also lead to variations in how these 'function' together. The varied
products that the brand-product companies, discussed above, bring to
market interestingly point to both variation and limitation in the ways
in which infant bodies and their functions are known, even when the
focus is solely on the shape of products. Rather than pointing to infants

quickly becoming habituated, and as developing fixed preferences in their approach to getting food, product variation suggests that infants demonstrate embodied flexibilities and resilience exactly because different infants apparently manage very well to procure their food from products with different designs. Whilst there is little doubt that these brand-companies know all of this very well, it confirms sales narratives as specific 'mobilizations of the world' (Latour 1999: 99–100), designed not so much to prove that their products do the job, but to locate themselves in relation to the competition and to shift cultural narratives on infant feeding in favour of tool use.

Finally, this chapter has offered illustrations of the ways in which the teleoaffective qualities of child caring are brought together in the constitution of different sales narratives. As was the case in the last two chapters, whilst the emphasis was on child purity, the investigated sales narratives demonstrate nuanced variations through the entanglement of teleoaffective priorities. In NUK, MAM and Phillips Avent, the natural child is also a lovable child, a child that is deserving of the carefully designed products these companies offer. Moreover, NUK places emphasis on child development, whilst MAM speaks about the child's innate interest in learning in multi-sensory and embodied ways, giving voice to the importance of the feeling of touch and closeness. The narratives these companies construct are also overwhelmingly positive in their tone. They have clearly decided to make their sales pitch around the lovable qualities of childcare, instead of driving messages through anxiety narratives. Especially in the NUK example, the optimisation narrative offers a progression from the traditional emphasis that bad tools and certain habituated embodied practices cause embodied abnormalities (see also Coutant et al. 2011).

Bibliography

Apple, R.D. 1987. *Mothers and medicine: A social history of infant feeding, 1890–1950*. Madison: University of Wisconsin Press.

Beck, U. 1992. *Risk society: Towards a new modernity*. London: Sage.

Beck, U., A. Giddens, and S. Lash. 1994. *Reflexive modernization: Politics, tradition and aesthetics in the modern social order.* Palo Alto: Stanford University Press.

Boyer, K. 2010. Of care and commodities: Breast milk and the new politics of mobile biosubstances. *Progress in Human Geography* 34 (1): 5–20.

Boyer, K., and M. Boswell-Penc. 2010. Breast pumps: A feminist technology, or (yet) "more work for mother"? In *Feminist technology*, ed. L. Layne, S. Vostral, and K. Boyer. Urbana: University of Illinois Press.

Brownlie, J., and V. Leith. 2011. Social bundles: Thinking through the infant body. *Childhood* 18 (2): 196–210.

Burningham, K., and S. Venn. 2017. Understanding and practising sustainable consumption in early motherhood. *Journal of Consumer Ethics* 1 (2): 82–91.

Burningham, K., S. Venn, I. Christie, T. Jackson, and B. Gatersleben. 2014. New motherhood: A moment of change in everyday shopping practices? *Young Consumers* 15 (3): 211–226.

Castree, N., and B. Braun. 1998. The construction of nature and the nature of construction. In *Remaking reality: Nature at the millenium*, ed. B. Braun and N. Castree, 3–42. London: Routledge.

Cook. 2009. The ingratiating child: Conundrums and questions in the commercial depiction of childhood. Unpublished paper for "The Ethics of Representing Childhood: Popular Culture, Performance, and Pedagogy," 1–19, March 5–7, Arizona State University.

Coutant, A., V.I. de La Ville, M. Gram, and N. Boireau. 2011. Motherhood, advertising, and anxiety: A cross-cultural perspective on Danonino commercials. *Advertising & Society Review* 12 (2): 1–19.

Dombroski, K. F. 2012. Babies' bottoms for a better world: Hygiene, modernities and social change in Northwest China and Australasia. Doctor of Philosophy, University of Western Sydney.

Douglas, M. 1993. *Purity and danger: An analysis of concepts of pollution and taboo.* London: Routledge.

Douglas, M. 2003. *Purity and danger: An analysis of concepts of pollution and taboo.* London: Routledge.

Halkier, B. 2013. Contesting food–contesting motherhood. In *Motherhoods, markets and consumption: The making of mothers in contemporary Western cultures*, ed. S. O'Donohoe, M. Hogg, P. Maclaran, L. Martens, and L. Stevens, 89–103. London: Routledge.

Halkier, B., and I. Jensen. 2011. Methodological challenges in using practice theory in consumption research. Examples from a study on handling nutritional contestations of food consumption. *Journal of Consumer Culture* 11 (1): 101–123.

Harris, D. 2000. *Cute, quaint, hungry and romantic: The aesthetics of consumerism*. Cambridge, MA: DaCapo Press.

Iovino, S. 2012. Material ecocriticism: Matter, text, and posthuman ethics. In *Literature, ecology, ethics: Recent trends in ecocriticism*, ed. Timo Müller and Michael Sauter, 51–68. Heidelberg: Winter Verlag.

James, A. 1993. Eating green(s). In *Environmentalism: The view from anthropology*, ed. K. Milton, 205–218. London: Routledge.

Keenan, J., and H. Stapleton. 2013. 'It won't do her any harm' they said, 'or they wouldn't put it on the market'. In *Motherhoods, markets and consumption: The making of mothers in contemporary Western cultures*, ed. S. O'Donohoe, M. Hogg, P. Maclaran, L. Martens, and L. Stevens, 71–87. London: Routledge.

Latour, B. 1993. *The pasteurization of France*. Harvard, MA and London: Harvard University Press.

Latour, B. 1999. *Pandora's hope: Essays on the reality of science studies*. Harvard, MA and London: Harvard University Press.

Law, J. 2004. *After method. Mess in social science research*. London and New York: Routledge.

Lee, E. 2011. Breast-feeding advocacy, risk society and health moralism: A decade's scholarship. *Sociology Compass* 5 (12): 1058–1069.

Lupton, D. 2013. Precious, pure, uncivilised, vulnerable: Infant embodiment in Australian popular media. *Children and Society* 28 (50): 341–351.

Martens, L. 2012. Practice 'in talk' and talk 'as practice': Dish washing and the reach of language. *Sociological Research Online* 17 (3): 22. http://www.socresonline.org.uk/17/3/22.html.

Martens, L., and S. Scott. 2006. Under the kitchen surface: Domestic products and conflicting constructions of home. *Home Cultures* 3 (1): 39–62.

Mepham, T.B. 1993. " Humanizing" milk: The formulation of artificial feeds for infants (1850–1910). *Medical History* 37 (3): 225.

Murcott, A. 1993. Purity and pollution: Body management and the social place of infancy. In *Body matters: Essays on the sociology of the body*, ed. D. Morgan and S. Scott, 122–134. London: Falmer Press.

Murphy, E. 1999. 'Breast is best': Infant feeding decisions and maternal deviance. *Sociology of Health & Illness* 21 (2): 187–208.

Murphy, E. 2007. Images of childhood in mothers' accounts of contemporary childrearing. *Childhood* 14 (1): 105–127.

Nimmo, R. 2010. *Milk, modernity and the making of the human: purifying the social. CRESC: Culture, economy and the social.* London and New York: Routledge.

Rosen, R. 2015. 'The scream': Meanings and excesses in early childhood settings. *Childhood* 22 (1): 39–52.

Stevens, E.E., T.E. Patrick, and R. Pickler. 2009. A history of infant feeding. *The Journal of Perinatal Education* 18 (2): 32–39.

Taylor, A. 2011. Reconceptualising the 'nature' of childhood. *Childhood* 18 (4): 420–433.

Taylor, A. 2013. *Reconfiguring the natures of childhood.* London: Routledge.

Verbeek, P.P. 2006. Materializing morality design ethics and technological mediation. *Science, Technology & Human Values* 31 (3): 361–380.

Verbeek, P.P. 2011. *Moralizing technology: Understanding and designing the morality of things.* Chicago: University of Chicago Press.

Waight, E. 2013. Eco babies: Reducing a parent's ecological footprint with second-hand consumer goods. *International Journal of Green Economics* 7 7 (2): 197–211.

Waight, E. 2014. Second-hand consumption among middle-class mothers in the UK: Thrift, distinction, and risk. *Families, Relationships and Societies* 3 (1): 159–162.

Weaver, L.T. 2003. Improving infant milk formulas: Near the end of the trail for the holy grail? *Journal of Pediatric Gastroenterology and Nutrition* 36 (3): 307–310.

8

Marketised Pedagogy and the Moralities of Child Caring

Introduction

The previous three chapters focussed on the teleoaffective structuration of child caring through practices of knowing the young child in distinct ways. This chapter is about the moralities of child caring, and connects the teleoaffective structure and the rules and principles of this practice, for whilst the teleoaffectivities point to why child caring is important, the principles and instructions map out how the practice ought to be done. This chapter moves through two interconnected arguments. I start by discussing a phenomenon I call the marketisation of child caring pedagogy, by drawing out a set of features of the ways in which information and instruction are evident in the business of child caring. Two of these features: pedagogic merging and the production of brand-company websites as a one-stop-shop are further explored. My concern is to develop an understanding of the marketisation of pedagogy so as to clarify the implications of this phenomenon. As argued in Chapter 3, practices can be carried by different entities and carrying a practice is always a moral and politically infused performance. Here, I therefore focus primarily on the question what the process of

© The Author(s) 2018
L. Martens, *Childhood and Markets*, Studies in Childhood and Youth,
https://doi.org/10.1057/978-1-137-31503-8_8

pedagogic marketisation conveys about the position and positioning of commercial interests in the field of child caring. I then move onto the second part of the chapter, where, based on the semi-structured interviews with new and prospective parents, I present a three-fold typology of parental moral-selving (Barnett et al. 2005: 30). I conclude by thinking through how effective the marketisation of pedagogy is in governing new parent consumers in accordance with the principles of neo-liberalism.

Chapter 3 described new parents as a particular group of adults in the sense that they have been conceived of as essentially 'in-the-making' and on a trajectory of becoming (e.g. Bailey 1999; Lawler 2000; Miller 2005; Thomson et al. 2011). The voluminous amount of information, advice, guidance and instruction that is directed at new parents today, and that I encountered during my research, may be seen as confirming the significance of this characterisation. Not surprisingly, the pedagogy that lies at the heart of parenthood has already been subject to considerable scholarly interest (e.g. Apple 2006; Arnup 1994; Ehrenreich and English 1979; Furedi 2001; Hardyment 1995, 2007; Lawler 2000; Marshall et al. 2013; Martens 2009; Murphy 2003; Thomson et al. 2011). These early discussions are connected with 'scientific motherhood', which Rima Apple (2006: 2) offers as a historical process, evolving over the course of the past century, whereby motherhood transformed over time as childcare came to be increasingly mediated by scientific-medical-health know-how and instructional devices. Scientific motherhood is therefore an analysis of childcare moving more into the public domain, with parents directed to follow the advice of experts rather than that which comes from their personal lay network.

Contemporary parenthood means that those involved are caught up in a field of powerful and authoritative voices that formulate 'best' doing-scenarios that are *strongly directional* in their content, and that formulate and feed narratives of good parenthood, motherhood, and fatherhood (Lee 2007; Miller 2005). In Murphy's (2003) Foucauldian analysis, for instance, the strong directive on 'breast is best' is related to the generation of self-governing good mothers, who breast-feed their babies (see also e.g. Lee et al. 2014). During my research on the business of child caring, I came across a range of best doing-scenarios, including the imperative (discussed in Chapter 4) to maintain good health before and during pregnancy, with prospective mothers and fathers being discouraged from smoking, alcohol consumption, and with folic acid prescribed as a standard supplement for women during early pregnancy to prevent the development of brain and spine abnormalities in their babies. Another example is the relatively recent directive to place the baby on its back to sleep, and together with the imperative to monitor the baby's body temperature when asleep, this functions as means for preventing baby cot death.

Whilst these examples may be seen as feeding the highly moralistic quality of contemporary child caring, parents are said to now also face considerable quantities of information as well as pedagogical contradictions, with evidence that contemporary child caring advice lacks consensus (Halkier 2014; Thomson et al. 2011; Warde 1997). Sociologists have pointed to the complexities inherent in child caring advice as this shift over time with changes in scientific and medical know-how (e.g. Furedi 2001; Hardyment 2007). This was expressed by one of the new parents in my study:

> I think as you get on, you listen to everything everyone says, as people seem to go by the book. It says you have to do this and you have to do that, and then I think, you do listen to everything from when you first have a baby, you have people telling you all different things, and you get 3 different midwives coming round your house or something, and they will all tell you 3 different things. You don't know where to go! (Charlotte, couple, 6 months old daughter, first time parents, 20s, white, working class)

Whilst shifts and changes in medical-science knowledge may well go some way towards explaining this phenomena, I have argued for the importance of deliberating whether and how the complex and contradictory nature of contemporary childcare advice is related to the marketisation of pedagogical content and resources (Martens 2009). Thought through from a practice perspective, this question may be translated as follows: if commercial actants are recognised as carriers of child caring, what role do these play in the structuration of the rules and principles of the practice? Moreover, what commercial priorities inform practices of child caring pedagogy? This calls to attention the relationships between different carriers of the practice of child caring, including those between commercial players, those with medical-science practitioners and with new and prospective parents. Before such questions may be addressed, there is a need to know more about the marketisation of child caring pedagogy.

Pedagogic Marketisation

I start by outlining five interconnected features of the marketization of pedagogy:

1. The provision of information, educational resources and advice must be recognised as a ubiquitous element in the organisational mix of contemporary commercial encounter practices. By coining the phrase *organisational mix*, I am pointing to the way in which especially larger commercial entities 'fill out' their encounter practices by adding different 'ingredients' into the mix. For instance, parenting magazines explicitly declare that they employ child caring experts in their staff group; they include celebrity narratives in their publications and thus achieve a level of edutainment (Buckingham and Scanlon 2005), and recent years have seen a growth in the reporting and sharing of everyday parenting practices and ideas, drawing on 'communities of interpretation' (Thomson et al. 2011: 127) or 'communities of parenthood' (Martens et al. 2005). There are interesting parallels between consumer exhibitions, retailers, magazines, and brand-company websites in the manner in which a range of pedagogic materials are brought together. As touched on briefly in Chapter 4, The Baby Show operates very much as an informational environment through the opportunities it offers parents to gain advice on aspects and experiences of pregnancy and early parenthood/childhood from a diversity of experts, ranging from certified midwives to sales staff. Magazines and brand-company websites essentially offer the same pedagogical mix as can be found at the consumer exhibition, with

one difference being that the consumer exhibition operates more as a face-to-face interactional forum (though also see Chapter 9).

2. The information and advice provided in this commercial world concerns two distinct things. As discussed in Chapter 4, on the one hand, there is obviously substantial information on child caring *products* and *services*. At The Baby Show, product information comes in different forms: as verbal communication between stand representatives and the visiting public; as visual displays on exhibitors' stands; and as product brochures and company magazines. Chapter 4 highlighted how visitors can accrue a wealth of plastic bags during a day at The Show containing product samples and leaflets. On the other hand, there is information on child caring *practices*, and on the practicalities and symbolic consequences of family life in contemporary affluent societies. How these categories of advice come together is of considerable interest! The sceptic might quickly reach for the straightforward and simple explanation that the informational content on child caring practices is selected to best demonstrate the uses and usefulness of the products on sale. This is explored further below through an examination of the Cow & Gate website, which suggests that a more subtle analysis may be needed.

3. Whilst the earliest forms of advice were either free of charge, supplied by public bodies,[1] or came at a price in the form of expert advice books and parenting magazines, in the contemporary period, there has been a distinct growth in advice and informational resources that come 'free of charge'. Internet-based encounter platforms and consumer exhibitions offer excellent illustrations of this, raising the question why commercial practitioners invest in such copious instructional content? I will examine this further below, where I will ask why a company like Cow & Gate, which effectively sells food for young children, has such extensive informational material on its site, including a broad based discussion on pregnancy.

---

[1]For instance, Rima Apple (2006) points out that the American childcare advice publication with the greatest historical impact in the twentieth century was *Infant Care*, which was handed out to mothers by the U.S. government, suggesting that pedagogical resources have come free of charge.

4. As I have argued earlier (Martens 2009), it has become increasingly difficult to distinguish state-medical-science instructions from content constructed and provided by commercial practitioners. In addition, non-commercial and commercial pedagogic practices and content merge in different ways, and suggest that perhaps the distinction between these actants is becoming too laboured. I called this phenomenon pedagogic merging and it is a salient quality of the marketisation of pedagogical resources. It is illustrative of the ubiquitous utilisation of medical-health-science know-how and practices in this commercial world, as was already demonstrated in previous chapters.

5. Talking about the Cow & Gate website, which now exists as one site amongst a multitude of others, the past decade has seen the exponential growth of digital pedagogical media content, provided through Internet-based encounter platforms including brand-company websites, 'life course' websites addressed at new parenting, online discussion forums (e.g. Mamsnet), and the parenting clubs that are hosted on almost all of the sites. Using the website of Cow & Gate as example, below I discuss the organisational features commonly found on the websites of larger brand-companies.

Using the example of The Baby Show, I first discuss the phenomenon of pedagogic merging, and then move on to discuss the pedagogic organisation of the brand-company website, using the Cow & Gate website as example.

Pedagogic Merging as an Element of the Marketisation of Pedagogy

The Baby Show is illustrative of a commercial encounter platform in which non-commercial information, commercial pedagogies and entertainment are merged. The Show itself is a space for commercial as well as non-commercial and semi-commercial exhibitors. Over the years, I have come across the UK National Health Service (NHS) and the National Childbirth Trust. As a registered charity, the latter is an example of a semi-commercial exhibitor as it offers merchandise in the form of information and other products. Exhibitors like The Baby Website and Midwives Online were examples of the growth of web-based informational services that are also semi-commercial. The midwives who started these companies spoke about their ethos of providing good parent information, and supporting this information work through advertisements. A representative Midwives Online asserted that only those sponsors considered to be ethically sound could advertise on their site. Websites frequently operate on a commercial basis, though that they do so and exactly how they do so was not always clear. Emma's Diary² and Bounty, for instance, are market research companies that gather information on new parents and provide them with services (such as websites and pregnancy guides) and goods (freebees) in exchange. In my discussion with a Bounty representative at one of the consumer shows I attended, I found out how hard it was to get a straight answer about the fact that they were a commercial operation. These market research companies now host popular websites that cannot be easily distinguished from others.

Non-commercial and commercial pedagogical elements and entertainment were also mixed on The Baby Show stage. Apart from the fashion and the Bob-the-Builder shows, the stage featured commercial and semi-commercial experts and celebrity experts talking about a range of early childcare and pregnancy concerns. Midwives and child nurses spoke about specific baby and childcare issues, such as nappy rash and sleep. Their advice blended in with equally confident, assertive and expert sounding commercial advisers. The founder of the Plumb baby organic foods range, for instance, came onto the stage with the company's food scientist to expound the ethos and science behind the company's products. They were likeable

---

²According to the small print on the website's terms and conditions of Emma's Diary, this company is a division of Lifecycle Marketing (Mother & Baby) Limited. Mother & Baby is a well know early parenting magazine. According to one of The Baby Show exhibitors I spoke with, Emma's Diary is also financially supported by Lloydspharmacy, which provides a free gift pack for all members of Emma's Diary.

people, had an easy interactional manner, and sounded authoritative in a positive way about their range of organic infant foods. Over the years, the stage has offered a sounding space for experts like Jo Frost, Annabel Karmell, Clare Byam-Cook and Dr. Robert Titzer, who have respectively offered advice on how best to deal with 'disobedient children', how to feed babies and infants, and how to teach babies to read. When, during The Earls Court Show in 2009, experts were invited to talk on The Expert Advice and Information Theatre, their half hour lectures gave a distinct feel for the 'pedagogicalisation' Aarsand (2014: 627) talks about, whereby 'the techniques of teaching and learning, initially designed to fit formal education, are taken beyond that particular setting to be applied in other situations'.

Health professionals' stands, sponsored by brand-companies, offered open access to visitors who wished to speak with midwives and health visitors at every show I visited. During the course of my fieldwork, I also spoke with quite a number of midwives, either registered, or no longer so, working as NHS midwives, or working independently from the NHS, with some now working in their own businesses (e.g. providing commercial anti-natal classes), whilst others had moved on a full time basis to company work. Midwives were also present on commercial stands, where they were 'on hand' to speak with visitors who had health related questions in relation to their pregnancy, their young child, or early parenthood. Midwives are registered if they engage in professional midwifery practice, and those who were registered and working at The Show, wore a badge stating this. Their presence at The Show meant that they mixed their midwifery work with commercial work like this.

Pedagogical Content and the Brand-Company Website

These elements of pedagogic merging may be witnessed in the newly emergent online informational and networking environment, which has developed over the past 15 years. The growing presence and salience of online platforms are documented in my fieldnotes as the research progressed from 2005. Retailer Mothercare and The Baby Show were already working with websites in 2005, whilst in 2008–2009, new website-based companies and initiatives, like Midwivesonline.com and NHS Choices, first exhibited at The Baby Show, making visitors aware that these new online provisions were there for them to tap into. Today, no product or service in this commercial world exists without an online presence in the form of a website, a Facebook page and a Twitter account. As relatively new kids on the block of commercial pedagogical literature, brand-company websites have now taken their place amongst more established modes of commercial communication, such as advertisements, magazines, advice books, informational brochures and product packaging (Fuentes and Brembeck 2017). These commercial online environments, especially those produced by well-known brand-companies, are made to do a lot of work. They are avenues for market research and product testing, and they create at least some form of brand awareness. By providing comprehensive information, expert support, freebees and free resources, and a range of opportunities for new parents to join Internet-based life-course networks and resources, it may be argued that ultimately a primary aim of these commercial online environments is to 'tie' prospective parents into the brand at an early stage. Below, I argue that the larger sites produce 'one-stop-shops,' where, when it concerns becoming informed about all of the stages of transitioning into parenthood, there really is no need to look beyond some of the websites that currently exist.

Turning to the Cow & Gate website from 2013,[3] I develop an analysis of commonly found conventions on these faceless encounter platforms. The features introduced above may all be found on this site. So, in addition to the introduction and recommendation of the commodities the company sells, an extensive array of childcare information is provided. A typical way in which this information is organised is

---

[3]The Cow & Gate website is a UK Internet platform. The website was accessed in 2013 (June 2013 @ http://www.cowandgate.co.uk/) and 2016. Using screen prints and copying website text alongside these to enable textual analysis, the 2013 webpages were individually archived, leading to a data resource with 170 pages. In 2016, the site was checked for changes, and these are discussed in the text.

through the time-lining or staging of life-course experiences. This lends the 9 months of pregnancy and the first years of infanthood and parenthood 'tell-able' in minute detail, as there is always 'something happening' in the developing foetus, the maturing pregnant body, and the growing infant child, that is worthy of discussion. Time-lining information allows companies to locate their specific products and services in relation to these various developments, and may be used in parental planning work on 'the next stage'. Staging information in this fashion was an organisational device used by Mothercare on its website as early as 2005. Today it may be found on the Cow & Gate website, and a host of other sites.

Visiting a range of websites, the amount of information provided free of charge does vary. On some sites, commodities are moved into the foreground, whilst on others, the informational resource is made more visible in the first instance. The Cow & Gate website of 2013 was interesting for doing exactly this, and for providing what I earlier called a 'one-stop-shop' for prospective and new parents. As a company that sells infant foods and infant formula, there is no obvious reason for supplying extensive information on the phase of pregnancy, other than, as just argued, a desire to 'tie' prospective customers into the brand at an early stage. Access to information on the company's range of products was provided through one tab sitting on the left hand site of the screen, and amongst a series of other tabs that moved the visitor to information pages on the themes listed in the title row of Table 8.1. In 2016, the company has reorganised its website slightly to move its products into the forefront, with the informational resource embedded in a tab for its Baby Club.

The informational materials on the 2013 site are organised in, what may be called an information cascade. Table 8.1 represents this cascade through the organisation of materials under top-level themes (lined up on the left hand side of the main welcome page), followed by sub-themes, with a set of further themes following on from these. The top-level themes on the website are pregnancy, new mum, my baby, my toddler, dads and feeding & nutrition, with feeding & nutrition suggesting that informational content is shaped in accordance with the business' main child caring pathway of feeding (see Table 4.2). The

Table 8.1 Information pages on the Cow & Gate website (2013), organised by themes

Pregnancy	New mum	My baby	My toddler	Dads	Feeding & nutrition
Conception and the early pregnancy signs	My health and nutrition	My baby's health	Toddler feeding and nutrition	Dads' health and nutrition	Weaning advice
My pregnancy calendar week by week (perk)	Practical information and advice for the first few weeks	My baby's routine	My toddler's health	Practical info and advice for dads before the birth	Good nutrition during pregnancy
Labour and birth	Emotional wellbeing and relationships	Baby feeding and nutrition	My toddler's development	Practical info and advice for new dads after the birth	Bottlefeeding advice
Practical info and advice	My growing family	My baby's development stage by stage	Playtime Planner (perk with 55 ideas)	Emotional wellbeing and relationships	Toddler nutrition
Your emotions and relationships			Lets Toddle! App (perk)		Breastfeeding advice
Nutrition and health					Feeding problems and allergies
Pregnancy due date calculator (perk)					
Common health worries					
Pregnant again					
9 & 87	4 & 28	4 & 37	5 & 59	4 & 19 & 12	6 & 81

sub-level themes are then listed in Table 8.1, and enumerated in the first number at the end of the list. The second number represents the number of informational items or pages that are sub-topics of each of the listed sub-themes. For instance, the sub-theme of 'Practical Information and Advice for the First Few Weeks', which is a sub-theme in the informational category of New Mum (second column in Table 8.1), has a further 10 information pages cascading off this topic on 'establishing a routine', 'breastfeeding advice', 'bottle feeding advice', 'common feeding concerns and what to expect', 'holding your baby', 'how to change a nappy +video', 'how to bathe your baby +video', 'identifying cries', 'sharing the workload', and 'what happens if you have a premature baby?' Altogether, there are 355 information topics and videos organised under the 6 top-level themes on this website. This is a lot of information! And it is by no means all about food, though as can be seen in Tables 8.1 and 8.2, this is certainly covered.

Turning now to the way the information is presented, it becomes clear that each page is organised in the same way. When opening a page, it remains embedded in the website's navigational environment, enabling visitors to quickly navigate to other pages if they wish, either by selecting from the thematic menu on the left, or by visiting the 'timeline' menu that runs along the top of the page. The topic's title sits as a heading at the top, and below this is an introductory text provided by one of the Careline's childcare experts, whose picture is included alongside the text. The text is 'signed off' by this expert, and 'her' specialism is listed, along with information about 'her' parenthood status (see also Chapter 9, where I return to this feature). Most of the experts are mothers and all are female! In 2013, the experts are all white; in 2016, they are all non-white. A visual image that reflects the discussion theme is also included. For instance, the topic on bottle-feeding has an image of a bottle-feeding mother with feeding baby; the topic on breastfeeding has a breastfeeding mother and baby. The site's various social networking services are listed in communication boxes on the right hand side. The visitor is invited to join the Cow & Gate Baby Club. There is also a text box announcing what 'mums are chatting about', which displays a small word cloud that indicates the most popular topics. For instance, on the breastfeeding advice page, mums are chatting about

Table 8.2   Online discussion forum topics on the Cow & Gate website (2013)

Pregnancy forums	Mums forums
Diet and fitness	Childcare
Introduce yourself	Losing a baby
Morning sickness	Postnatal depression and baby blues
Pregnancy pains and problems	Postnatal health, diet and fitness
Trying for a baby	Postnatal relationships and sex
Weight gain	Single parents
Scans & tests	Special events
General concerns	Travelling with your baby
Pregnancy fashion & beauty	Working mums and going back to work
Changing moods	Young mums
Pregnancy blues	Advice and information
Labour worries	Allergies & intolerances
Home birth	Baby development & behaviour
Caesarean sections	Bottlefeeding
Pain relief	Breastfeeding
Relationships during pregnancy	Dads
Working when pregnant	Feeding problems and questions
Young or single mums-to-be	General baby health
Dads-to-be	Immunisations
Travelling during pregnancy	Introduce yourself
Baby equipment	Items for sale
Baby names	Other
Feeding your new baby	Premature babies
Miscarriage	Weaning
Other	Your baby
	Special baby diets
	Sleeping
	Teething
	Toddler talk
	Useful information
	Toddler feeding ideas and concerns
	Toddler potty training
	Toddler activities and games
	Toddler tantrums
	Toddler health worries

breastfeeding, colic, milk, weaning and intolerance. Less popular chat topics are: allergy, finger food, fussy, meals, night feed, pregnancy diet, routine and vegetables.[4] Table 8.2 offers a list of forum topics, which visitors to the 2013 site can join.

Interpreting the Marketisation of Pedagogy

Following this discussion of the marketisation of informational, educational and instructional materials directed at new and prospective parents, how can this phenomenon be made sense of? One conclusion is that there is a fairly dominant for-profit presence in the shaping and delivery of instructional and informational resources in this life course phase. Of course, there always was a commercial presence, as magazines and parenting guides have usually come with a price tag (Thomson et al. 2011), though ignoring this in my view weakens an understanding of the governance of child caring. In the contemporary context just discussed, the move to freely given information is particularly interesting, as it provides insight into the relationship between different sectors of the business of child caring. In the drive towards the Internet as the location for increasingly popular communicative platforms, it is likely that traditional instructional and entertainment resources, like pregnancy and parenting magazines, have been facing challenging times. During the course of my research, it became clear that magazines were changing direction by joining this Internet revolution with the development of websites. But the provision of freely given information and advice, especially in the form of brand websites of the larger companies I looked at, may be seen to serve different purposes. As I suggested above, it is a way of making and maintaining contact with a potential clientele in circumstances where customers move through the stage, where products are 'relevant' to them, relatively quickly. From this perspective, extensive information on the experiences of pregnancy

---

[4]From https://www.cgbabyclub.co.uk/feeding-and-nutrition/breastfeeding, accessed on 19 July 2016.

certainly makes sense, especially if pregnancy is marked out as a time when prospective parents spend a lot of time researching their experiences and prospective parenthood. A well-resourced web site is thus a tool to recruit customers and keep them away from the competition. It is probably true to say that the Internet has revolutionised marketing in this field.

Pedagogic merging may be related to my earlier discussion, especially in Chapters 6 and 7, of the ways in which techno-medical-science density benefits sales practices in this field, and I will return to this in Chapter 9. In relation to the concerns of this chapter, pedagogic merging calls into question the binary distinction between state-medical-health instruction and that, which comes from commerce. One of questions which is of considerable interest, but which I cannot do justice to here, concerns the dynamic between the advice that is driven by the state-medical-science complex and that provided by commercial practitioners. For instance, does pedagogic merging challenge or support the maintenance of the *strongly directional* principles that were identified earlier, and what gives rise to complexity and contradiction in recommended principles? Drawing on the analysis of the Cow & Gate website and on the earlier analysis of infant orality tool brand-companies (see Chapter 7), it would appear that directional principles, informational complexity and contrasting advice can also co-occur, though not necessarily within specific sites, but certainly across sites where similar products are sold (see also Martens and Scott 2006). The fact that, in relation to child caring, strong directional principles can co-exist with a pluralisation of advice is again of interest. Future research could address how this is managed from a regulatory perspective.

These questions may be connected with some of the other qualities of pedagogic marketization: the ubiquitous quality of child caring advice, and the fact that information is often as much about child caring practices as about products, whilst simultaneously promulgating some dominant values around, for instance, keeping bodies healthy, and young infant bodies safe. As marketization is an aspect of consumer culture, I briefly turn to the work of Barnett and colleagues (2005), who develop an analysis of the role played by information in communications between businesses and consumers of so-called 'ethical' products.

They conceptualise commercial practices (and those of others) as the 'governance of consumption', which is defined as follows:

> There is an organisational dimension, referring to the strategies used by campaigning organisations, policy makers, and businesses to facilitate the adoption of ethical consumption practices by consumers. This dimension ... involves *governing consumption*, where this refers to an array of strategies that aim to regulate the informational and spatial contexts of consumer 'choice'. ... these include market research and marketing, advertising, ... and the dissemination of the discourse of consumerism more generally. (2005: 31)

Rather than seeing consumer pedagogy as a simple process of passing on knowledge to consumers, like Murphy (2003), discussed earlier, they adopt the Foucauldian notion of 'governance' to build upon earlier arguments, especially those developed by Miller and Rose (1997) and Du Gay (1996), that link the growth of a neo-liberal ethos with the idea of a self-governing subjecthood that pursues informed choices, wielded through consumption in the market place. They argue that consumption is 'one key site of ethical self-formation in the contemporary period... that ... serves as a key arena in which people are made up as selves who can exercise freedom and responsibility by exercising their capacity to choose' (Barnett et al. 2005: 30). The instructional quality of early parenthood may thus be interpreted as a stimulus for parental subjects to engage in 'ethical self-formation' or 'moral selving,' which is defined as:

> ... the mediated work of creating oneself as a more virtuous person through practices that acknowledge responsibilities to others. Moral selving might take the form of explicit performances, or displays, of virtuous conduct. But it also refers to a range of more humble, perhaps even anonymous modes of conduct. (Barnett et al. 2005: 30)

As was shown in Chapter 3, much social scientific commentary on parenting focuses on moral questions that often flow forth through the imposition of public concerns onto private lives. Whilst on the one hand, this has fed debate on the intensification of parenting (e.g. Afflerback et al. 2013; Faircloth 2013; Hays 1996; Song and Paul 2015; Vincent and Maxwell 2015), recent interest in child caring and consumer culture may be seen to join the intensification debate with the evolution of a neo-liberal ethos and environment (Cairns et al. 2013; Fuentes and Brembeck 2017; MacKendrick 2014). At the same time, consumer culture is recognised as a domain in which moralities feature highly (e.g. Miller 2001; Sayer 2003; Wilk 2001). Consumption related moralisations connect a diverse set of concerns with specific consumption practices and specific sets of consumers, and leads to binary categories of good and bad consumption and morally honourable and suspect consumers (Casey 2007; Martens and Casey 2007). Early parenthood thus raises the question how the highly moralistic character of this phase of the life course 'meets' moralities of consumption. After discussing the marketization of pedagogy, I therefore now turn to the narratives of prospective and new parents to examine how they enacted a moral sense of self. I argue that these reflect different consumer concerns and priorities, and also illustrate different mobilisations of the teleoaffective qualities of 'the young child'.

Becoming a Moral Parent-Consumer

> There is a definite learning process, as watching other people do it is very different to doing it, and suddenly being there yourself! … I used to stay at Terry's sister's house, so I was there when she had her first children, and when she was due her second. So nappies and toilet training, and things like that, I saw almost hands on, but I would say, even though there were all those children around, I still feel very … like I have to go and read a text book. (Sarah, 23 weeks pregnant, first time parent, 30s, professional, white)

New and prospective parents in this study unanimously spoke about their journey into parenthood as a learning experience. Most of the new parents I spoke with did not have much personal experience with young children, but a number had, either because they had older children (and thus were not first-time parents) or because they had close friends and family members with young children. Sarah, whose narrative opens this section, had 'almost hands on' experience with the young children of her sister in law. Even so, in becoming a new parent, participants like her experienced a compelling need to consult books, magazines and websites, and to listen to the advice of child caring experts, like midwives. There was ample discussion in the interviews about picking up and reading books, and reflections on the preference for magazines or Internet content, and some (including Jasmine, whose narrative is presented below) elaborated on the different models of child caring that circulate in this mediated realm. With the ubiquitous presence of child caring and product information, in mediated form, and the plethora of expert voices and advice, it could easily be assumed that new and prospective parents are a captivated audience. Indeed, when mediated content is taken as the sole element in the analysis, this is indeed what is often argued (e.g. Hardyment 1995, 2007).

I continue to present a three-fold typology that represents different priorities and models of moral-selving, enacted by people who are on a trajectory of becoming parent-consumers. I am coining the term parent-consumers, as our conversations took place in a commercial environment and all included consumption and consumer culture as dimensions of the narration of a moral self. The ideal types are 'neo-liberal' parenting, 'balancing the budget' parenting, and 'respectable' parenting. They reflect different stances towards the child caring pedagogies that circulate in this environment. Indeed, they also illustrate how the very definition of 'the young child', which was explored in the first part of the book, is made malleable by parents as they make a case for their specific concerns. These offer a firm glance into performances of consumer culture as profane, and of the binary opposition of the sacred and the profane.

Neo-Liberal Parenting: Researching, Guardianship and Symbolic Moderation

Jasmine, and her 5-week old daughter Iris, visited The Baby Show in May 2006, and she offered to speak with me after approaching our little exhibition stand at this show. Being well-to-do and university educated, and with a professional career 'behind her', Jasmine performed a strong middle-class professional sense of self in terms of the topics she brought to the interview. These, in turn, intersected with ethnicity (Jasmine was from Asian descent), gender (Jasmine, rather than her husband, had decided to give up work and become a full-time parent) and generation. Much of the discussion centred on Jasmine's experiences of, and plans for, her new 'role' as full-time mother. The transition to mothering was a life course change that she was working on in an active and conscious way, and approximated the idea of an 'explicit project of self' (Thomson et al. 2011: 149) in a neo-liberal environment (Cairns et al. 2013). She experienced this transition with strong personal emotions of love towards her daughter and her husband, and conceived her new role as about creating the kind of family and childhood for Iris that cohered with the values of both parents. In Jasmine's account, her moral selving exhibited the specific task of researching as a salient element of mothering, as information gathering and sifting through the various alternatives were seen by her as providing the means for making decisions about 'best' child caring practices and tools (see also AbiGhannam and Atkinson 2016). This discussion was located in an understanding of 'the young child' and 'their needs' that generated a stance on consumption and consumer culture that coheres with Alison Pugh's (2009) notion of 'symbolic moderation' as characteristic of middle class parenting.

The transition from working professional woman to full-time mother was very much at the forefront of Jasmine's narrative. Prominent in this discussion was her learner self-positioning. Jasmine spoke at length about how active she was in gathering information that allowed her to become familiar with 'everything under the sun' concerning mothering, her daughter and their young family. She grew up understanding the importance of learning and education in life. Coming from a migrant Asian family, she described how her parents ensured that she and her siblings 'enjoyed' a good education, and so, Jasmine attended university and became a professional working woman. In becoming a full-time mother at the age of 37, she spoke about applying her skills of researching, reading and information gathering to the task and challenges of mothering a young child:

Lydia: Do you consider yourself as going through some kind of learning process?
Jasmine: Yeah, every other job you have you have training for, you get manuals, and.., right motherhood, I don't see why you shouldn't inform yourself in the same way, so I went to the library and got loads of books, and websites, I really wanted to go into it informed...

The importance Jasmine attributed to learning is evident throughout the interview. Like other professional interviewees in the study, she managed to verbalise, with some measure of detail, mediated approaches to child caring she had picked up through her research, and she spoke about sifting through information as a means of selecting that which she felt was best for her, for her child, and for her family. Here, she speaks about learning about different child caring approaches:

... I am very pro attachment parenting and there is stuff I read about training your child, getting them into routines, is it ... I don't know her name, Gina Ford? In fact, Gina Ford is all about training them, regimenting them, getting routines. And then there is the continuum... concept, yeah, and then there is attachment parenting in between. And I think I am, I am very interested in knowing about both, all of them, and I take the bits that I want.

She also spoke at length about learning about the products that facilitated child caring practices, pointing to the distinctiveness of learning about practices and products. As was the case for some other interviewees, Jasmine really appreciated the fact that The Baby Show offered a broad range of products and information 'under one roof', and, as was the case for pregnant couple Cheryl and Liam discussed in Chapter 7, she treated this as helpful in making decisions about what she wanted, and importantly, what she did not want. In coining the phrase 'I take the bits that I want' above, Jasmine did not sketch herself as in any way perturbed by the variety of information and products that she was confronted with, but spoke on several occasions about making decisions that made sense to her at the time these were made.

The prospective parents in this study were on the whole not very articulate about what a young child is like, and by extension, what their needs are. Parental narratives thus did not illustrate the minute descriptive detail and 'child lore' that may be found in the commercial literatures that were discussed in previous chapters. There was, however, a clear and underlying sense of the importance of the young child, and especially one's own young child, which was infused with the emotion of love. This feeling of love was the driving force behind child caring activities, including, for Jasmine, this visit to The Baby Show. In my discussion with Jasmine, the idea of the loved child sat alongside other understandings of the young child, including a reference to the *natural* quality of their loving familial bond, and the idea that broad-based and *natural* experiences were the road towards her child's future happiness, confidence and the acquisition of the right social values. In Jasmine's account, therefore, the teleoaffective qualities of loving and purifying merged and took on a particular primacy, along with the teleoaffective quality of nurturing through stimulation. Infantile vulnerability made an appearance especially when the discussion turned to the invasive qualities of a consumer world, against which Jasmine sought to protect her young child. Let's illustrate these points.

All of Jasmine's energies were now going into mothering and family life, and she described this effort as 'a labour of love'. Jasmine indicated her affinity with 'attachment parenting' (Faircloth 2013), and in describing her child caring practices—breastfeeding, carrying daughter Iris in a sling wrap, and sleeping with her in the night—suggested how she was putting the ideas of attachment parenting into embodied practice that speaks to Lupton's (2013) notion of interembodiment. Jasmine was seeking out caring practices that involved embodied closeness, and in this context, she defended the multidimensional benefits of her breastfeeding practices as follows:

> …You know, someone will say, reading some books on how not to be used as a dummy yourself, well I have learned that babies use your breast for milk AND for comfort AND for closeness and you know, it's all those things, so why are we cutting that out saying: 'I am merely a feeding machine'? I am more than a feeding machine! You know, I feed but I also give her safety and comfort, and that's what my breasts are for, and ehhmm, it is only other people who don't breastfeed that say that to you. So that's what I am learning (capital 'AND' reflects emphasis in the talk).

Jasmine also described their familial love for one another as 'natural', thus essentialising and purifying their mutual adoration towards one another:

> Jasmine: ... you become selfish, you're a family unit. I suppose the most important thing is my husband and my baby and then me, collectively, and our happiness is paramount, and everybody else comes second (pauze) ...
> Lydia: do you think that is positive or negative, or...
> Jasmine: I think it's nature... I think nature does something to you, because my husband and I talked about it when we heard her cry, and she is like this (copies the cry of her baby) and you think, my god, she has got wind, she suffers from wind a bit, and we both said, there is this natural instinct in you that wants to comfort her, and never wants her to experience any pain, and your devotion to her is just innate. And it's nature and biological, it is something that society doesn't do, environment doesn't do that, it's just something that we are biologically born with, to care and nurture. Life!

The ideal of natural parenting Jasmine aspired to also involved the purchase and consumption of organic foods, and continuing in this line of thinking, she described the idea that baby needs are very basic:

> She's got food in the belly and she's got shelter and she's got something on her back, to keep her warm, and the rest of it she can learn, she can play with leaves, she can look at the sky, and ehhmm ... she needs, she needs us ...

Like some other interviewees in this study, Jasmine's enactment of the young child as pure and natural happened alongside and in close proximity to the enactment of 'pure nature' (Taylor 2011), engendered above through the reference to leaves and the sky. These understandings of the young child were the very foundation upon which Jasmine enacted the opposition between nature and culture, between the sacred and the profane (Zelizer 1985), and between the natural child and natural childhood, and the reprehensible qualities of consumer culture. This juxtaposition was one of Jasmine's most prominent volunteered priorities during our conversation! It started as soon as she had taken her seat to talk with me, and turned into and on a narrative of 'moderated consumption' (Ellis 2011) or 'symbolic moderation' (Pugh 2009). In the following, the quality of the young child as in need of the right kind of stimulation is developed alongside a specific critical rendition of 'consumer culture'.

Jasmine returned several times to the importance of experience. Gathering experience was seen as important for her education as a mother, and in a similar way, experience was seen to be good for her daughter. Below, gaining experience is sketched as a positive thing, in juxtaposition to some iconic negative features—the 'pink flashing lights' and 'lots of toys'—of children's consumer culture:

> … yeah, do we want to have, do we want to have everything? My husband is very pro spoiling her with experience rather than things. And he is a big traveller so he thinks the best education and the best thing for her would be to go on holiday. To see the world and get as far, you know, and I agree with him. … I read in the Sunday Times about how we are making children lazy now, and sort of limiting their creativity, their personal creativity, by organising things for them… putting lots of toys in front of them, whereas years ago, children would, their imagination was far more innate. Because they were given a box or napkins to play with and their vivid imagination would be going off in all sorts of directions. Whereas now it is like, pink flashing lights, and Fisher Price, and Tomy (pauze) …

So, their time together was very much organised around, what may be described as, experiential consumption that also involved market exchange. Jasmine and her daughter went swimming every week, organised by a company called Water Babies, and they joined in the singing and signing classes provided by a company called Tiny Talk. Moreover, Jasmine took Iris to her weekly sewing class. For Jasmine, experiences were not simply sought out for their own sake, they had a specific purpose—the sewing class, in specific, nurtured Jasmine's mothering qualities and allowed her to reconnect with her Indian cultural heritage, whilst offering Iris experience of cultural diversity:

... and I let all the Indian women, who don't speak any English, Pakistani and Muslim women, to cuddle her and to hold her and speak to her in their own language. Ehhm that's another of these, that I want her to be exposed to different cultures and different languages ...

Whilst embracing experiential consumption, in other respects Jasmine's position on consumption was highly ambivalent, informing the specific way in which 'parent' and 'consumer' were merged in the moral work exhibited in her transition into motherhood. Thus, Jasmine explicitly rejected the kind of consumer she had been before she embraced motherhood:

Lydia: So how would you describe yourself as a consumer?
Jasmine: Three years ago, yeah, I was single, middle income, professional, good income, high tax bracket payer, and yet spending money like no tomorrow (pauze), on myself and my nieces and nephews, and I bought brands for other people's children. I spoiled other people's children, nieces and nephews, and yet I don't want anyone to spoil mine.
Lydia: But are they? Have you been given toys and things like that?
Jasmine: Yeah, and I have done the same for other people's children, you know, I have bought, and I have got, one of the reasons why I was here is because I have a first birthday party to go to, not yes cousins, yeah cousins, and I don't really know what to give, because I don't think he needs a thing, he is one. And I was just going to get some vouchers and let the mother choose, cause I know the mother ... may get something which is practical and its needed, whether its nappies or extra teats for a bottle. So that's what we will probably do...

If, as discussed above, Jasmine mobilised specific child qualities and needs in order to outline her criticism of children's consumer culture, she here moved onto an associated ideology of good parenting, where a moral stance towards consumption hinges on the development of frugality and 'a practical stance' towards expenditure. This is the primary theme of the next ideal type.

In this study of Jasmine's narrative work of moral selving, associated with her new mothering role, three salient facets were interwoven.

First, Jasmine was enacting what may be seen as a model of neo-liberal subjecthood, in which research and education are regarded as offering a route towards making informed decisions in everyday life. Jasmine very much spoke the language of choice, unfettered by material constraints, where she was free to decide in what way she parented her daughter, and what products she would use in the process. Second, one of the lessons about mothering and its responsibilities learned by Jasmine was the importance of her role as guardian of her family and of her child. As mother, she regarded it her duty to engage with the world of products and shopping, and to be a go-between between her daughter and her husband on the one hand, and the market place on the other. These two facets informed Jasmine's consumption hierarchy, in which expenditure on 'good experiences' were effectively excluded from 'consumer culture', and where products targeted at young children ('I don't want her to be necessarily drawn to lots of things that,… you know, all glitches of gold sort of thing, and that will be short term impact, short term stimulus for her, and that is consumerism, isn't it?') were positioned as 'bad' and equated with consumer culture. Third, Jasmine's enactment of this specific critical stance towards consumer culture may be recognised as similar to the symbolic moderation enacted by middle-class American parents in Alison Pugh's study (2009). It is, importantly, organised through a specific narrative mobilisation of the teleoaffective qualities of child caring; those of loving, purifying and nurturing through stimulation, which provided a rationale for why the young child needed to be protected from the negative qualities of consumer culture.

'Balancing the Budget': Practical Moderation and 'All They Need Is Love'

Becoming a thrifty and practical parent-consumer was a common theme in my conversations with new and prospective parents. We just saw how Jasmine verbalised this moral position, but that she did so by connecting motherly thriftiness with ideas of 'how best to raise a child' in which child love, purity and stimulation were dominant in the teleoaffective mix of child caring. In Jasmine's enactment of a neo-liberal moral sense of self, she also conceived of 'family' in a narrow 'nuclear' way, where the relationship between mother, father and child was paramount, thus giving power to her motherly self as individually sovereign in the context of information management and decision making. Consequently, one of the characteristics of the neo-liberal ideal type of the moral parent-consumer was hesitancy about intergenerational 'involvement' in the care of the child. In Jasmine's narrative, this came out as an opposition between her views and those of her mother on child caring 'best practice'. In the ideal types of 'balancing the budget' and 'respectable parenting', the extended family was rendered more important—both as a model of moral practice and as a general support structure (involving support with care and resources)—with 'the child' moving more into the background into a location as a family member. Therefore, here we have two positions that move away from the neo-liberal morality of early parenthood, especially in terms of its emphasis on the necessity of individual research and decision making, and in the complex realisation of 'the child' and its needs.

I here present the narrative of Carol as an example of the ideal parenting type of 'balancing the budget'. Carol was in her 20s, and was visiting The Baby Show with her mother Sue (40s). She had recently married husband Mike and they were a working class couple, with Mike working as a motor technician and Carol working full-time in sales, whilst also holding a part-time job and doing voluntary work. Carol was only 15 weeks into her pregnancy, and this was to be the first grandchild in both families. Because of the early stage of her pregnancy, Carol and her mother were at The Baby Show to find out about things, rather than to buy. Unlike a number of other prospective parents, Carol did not vocalise the need to read books and magazines, but did say that she was talking about her pregnancy with her family and best friends, and she had recently spoken for the first time with a midwife.

The interview with Carol and her mother was interesting particularly for the 'practical' focus of the two mothers. Both came out strongly against the idea that expecting a child should mean excessive expenditure. Both reflected on their upbringing and the *moderated consumption ethos* characterising their family lives. For Carol, becoming a mother was verbalised as a transformation, in which she juxtaposed the 'excessive' consumption desires of her teenage years (and which had been actively curtailed by mother Sue), with a moderated consumer self and child caring ethos that was modelled on her mother. Especially prominent in Carol's narrative was the opposition between needs and wants, of herself and of her expected child. The following exchange illustrates how Carol was weighing up the contradictory demands in early parenthood to 'do the best for your child' by purchasing 'the best stuff' and 'to purchase wisely and within budget':

Carol: … I think that there is a lot of pressure. Here (at The Baby Show), for example, everything is really nice but there is a pressure on parents, new parents, to buy the best and that you have to have this, as it is fantastic, that you don't really need. For example, I was looking at furniture for the nursery. If you buy purpose nursery furniture from anywhere, Argos, Toys-R-Us, anywhere, it is really expensive, and it is tiny. In Argos, I saw the same wardrobe we had in our new house, was in the sale, so I bought it, as at the end of the day, you don't need a tiny wardrobe. I think there is pressure on new parents to buy everything new and everything special, because it is your child and that is what you should do. I don't think that is needed but I think there is a lot of pressure on new parents to buy everything and you need this. But you don't really need it. Like nappy buckets, for example. Well, all you need is a bucket with a lid, you know. It is exactly the same thing, just not as pretty. I think that is the kind of consumer pressure on parents, I think, I find.

Lydia: And you feel that yourself?

Carol: Yeah. If you have got the money, then fine, but I don't think you need to spend as much as people think you do, to have a baby. Like before it was: 'Oh, I don't know if I can afford to have a baby,' but now, half the stuff here is lovely but you don't need it. That is the worry, in that you just go out and buy, buy, buy, and then you wonder why you are in debt.

Lydia: But it doesn't work for you?

Carol: No! [laughs] When I walk away, I actually think I am really glad I walked away, as I didn't need it. Some things… some things would be lovely, but not if you haven't got the money.

What is interesting here is how Carol turns a number of common understandings around. The first follows at the end of the first passage, where she is presenting the idea that good parenthood may be about *not* spending rather than spending. The second is in highlighting how a baby's needs are very basic, and importantly, includes love and affection rather than more and more stuff. In doing so, Carol even goes as far as to downplay the dichotomy between adult and child – children's needs are not any different from that of an adult, which was especially interesting:

Lydia: So what does a baby need?
Carol: I think if you are going think what a baby needs, I think it needs love and the main thing that an adult needs, which is a roof over their head, to be fed, and love, and apart from that …

As an example of the moral position of 'balancing the budget', Carol's narrative is demonstrative of a rejection of the detailed descriptions of 'what young children are like' in commercial texts, that give rise to a multitude of young child needs and is suggestive of child-caring attentions that involve endless expenditures. In Carol's narration, this rejection was vocalised through the juxtaposition of products that are 'nice' because 'purposely designed with the young child in mind' and those that are practical and cheaper and not designed specifically for the young child. Carol's advocacy of moderated consumption is distinct from that of Jasmine, in the sense that her discussion was more focused on 'practical' goods and a rejection of the multiple symbolic meanings of childhood, with the exception of loving, couching the best interests of 'her child' as about the proper management of her budget.

Respectability, Familial Love and Social Belonging

When I spoke with Veronica and her mother Sally, she was 26 weeks into an unplanned pregnancy. Veronica was 18 years of age; she was white; and working in a care home for the elderly. Our conversation was interesting for the very distinct priorities that were embedded in the narrative accomplishment of these two mothers, resulting in a conceptualisation of learning to become a parent, 'the young child', and consumer culture, that were very different from the ideal types discussed above. Veronica and her mother were aware of the child caring lessons that were circulating in the commercial environment of The Baby Show, and mother Sue, in particular, marvelled at the inventions that were now available to make child caring easier compared with when she was a mother with young children. But they were also paying lip service to elements of this culture. The mothers did not vocalise the importance of pedagogic materials and expert models on how to care for the expected baby. In response to the question where she would find answers to questions she might have about her pregnancy, Veronica's direct response was: 'I would go to my mother'. Unlike the professional and middle class parents in the study, for Veronica and her mother, realities associated with being young, working class and going through an unplanned pregnancy, were salient elements of experience that informed their moral becoming.

Veronica and her mother thus used the conversation primarily for the purposes of 'respectability work', to deflect possible accusations of a pregnancy associated with teenage selfishness, bad mothering and child neglect. Repeated expressions of mutual love and affection for one another, and a narrating of a family rallying behind Veronica in support, were also part of this work. Veronica did considerable respectability work during the interview, distancing herself from the idea that she was a teenager (I am not a teenager any more, I am a young woman, do you know what I mean?), whilst narrating her personal growth process since discovering that she was pregnant. Here, she juxtaposed a conception of her younger self as selfish and inward focused, and a lack of respect for her own parents, with a conception of becoming a mother who would put her baby first, who would carry the responsibility of looking after it, and who was happy to model her own parenting on the example of her parents:

Veronica: Don't get me wrong, when I first found out I was pregnant I was: 'Wow!', as it was going to be a big change in my life, it is not just going to be me. I can't just think about me, I have got somebody else to think about who is going to depend on me 24/7. It is not like I can just say: 'Oh, go away I don't want to know.' I can't do that. I am not having this baby to dump on my mum, like a lot of teenage parents probably would. This is my child, and I know what I have got myself into, and I have got to look after it how I have been brought up, so...

She also sketched herself as an affectionate person, who loved children generally, who was enjoying the embodied experience of being pregnant, but also worried for the child that was growing inside her:

Veronica: And just before my scan, cause I was scared, as I hadn't seen the baby from 8 weeks, and then I seen it, when it was 20 weeks, and it was just like 'Wow!' ... from seeing the little heart beat, seeing this baby... that completely... it was just an amazing feeling. I was really quite ill, weren't I, the day before I had my scan, wasn't I? I stress myself out too much.

Sally: Yeah, when she is not feeling well, the baby seems to let her body know and she is sick and she gets dehydrated, so she suffers that way.

Veronica's pregnancy had been unexpected. It was clear that members of the family had got a bit of a shock. Veronica was the youngest of three, and her older siblings (a brother and a sister aged 25 and 22) had not yet started families. The feeling that this pregnancy came too early was expressed by both Veronica and her mother: at some point Sally said: 'it was quite a shock like at first when she said she was pregnant to all of us because of her only been 18 and we wanted more for her...' But this was followed immediately by:

But... as long as the baby is okay, and she is okay, she has got the full support of all of us, including her brother and her sister, which is good. Cause there is not many families who do stick by young ones when they are so gutted that they have got pregnant. But no, quite looking forward to it.

Mother and daughter showed their love and respect for one another as the interview progressed. Veronica's language was peppered with expressions of love—'I couldn't ask for better parents, to tell you the truth' and 'I would be lost without my mum', whilst voicing her recognition of the worth of her own upbringing in the quote above. Mother Sally, in turn, carefully negotiated her contribution to the narration by Veronica of her selfish teenage years, leaving the truth telling to her daughter, and backing this up with carefully selected comments. Both spoke about how the pregnancy had brought them closer together, with Veronica clarifying that her mother had been there for her during her pregnancy, and supportive throughout. And the fact that her father and her brother had bought some baby gifts was put forward as evidence that the family was strongly behind her.

Of interest is how, in this narrative, the expected child is not analysed beyond the idea that it is loved and precious. The importance of this loved child was narrated by Veronica through the need of growing up and out of her teenage selfish phase, and developing and actively accepting the qualities of a motherhood that would be child-centred, in which she would take second place. This was also a motherhood tied into a specific consumer self, as she was adamant that she would be financially resourcing the needs of her child and its care, in the short and the long run ('I want to get back to work, as I want to give my child everything that I have always been able to have'). At the time of the interview, being able to make purchases for the baby, with the money she earned, was put forward as an important element of her growing independence and responsibility. Moderated consumption was not a part of this narrative, though there was a language of being careful with money, with small expenditures made on a regular basis making resourcing for the baby very much manageable. Both mothers spoke about the importance of buying things cheaply, with Asda and Primark mentioned along the way as places to go, and Mothercare described as often too expensive. But the mothers clearly preferred new goods, rejected second hand goods, and signalled the importance of a good outward visual appearance ('you don't want your child to look a mess and you want the best for your child and you will do anything'), confirming the importance of being seen to be respectable in a watchful outside world. Her claim to independence was probably behind the reason why Veronica was rejecting gifts for the baby from the father at the moment, though she was happy to receive gifts from her family, as this was indicative of familial support and the future social belonging of Veronica and her baby child in her extended family. Familial embeddedness and closeness was there to ensure that Veronica and her child would be safe in a local community where teenage mums were easily criticised and ostracised, and located at the bottom of the social hierarchy.

Conclusion

The three-fold typology of moral-selving that I have just presented suggests that new parents are negotiating between a range of moral concerns and priorities, amongst which are the need to balance the budget and the need to secure moral acceptability in a broader social environment, which is critical of certain types of parents. Jasmine's narrative may be seen as sitting most closely to the kind of subjecthood that may be regarded as neo-liberal, in the sense of 'making life a project of self-cultivation' in which market-based information gathering and analysis (part of the project of shopping) were seen as crucial parts of the work of parenting (Kehily 2014). But, as Jasmine enthusiastically took up various responsibilities in her new role as mother, and refuted the negativity that comes with informational complexity and the need to make choices, her account veered away from the idea that mothering is intense and full of anxieties and contradictions. Her narrative also accentuated the love that formed the strong bond between her, her young daughter and her husband. Finally, her account conveyed the priorities and values of her position as an educated and well-to-do woman. In all three typologies, consumption practices and preferences were informing, and informed by, the specific moral work the new parents in this study did in and through their narrative interaction with me. In Jasmine's account, the transition to motherhood was also informing a transition to a more moderate consumer subjectivity, though, as indicated also in the work by Pugh (2009), this was very much a symbolic practice, rather than something driven by real necessity. The 'balancing the budget' moral typology was much more clearly about the necessity to spend money wisely, and in the argument to support this, the child and its needs were narrated in ways that were different from those found in the first typology, and were positively posited against the elaborate narratives of child needs in commercial narratives. Whilst the marketization of child caring pedagogy may be interpreted as signalling the governance of consumption, the discussions with new and prospective parents illustrate that moral selving is a complex set of practices that perhaps a more revealing of the 'particular forms of social distinction' that are demonstrated in the narrative displays of the parents I spoke with (Barnett et al. 2005: 30), rather than as straightforward demonstrations of a neo-liberal subjectivity. It may therefore be more fruitful to think about the marketization of pedagogy as an element in the normalisation of consumption, in the competitive practices of different carriers of child caring, and as a manifestation of the institutionalisation of elements of the organisation of the sales culture in this field that is associated with the discourse of childhood. I will develop this further in the next chapter.

It is interesting to see new parents performing the teleoaffective qualities of child caring, but doing so in ways that are different from the commercial performances encountered earlier on, in Chapters 5, 6 and 7. New and prospective parents essentially confirm the importance of the young child, and especially the idea that young children are deserving of love and affection. Love and affection were found to be salient elements in all three typologies of moral selving. Other than that, the qualities of the young child were organised in such a way as to rationalise the specific stance adopted by new parents in relation to child caring and consumption. Here too, the qualities of children are both sedimented and flexible. Like commercial practitioners, parental narrative work converges on a limited range of qualities (those of lovable, vulnerable, pure and nurturing were all present), with the flexible element representing the opportunities for 'personal nuances', which reflect and undergird variations between parents, and between parents and commercial practice carriers. One such nuance was parents sketching 'the market' as a threat to their young offspring, as an element of the young child's vulnerability, for which the parent took on the responsibility of protection. This was one example in the study where 'the young child' and 'the market' were distanced, and the binary opposition between the sacred and the profane culturally enacted. A final observation: it would seem that the cultural work that splits the sacred and the profane in this field is done with the most verve by those new parents who sit most closely to a neo-liberal subjecthood, which, as was seen earlier, is also most closely related to a consumer ethos.

Bibliography

Aarsand, L. 2014. The knowledgeable parenting style: Stance takings and subject positions in media encounters. *International Journal of Lifelong Education* 33 (5): 625–640.

AbiGhannam, N., and L. Atkinson. 2016. Good green mothers consuming their way through pregnancy: Roles of environmental identities and information seeking in coping with the transition. *Consumption Markets & Culture* 19 (5): 1–24.

Afflerback, S., S.K. Carter, A.K. Anthony, and L. Grauerholz. 2013. Infant feeding consumerism in the age of intensive mothering and risk society. *Journal of Consumer Culture*. https://doi.org/10.1177/1469540513485271.

Apple, R.D. 2006. *Perfect motherhood: Science and childrearing in America*. New Brunswick, NJ: Rutgers University Press.

Arnup, K. 1994. *Education for motherhood: Advice for mothers in twentieth-century Canada*. Toronto: Toronto University Press.

Bailey, L. 1999. Refracted selves? A study of changes in self-identity in the transition to motherhood. *Sociology* 33 (2): 335–352.

Barnett, C., P. Cloke, N. Clarke, and A. Malpass. 2005. Consuming ethics: Articulating the subjects and spaces of ethical consumption. *Antipode* 37 (1): 23–45.

Buckingham, D., and M. Scanlon. 2005. Selling learning: Towards a political economy of edutainment media. *Media, Culture & Society* 27 (1): 41–58.

Cairns, K., J. Johnston, and N. MacKendrick. 2013. Feeding the 'organic child': Mothering through ethical consumption. *Journal of Consumer Culture* 13 (2): 97–118.

Casey, E. 2007. Gambling and everyday life: Working class mothers and domestic spaces of consumption. In *Gender and consumption: Material culture and the commercialisation of everyday life*, ed. E. Casey and L. Martens, 123–140. Aldershot, UK: Ashgate.

de Laat, K., and S. Baumann. 2014. Caring consumption as marketing schema: Representations of motherhood in an era of hyperconsumption. *Journal of Gender Studies* 25 (2): 183–199.

Du Gay, P. 1996. *Consumption and identity at work*. London: Sage.

Ehrenreich, B., and D. English. 1979. *For her own good: 150 years of the experts' advice to women*. London: Pluto.

Ellis, L. 2011. Towards a contemporary sociology of children and consumption. Durham theses, Durham University. Available at Durham E-Theses Online: http://etheses.dur.ac.uk/3206/.

Faircloth, C. 2013. *Militant lactivism? Attachment parenting and intensive motherhood in the UK and France*. London: Berghahn Books.

Fuentes, M., and H. Brembeck. 2017. Best for baby? Framing weaning practice and motherhood in web-mediated marketing. *Consumption Markets & Culture* 20 (2): 153–175.

Furedi, F. 2001. *Paranoid parenting*. Chicago: Chicago Review Press.

Halkier, B. 2014. Contesting food—Contesting motherhood. In *Motherhoods, markets and consumption: The making of mothers in contemporary western cultures*, ed. S. O'Donohoe, M. Hogg, P. Maclaran, L. Martens and L. Stevens, 56–67. London: Routledge.

Hardyment, C. 1995. *Perfect parents: Baby-care advice past and present*. Oxford, UK: Oxford University Press.

Hardyment, C. 2007. *Dream babies: Childcare advice from John Locke to Gina Ford*. London: Frances Lincoln.

Hays, S. 1996. *The cultural contradictions of motherhood*. New Haven, CT: Yale University Press.

Kehily, M.J. 2014. For the love of small things: Consumerism and the making of maternal identities. *Young Consumers* 15 (3): 227–238.

Lawler, S. 2000. *Mothering the self: Mothers, daughters, subjectivities*. London: Routledge.

Lee, E. 2007. Health, morality, and infant feeding: British mothers' experiences of formula milk use in the early weeks. *Sociology of Health & Illness* 29 (7): 1075–1090.

Lee, E., J. Bristow, C. Faircloth, and J. Macvarish. 2014. *Parenting culture studies*. Basingstoke: Palgrave MacMillan.

Lupton, D. 2013. Infant embodiment and interembodiment: A review of sociocultural perspectives. *Childhood* 20 (1): 37–50.

Mackendrick, N. 2014. More work for mother: Chemical body burdens as a maternal responsibility. *Gender & Society* 28 (5): 705–728.

Marshall, D., M. Hogg, T. Davis, T. Schneider, and A. Petersen. 2013. Images of motherhood: Food advertising in Good Housekeeping magazine 1950–2010. In *Motherhoods, markets and consumption: The making of mothers in contemporary Western cultures*, ed. Stephanie O'Donohoe, Margaret Hogg, Pauline MacLaran, Lydia Martens, and Lorna Stevens. London: Routledge.

Martens, L., S. Scott, and E. Uprichard. 2005. 'Safety, safety, safety for small fry': Children and safety in commercial communities of parenthood. Unpublished paper presented at The Norwegian Institute for Consumer Research, June.

Martens, L. 2009. Creating the ethical parent-consumer subject: Commerce, moralities and pedagogies in early parenthood. In *Critical pedagogies of consumption: living and learning in the shadow of the "shopocalypse"*, ed. J.A. Sandlin and P. McLaren. New York: Routledge.

Martens, L. 2010. The cute, the spectacle and the practical: Narratives of new parents and babies at The Baby Show. In *Childhood and consumer culture*, ed. D. Buckingham and V. Tingstad. London: Palgrave Macmillan.

Martens, L., and E. Casey. 2007. Afterword: Theorising gender, consumer culture and promises of betterment in late modernity. In *Gender and consumption: Material culture and the commercialisation of everyday life*, ed. E. Casey and L. Martens, 219–242. Aldershot, UK: Ashgate.

Martens, L., and S. Scott. 2005. "The unbearable lightness of cleaning": Representations of domestic practice and products in Good Housekeeping magazine (UK): 1951–2001. *Consumption, Markets and Culture* 8 (4): 379–401.

Martens, L., and S. Scott. 2006. Under the kitchen surface: Domestic products and conflicting constructions of home. *Home Cultures* 3 (1): 39–62.

Miller, D. 2001. The poverty of morality. *Journal of Consumer Culture* 1 (2): 225–243.

Miller, T. 2005. *Making sense of motherhood*. Cambridge, UK: Cambridge University Press.

Miller, P., and N. Rose. 1997. Mobilizing the consumer: Assembling the subject of consumption. *Theory, Culture & Society* 14 (1): 1–36.

Murphy, E. 2003. Expertise and forms of knowledge in the government of families. *The Sociological Review* 51 (4): 433–462.

Pugh, A.J. 2009. *Longing and belonging: Parents, children, and consumer culture*. California: University of California Press.

Sayer, A. 2003. (De)commodification, consumer culture, and moral economy. *Environment and Planning D: Society and Space* 21 (3): 341–357.

Song, F.W., and N. Paul. 2015. Online product research as a labor of love: Motherhood and the social construction of the baby registry. *Information, Communication & Society* 19 (7): 892–906.

Taylor, A. 2011. Reconceptualising the 'nature' of childhood. *Childhood* 18 (4): 420–433.

Thomson, R., M.J. Kehily, L. Hadfield, and S. Sharpe. 2011. *Making modern mothers*. Bristol: Policy Press.

Vincent, C., and C. Maxwell. (2015). Parenting priorities and pressures: Furthering understanding of 'concerted cultivation'. *Discourse: Studies in the Cultural Politics of Education* 37 (2): 269–281.

Warde, A. 1997. *Consumption, food and taste*. London: Sage.

Wilk, R. 2001. Consuming morality. *Journal of Consumer Culture* 1 (2): 245–260.

Zelizer, V.A.R. 1985. *Pricing the priceless child: The changing social value of children*. New York: Basic Books.

9

Child Caring Moralities and Market Organisation

Introduction

With every step taken, performances of child caring—whether by parents, commercial organisations or products—may be assessed and judged for adherence to the key understandings of the young child that 'feed' the teleoaffectivity of this practice. In the previous chapter, I discussed how the moralised and moralising process of becoming new parents is informed in and through commercial communications. This chapter also listened into narratives of parental moral selving, and presented typologies of parental concerns that show that parents connect 'understandings of the young child' with their own priorities and actions, and that also mobilise critical understandings of 'the market'. Of interest is that consumption and motherhood/parenting scholars have tended to focus solely on the implications of child caring moralities for consumers and parents. This may be defended on the political grounds that consumers and parents are 'subject' to the exigencies of techno-medical-science practices and the market. But this leads to a tendency to construct binary oppositions that hide underlying complexities. Thus, the analysis offered by Barnett et al. (2005) offers much food

© The Author(s) 2018
L. Martens, *Childhood and Markets*, Studies in Childhood and Youth,
https://doi.org/10.1057/978-1-137-31503-8_9

for thought, but it enacts the binary opposition between consumption and production through its focus on the governance of consumption, and to the exclusion of the governance of production and sales practices.

The analysis offered thus far suggests that the moralities of child caring manifest in varied ways, implicating commercial organisations and the organisation of their practices, along with their products. For instance, when presenting, in Chapter 7, the recent 'naturalisation drive' in infant feeding tools as a case-study in the moralisation of products, it becomes clear that the products in this world are under continuous scrutiny for whether these are acceptable. In the example I discussed, making orality tools 'fit for purpose' consisted in a process of aligning the qualities of the products closely with the qualities of the young child and the practice of breastfeeding. Chapters 5, 6 and 7 provide examples of how products are sold through alignment with aesthetic understandings of the young child; understandings of child embodied vulnerability; and concerns with child purity.

In this chapter, I discuss examples of how the moralities of child caring are evident in the interactions between commercial practitioners, and in the institutionalised qualities of sales/buyer interactions, which, as I argued in Chapters 3 and 4, are characterised by more-than-human saliences. I commence with a discussion of an episode of moral disruption, which started with the transformation of the chemical compound Bisphenol A into an infant health hazard in 2008, and which created upheaval in the business of infant feeding tools. In my analysis, I work through this 'episode' in a temporal way, attending to the issues that characterised the start of this new 'scare', the ways in which companies responded, and how moral stability returned in the aftermath. I then move on to discuss two other ways in which morality is evident in commercial practices. The first considers the interactions between commercial practitioners at consumer exhibitions, and reflects on how moral worth manifests itself through gossip. This is followed by a brief discussion of product standards, which evidences formal modes of governance of commercial practices and responsibility. In the final section of this chapter, I argue that the organisational features of commercial communicative practices—the informational content, the techno-medical-science density, and the faceless forms of interaction—that were discussed in previous chapters, may be read as institutionalised responses to the discourse of childhood.

Moral Disruption: The Case of Bisphenol A

In *The Politics of Plastics: The making and unmaking of Bisphenol A "safety"* (2009), Sarah Vogel provides a useful summary of the historical biography of this synthetic chemical compound, from its invention in the 1930s to the publication, followed by media coverage, of the UK National Toxicology Programme's report in April 2008 on the potential impact of Bisphenol A (BPA) on human reproduction and health. The conclusion drawn in this report is that 'the possibility that Bisphenol A may alter human development cannot be dismissed' (2007: 7). Vogel's article is important for its analysis of how 'safety' and 'risk' become concerns in and through the historically evolving scientific research process, and the entanglements of scientists, scientific knowledge, and commercial and political interests. Her paper gives voice to how the concern over Bisphenol A has converged on infants and the products used in their care, especially baby feeding bottles. At the same time, the scientific research Vogel discusses is opening up causal pathways of risk other than ingestion directly from bottles in which the pollutant has leaked. Scientists have, for instance, been asking research questions about the transfer of chemical compounds from the mother's body to the foetus and the baby, through the placenta and through breastfeeding. The parents NUK's representative spoke about, who said they did not mind so much about these pollutants for themselves, but that they were worried for their babies, may thus be seen to be misguided. Under the right conditions, scientific research on embodied transfers of this pollutant might turn into a future scare, though as this would then concern breastfeeding rather than bottle-feeding, this seems unlikely in the current moral context of infant feeding. In what follows, I reflect on how the events discussed by Vogel evolved into a moral disruption in the business of child caring. I call the disruption 'moral' because at its foundation is the 'stable' teleoaffective structure of infants as precious, vulnerable and pure, and it is this teleoaffective structure that is mobilised in the morally infused interactive work of carriers of child caring.

It is May 2008 when I visit The Baby Show again. At this event, there are 220 exhibitors, ranging from small entrepreneurs through to common and well-known brands, such as Pampers, Persil and Volvo. During this three-day visit, I have decided to focus on products that are related to 'mouths' and 'ingestion'. This includes the product categories of foods, food supplements, medicines, and orality tools. Exhibitor presence in this product group is not substantial, I write in my notes, especially considering the everyday quality of food and eating. In the product group of orality tools, brand companies NUK, Phillips Avent, Tommee Tippee, MAM and Playtex are exhibiting. For convenience sake, I use the term 'orality tool' for any tool that enters the mouths of babies, infants and toddlers. This includes products ranging from the teats that sit on top of infant feeding bottles, used to feed babies expressed milk or formula products, through to early toothbrushes and specialised cutlery for 'early users'. Other common tools that enter baby mouths are soothers (also known as pacifiers or dummies) and teethers (tools that may be used by babies who are in the process of producing teeth, and that are typically sold as tools for gnawing and cooling of the gums).

Foods, food supplements, medicines and orality tools are common everyday products used in the accomplishment of mundane everyday life in families with young children. These items are typically relatively cheap, used up relatively quickly (or not used at all), and are not particularly striking for their potential as symbolic resources that garner status for parents, in the way that larger items, such as child carriers, are argued to do (VOICE Group 2010a, b, see also Chapter 4). Following this through, one might be lulled into a false sense of security that this is a commercial terrain in which nothing much happens. After all, what can be so exciting about infant foods, food supplements or orality tools? Behind the apparent 'mundane', 'matter of fact,' and 'practical' facade of these common everyday products resides a degree of restlessness and commotion that is a typical quality of market practices (Beckert 2009). This, I go on to argue, touches at the very heart of one of the main concern in this book, which is the connection between childhood, moralities and markets.

On my first day at this event, I start a conversation with a sales representative from the German company NUK, whose webpage narrative was discussed in Chapter 7 alongside those of other food and feeding tool producers. She tells me that NUK's orthodontic feeding tool is stocked in UK hospitals, but that it was, until 2008, not widely available in retailing outlets. She talks about the growth of their online sales as a useful answer for new parents who are looking for their product following their introduction to the product in those early days. From here the discussion turns to a new safety concern around the chemical compound Bisphenol A, which is present as a plasticiser in the most commonly used plastic in the industry, PVC. This includes infant feeding bottles, a range of other infant products and toys. At the time of this discussion, the bottles are mostly made of see-through PVC plastic, which replaced the glass used in bottles in the past, but that are still stocked by some companies, including NUK. With a line running down the side with numerical volume measures, these bottles make it possible for the child carer to monitor how much the baby is drinking. There are also screw-on-tops that hold the teat in place, and bottles typically come with caps that prevent the milk from leaking out when the bottle is filled but not in use. Whilst these basic bottle features are shared between brands, diversification is achieved through bottle shapes, overall designs, the materials used in their production, and product decoration. 'Accessories' facilitating the practice of bottle-feeding infants are also multiplying, as is clear when you look through the extensive range of products on offer by Phillips Avent. Apart from its see-through quality, the NUK representative informs me, PVC plastic also came into use for its shatterproof qualities, something lacking in the earlier glass bottles.

She goes on to talk about how concerns about Bisphenol A leaching from feeding bottles, and leading to the ingestion of this chemical compound by babies, had recently grown. She discusses how her company has responded immediately by changing the plastic in its bottles, and she shows me the milky coloured plastic bottle that they are selling now, having withdrawn their original plastic bottles from sales. Since the concern around BPA has grown, the company had also been contacted by what she calls 'green retailers', who want to stock up on their glass bottles. The representative goes on to say that new parents are very worried about this compound. Being hypersensitive about anything that might harm their babies, she argues that parents are looking to go 'back-to-basics' in a move that coheres with the argument presented in Chapter 7 on purification.

In my discussions with orality tool company representatives in 2008, NUK was the only to have taken immediate action by bringing a new plastic bottle onto the market, and by continuing recommendation of their glass bottles. Other brand companies appeared to be playing the waiting game to see where the general consensus around Bisphenol A would go. Discussion with representatives suggested that companies were responding in different ways. One representative spoke at some length about how British parents were being sensible and reasonable about Bisphenol A and its consequences. She said that based on their own research, the amount of BPA that was released through the scratching of the material was so low, that babies would need to drink 4 times the amount of milk they did for them to ingest the daily recommended maximum. They were now advising parents on how to use and look after their feeding bottles to minimise the possibility of BPA leaking from the bottles. Their advice was not to put boiling water into the bottles and to discard those that were scratched. She also observed that parents were buying new bottles for a subsequent child, suggesting that the concern was already connecting with product longevity and second hand use. Another representative responded more despondently by blaming the anti bottle-feeding lobby for causing a stirring up of sentiment around BPA, contributing, in her view, to unnecessary parental anxiety, as, she assured me, levels of BPA leakage were so low that these could not be measured. A final exhibitor responded gleefully that their products had never contained BPA! This company was thinking through the potential competitive advantages that could be gained from this fact. However, because BPA had never been an issue before, the absence of this substance in their products was not visible anywhere in their promotional material and on product packaging. They now had sheets with small stickers they put on the packaging before sale, whilst their website proclaimed loud and clearly: 'Our conscience is clear: Bisphenol A-free products from (name of the brand)'. The concerns and frustrations that were displayed in these discussions are indicative of the emotions experienced by those involved, and suggestive of carrying the practice of child caring. It is not only the safeguarding of profit and the disruption to business routines, but also the moral obligation of safeguarding children, that was at the forefront of these accounts. The transformation of Bisphenol A into a safety issue had disrupted the commercial 'moral sense of self' of these companies.

When I attended the Earls Court Baby Show, in the autumn of 2009, the situation had changed. All exhibiting companies were now actively engaging with the Bisphenol A problematic, and there were more orality tool brand companies present at this exhibition than at others I had visited. From my discussion with a representative from a company I had not seen at The Show before, it became apparent that the companies were paying close attention to each other at this point in time, showing an interest in how they were responding to BPA and what they were doing by way of innovation. The two coordination problems of competition and cooperation (Beckert 2009) came together to make consumer exhibitions excellent sites for 'discreet' knowledge gathering of what was going on in the industry at this time of disruption. Of particular interest was how companies were innovating, and at this exhibition, various companies were displaying 'revamped' feeding bottles, made from plastics other than the PVC that contained BPA. Two plastics dominated in the innovations on show: Polyethersulfone (PES) and Polypropylene (PP), but neither was perceived to be the perfect replacement for PVC. The PES bottle was as clear and see-through as the PVC bottle had been, but had a yellow hue, a consequence of the sulphur used in the plastic. Phillips Avent attempted to 'cleanse' this bottle, by calling it their honey coloured bottle. The PP bottles had a milky appearance that made them less see-through than the PVC bottle, thus reducing the bottle's 'clinical look'. Product aesthetics clearly gives rise to contradictions. The PVC bottle, with its clean and appealing appearance, was now harbouring a polluting agent, and one company rep pointed out that the PES material contained a plasticiser called Bisphenol C, which she argued was safe, but which consumers could easily come to associate with its problematic cousin Bisphenol A.

Along with similar responses from the producers of other plastic infant tools (e.g. Lego), and following these initial teething problems with new product materials, peace has now returned in the industry. The materials used for infant feeding tools has shifted to Polypropylene, which, as explained by one of the exhibitors, is 6 times the price of PVC, bringing their bottle in at a show price of £10, though lasting only one year. It would seem that the price for BPA has been passed onto prospective and new parents. Promotional materials now proclaim loud and clearly that the products are BPA free, and BPA has taken its place amongst other past concerns in the history of infant feeding (see Chapter 6).

Gossiping Exhibitors

The transformation of BPA into a health hazard, and the consequent implications for companies, is interesting for illustrating the importance of interactions between commercial organisations. During the BPA episode, the competitive streak between exhibitors led to some sniggering behind the backs of other exhibitors for bringing 'morally questionable' product solutions to the show. The example of the PES bottle, with the yellow hue, was an example of this. During my visits to these shows, I listened into gossip amongst exhibitors about each other's sales practices and their products, and I heard stories that were enactments of moral selving (Bergmann 1993).

The sales tactics observed at The Show varied, as discussed in Chapter 4, and there were elements of the 'hard sell' and 'soft sales'. Exhibitors, who proclaimed loudly that *good* parents should use their products, because they had been clinically proven to be good for infants, received scorn from others. This was the case in Glasgow in 2005, with a company that sold early-learning cutlery for infants insisting that their product had been proven to help develop the young child's co-ordination skills, and that parents would therefore be mad to refuse to purchase the product. Exhibitors at The Show were gossiping about this sales representative as, so it was thought, this constituted unacceptable emotional blackmail. At the same Show, one of the products was highlighted in conversation as morally problematic. It concerned a new baby feeding bottle system that allowed a baby to feed itself. These kinds of moral musings were going on at every show. In 2010, when I spent some time in the corridor with smaller companies (see Chapter 4), I was asked for my views about Dr. Robert Titzer, who has created a business for himself in training babies, who have not yet the capacity to speak, to read. Whilst the idea behind this service was questioned, no concerns were raised about a similar company, Tiny Talk, in which young children are taught sign language. Needless to say, this specific commercial domain is guided by moralising practices that reflect the highly moral quality of childcare and the perceived value of young children.

There was further evidence of exhibitors engaging in forms of moral selving. Talking in particular with small entrepreneurs at The Show, it was apparent that many had started their companies after becoming parents. Most, though not all, exhibitors I spoke with proclaimed to be parents, and this information was volunteered readily during quite brief observations in discussions. In one instance, when I discussed the dubious safety credentials of cot bumpers[1] with a female sales representative, she said that as a mother she felt a moral obligation to tell prospective parents the truth and share with them their knowledge and opinions about products. Honesty, she said, sold better than dishonesty.

Product Standards and Institutionalised Governance

Fourcade and Healy (2007: 304) argue that governance is a cultural and moral process that writs equally highly in economic life, as it does in other public and private arenas:

---

[1]Cot bumpers are cushioned linings that may be used around the wooden sports of infant beds. These are in common use in the Nordic countries, where they are seen to counter drafts. In the UK, they serve more as decorative additions to bedding, and have been questioned as suffocation hazards.

The proliferation of agencies that monitor the behaviour of individuals, corporations, or nations with respect to debt, transparency, or honesty is an intensely moral project carried out in the name of rationalizing and expanding economic exchange and democratising society. (Political and economic liberalism are often two faces of the same cultural process.) The neoliberal economy is thus a governmentalized economy shaped by a myriad of surveillance organizations entitled to (but also with obvious material interests in) the rational application of technical means to govern the conduct of economic actors – be they small or large.

In Chapter 6, I introduced the idea that there has been growth in the product category of child safety. Here, I thought through how, in relation to products, *child safety consciousness* has become institutionalised in the form of formal standards (see also Martens 2014). Consciousness or awareness of child safety is illustrated through a questioning of whether a product or service is sufficiently safe to use, whether by the infant, or 'on' the infant and by those doing the caring. It is institutionalised through official British and international safety standards, which frequently appear as symbols on goods or guidelines on how to ensure the safe use of a product. An example is the toy for older children, which carries warnings about their danger for younger children (often based on them carrying small detachable items that are seen as potential suffocation hazards). At The Baby Show, a company selling playground installations displayed the European Safety Standard EN1176 in its product leaflet. Likewise, domestic products often carry warning labels to keep them out of reach of children. Some domestic cleaning products, deemed harmful for children, have in-built features that prevent easy child access, like bottle tops that cannot be easily unscrewed by young hands. These products have aspects of child safety incorporated into their design, some of which are legally required. Arguably, all products now in some way or other are implicated in the question of child safety.

As pointed out by Fourcade and Healy (2007), these formalised modes of governance are not necessarily about surveillance, and may be driven by material interests. In relation to child safety consciousness, an example where this was applicable was the child safety gate that may be placed at the bottom and tops of stairs on the home. Used widely in the UK, this product was covered with a standard from the British

Standards Institute in 1990. However, in a web-based discussion by the brand-company Belgray,[2] it was claimed that there was no statutory requirement to adhere to this standard and this brand-company therefore advised parents to check any product for information that it adhered to safety standards before purchase. Attaining safety standards for products can thus serve as a means for gaining advantage on the competition. The website further informed parents that in 2000, the UK had adopted the new European standard, the consequence of which was that the company had developed a new range of safety gates conforming to both the European and the British standards. With the adoption of the European standard in 2000, products adhering to the British standard and produced before the year 2000, might be conceived as embodying a set of out-of-date safety credentials, as those produced according to the new standards had added safety features to deal, for instance, with child entrapment. These 'new' gates were sold as containing important new innovations in their design, and are suggestive of the 'intensification' of child safety consciousness. I have previously linked this example of child safety consciousness, and the obviously shifting terrain of such consciousness over time, to the debate on the increasingly complex world that childcare practitioners are confronted with (Martens and Scott 2006). Changing safety standards, as pointed out by some of my interviewees, also leads to a speeding up of product obsolescence, and consequently, with greater turnover rates of products. This benefits pecuniary value creation, but to the detriment of the content of the consumer purse and the environment.

Organising the Face of Sales Encounters

One of the moral practices businesses need to engage in is attending to their 'trustworthiness' (Fourcade and Healy 2007). In sociology, trust has been theorised as prefiguring social relations: it is in and through social relations that trust becomes important (Giddens 1990; Kjaernes et al. 2007;

---

[2]http://www.beldray.com/gates/nat.%20standards.htm, accessed on 13 June 2005.

Luhmann 1982). Everts and Jackson (2009: 925) apply this to practices like shopping. They argue: … 'if we look at the enactment of trust in the light of a practice-oriented approach, trust has to be located not just in social relations but within practices.' Trustworthiness can thus be regarded as a quality of the relationship between carriers (human and more-than-human) of the practice of child caring, whilst simultaneously being tied up with the standards of this practice. Attending to the standards of a practice moves the discussion to the second dimension of Schatzki's (1996, 2002) ontology of practices, through which practices are socially organised: those of rules and principles. In the same way that parents are continuously confronted with *the standards* of their child caring practices through the expectation to reflect upon whether they are good enough parents, commercial players also need to attend to the standards of their practices. The commercial work of enhancing trustworthiness may then be seen as a continuous process whereby commercial players attempt to manage the ways in which they are publicly and culturally conceived and categorised. The work of trustworthiness is the problematic of how to attain and maintain the 'sacred' face of the *good commercial provider*, the conscientious carer whose products provide *true* aids to new families that are of *real* use and value, and that would never cause damage to young children. When talking about the maintenance of the standards of child caring, then, the concern is with the 'justificatory' practices through which the quality of standards are proven and defended (Fourcade and Healy 2007).

In view of this, in this final part of Chapter 9, I return to the question how companies frame—or organise—their actions (Callon 1998; Sayer 2006) in order to enhance their trustworthiness, and to safeguard against its opposite, which is the loss of trust imbued in their brands and products.[3] Two of these organisational components were

---

[3]That companies may loose the trust of consumers was illustrated in 2013, when Kimberly Clarke withdrew its disposable nappy brand Huggies from the UK market, after repeated complaints from parents that their nappies were producing skin rashes and inflammation on the brand's Facebook site. Huggies was present at early consumer exhibitions I visited, and was then, alongside Pampers, market leader in the disposable nappy market. The growth of social media, like Facebook, shows how it may have become easier for consumers to group together and question trustworthiness in brand-products.

discussed earlier: the techno-medical-science density found in sales narratives (highlighted especially in Chapter 6) and, related to this, the adopted role as pedagogue of child caring, which was discussed in Chapter 8. I will not repeat these arguments, but it is of interest how these organisational components of sales/buyer interaction serve a range of purposes, and that is partly why they have become conventions—organisational elements with substantial 'fixity'—across different interactional commercial practices, whether one considers parenting magazines, consumer exhibitions or brand-company websites. The multiplicity of purpose in techno-medical-science density should be clear from earlier discussions. In Chapter 6, for instance, I argued that techno-medical-science density is useful in the creation of pecuniary value, through knowing and describing the young child with a sense of authority, in offering ways for a group of businesses, whose area of sales overlaps, to find a niche market, but it simultaneously serves as a means for claiming trustworthiness. The adoption of a pedagogical role, especially in combination with techno-medical-science expertise, suggests 'professionalism' that can serve to draw in customers, but that at the same time makes a moral self-pronouncement that the firm speaks with a sense of authority and trustworthiness. There was evidence from my discussions with those exhibiting at The Baby Show that Mothercare operates what may be seen as a 'very tight ship'. Small commercial players, for instance, told me about the difficulties experienced in getting their products onto this retailer's aisles. One sales representative spoke about how their product had to adhere not only to the normal product safety requirements, but that Mothercare also had its own set of safety standards to which they had to adhere, suggesting a high level of care-full-ness on the part of this retailer.

I continue by presenting a discussion of another organisational element, which is how 'the face' is framed in exchange interactions. Recent commentary on the interactional dynamics between sellers and buyers in small markets, whether these are street markets (Cook 2008; vom Lehn 2014), charity shops (Gregson and Crewe 2003), or car boot sales (Crewe and Gregson 1998), is interesting for exploring some of the distinct qualities of face-to-face interactions in sales encounters (Brown 2004). Here, the skills of vendors and shoppers are explored,

and practices that involve a degree of deceit, such as playing customers, but also the haggling over price and the timing of the encounter,
are all explored. Two things stand out in this work. One is that these
studies tend to analyse one-off encounters of the sale and purchase of
products that carry little moral baggage; the other is that the concern
is with small players, rather than with big fish. The work by Everts and
Jackson (2009) on the corner shop differs from this as they focus on the
building of long-term relationships between shopkeepers and shoppers,
in which trust and communicative intercourse are important elements.
Everts and Jackson (2009) embed Giddens' (1990) analysis of trust relations in modernity as an element into their analysis. They sum up how
Giddens contrasts traditional and modern trust relations with reference
to face-to-face interaction:

> According to Giddens, there are two major forms of relationships that
> involve trust: 'facework commitments' and 'faceless commitments' (page
> 80). 'Facework commitments' refer to relationships, which are expressed
> and fostered in face-to-face interaction. This is found in settings where
> copresent people engage in various practices - they are present in the same
> place at the same time - whereas 'faceless commitments' refer to faith in
> 'abstract systems' as symbols or signs (e.g. certificates) or expert systems.
> … Giddens conceives of trust in relation to modernisation as faith in the
> "correctness of abstract principles" (1990: 34). (Everts and Jackson 2009:
> 924)

Their work on corner shop exchange relations offers a critique of the
mapping of facework and faceless commitments in simple ways onto
traditional and modern forms of social relations, where 'the modern' in
shopping is exemplified by the supermarket.

The business of child caring gives insight, not only in the different
kinds of encounter platforms through which exchange relations may
take place, but also into how, the larger the company that is considered, the broader the range of encounter platforms that may be found
in the marketing portfolio. Attending and doing exhibitions then
becomes one element in a broader portfolio of marketing devices, that
may also contain the design of product packaging, advertising, and
not to forget, a website presence (see also Chapter 3). Needless to say,

this makes an analysis of how 'the face' is mobilised in sales encounters more complex, with an expectation that both commitments—i.e. facework and faceless—may be found in the portfolio. In the analysis offered below, I pick up from the discussion on exhibitor conventions offered in Chapter 4. Here, I argued that even at what is, to all means and purposes, the most 'interactional' of market environments, there was a distinct lack of 'face-to-face' in the interactional organisation of especially the larger companies who attended. To sum up, small companies tended to communicate with visitors face-to-face, and where the purpose of the exhibition was demonstration or information, the face-to-face exchanges tended to happen between 'experts' and visitors. Where the purpose was to do marketing, interaction might be guided by facework and faceless exchanges, and where the purpose was brand positioning, there was a distinct lack of facework to be found at the exhibition stand. I will continue to explore reasons for whether and why face-to-face interaction may be used or avoided in exchange encounters in the business of child caring, and in doing so, I draw on the combined analysis of the consumer exhibition and brand-company websites. Of course, my analysis relates to the practice of child caring (of which shopping is one pathway), and how the teleoaffective qualities of this practice have become manifested not only in specific institutional (or organisational) qualities and modes of exchange that may be seen to be moral in relation to child caring, but also how 'the face' is incorporated as an element of such institutionalisation.

The presence of faceless commitments may be a consequence of the impossibility of face-to-face interaction, or, alternatively, the avoidance of direct communicative exchange. For larger brand companies, both may be argued to play a role. As argued earlier, products may have to 'speak for themselves' when they sit on a supermarket shelf. Where products are brought to customers via intermediaries, including distributors and retailers, the companies that produce them need to develop other means of bringing across their messages. But facework may also be avoided. One reason for this is that shoppers may not enjoy face-to-face encounters, experiencing the intermediation of a sales person an intrusion on their private considerations. This was expressed strongly by Julie (33 weeks, first time parents, 20s, white, white collar/technical), who was visiting The Show with her partner:

It is quite daunting really with all the different things here and all the people trying to sell you stuff if you see what I mean. I am not really into that kind of 'people-in-your-face' thing, which I am finding a bit daunting. Apart from that it is good, we have got lots of bags of stuff to take home and look at.

Another reason was given by Jasmin, whose observations were used to sketch out one of the consumer-carer typologies in Chapter 8, and who complained that retailing staff tended to lack knowledge. Undoubtedly, Jasmin's observation taps into the moralities of child caring, where the importance of the young child stimulates the need to be well informed. Jasmin's observation connects with discussions on markets and morality, and the consequent framing of action (Callon 1998). Whilst Hochschild (2003) has worried, following Fourcade and Healy's (2007) second strand of reactivity to markets, that the language of 'the market,' and *its* associated normativities and moralities are infusing intimate everyday worlds, Sayer (2006) points out that the 'everyday' norms and values of commercial practitioners, which he terms 'internal moral influences,' can be brought to bear on exchange interactions, and potentially disrupt the 'uniform' messages that commercial entities are attempting to bring across. As illustrated in Chapter 4, visitors for instance accounted of experiencing gender bias in their interactions with exhibition staff, who were seen as focusing on prospective mothers with bumps more than on prospective fathers. Internal moral influences, like these, are good reasons for limiting face-to-face interaction, especially where and when it is important that the content of the message commercial entities are trying to bring across needs to be coherent and of a certain standard. Child caring and its intrinsic moralities provide such a reason.

This also explains why brand-company websites have become such voluminous interactive technologies in this field. In exploring websites, common organisational elements in relation to 'the face' become apparent across commercial encounter platforms. Thus, whether we consider parenting magazines, brand-product websites, or the consumer exhibition, there are two organisational conventions that involve 'the face' that are welcome. These are the face of 'the expert' and the face of 'the child carer' (and these are mostly mothers).

The development of websites is interesting as these are essentially 'faceless' commitments through which content can be carefully constructed and conveyed. Yet, in the business of child caring, efforts are made to (re-)introduce the 'personal.' Examples include the introduction of parenting clubs and experts. With experts, 'the face' must be seen as re-introduced, if not necessarily in a streamlined fashion, then certainly for the capacity to answer customer questions with a sense of knowledgeability. In my work on commercial parenting pedagogy (Martens 2009), I discuss how child health and development professionals may move from the public to the private sphere, and make 'expertise' their occupation. Doing this successfully means establishing expert charisma, which includes the successful identification of knowledge innovation or knowledge needs, but above all is the need to package 'the goods' in appealing and authoritative ways. The Baby Show offers one avenue where such expert personalities are nurtured, as I for instance witnessed Annabel Karmel do over consecutive appearances at The Baby Show, as speaker on the stage, as 'celebrity' expert on the stands of exhibitors other than her own, and as the person cutting through the ribbon at the Scottish Show, to open this officially in the year I was there early enough to witness it. Practitioners in child caring clearly share in the quest for authority, reputation, and trustworthiness.

The example of Annabel Karmel is indicative of another convention that demonstrates the personal face; this is the face of the mother. As argued earlier, 'being a mother' seems to be an important credential for offering 'good' advice and products to other mothers. In this sense, The Baby Show works as a community of parenthood, as it does not matter whether you are seller or buyer, exhibitor or visitor; parenthood gives participants an 'easy' authority to advise others and a reason to place trust in the advice given. Thus, one convention in parenting magazines, which is repeated in the introduction of experts on the Cow and Gate website, is a mention of their parental status. Being a 'real life' child carer clearly serves more than one purpose, for in addition to the resultant acknowledgment of personal understanding, there is the added bonus that the mother-entrepreneur collapses the distinction between the profane market and the sacred qualities of intimate familial life.

Conclusion

I have here examined the implications of being a commercial practitioner in a field where moralities feature strongly, precisely because the teleoaffective structuration of child caring, in which commercial agents play an active role, leads to the 'fixing' of distinct understandings of the young child, that in turn govern the possibilities for economic action. The analysis presented shows how the practices of commercial organisations are infused with the moral concerns of child caring. This was supported with different examples. One example was the moral scare that followed the transformation of Bisphenol A into a baby health risk in 2007–2008, and that let to considerable disruption in the routines (in production and sales) of companies that deal in plastic products, and especially, those that enter the infants mouth through which the compound could be ingested. Another is the more mundane example of gossip amongst exhibitors and that may serve as a reason for cutting, or carefully organising, of staff at exhibition stands. Consequently, the work of trustworthiness is important in the business of child caring, and we saw how this was attended to through formalised standards and regulations, but also in the very organisation of sales encounters. Thus, the various organisational elements that were identified and discussed in earlier chapters, may be related back to the normativities of child caring and the discourse of childhood. Notably, the techno-medical-science density of this field, the pedagogical/information content, as well as the management of 'the face' in exchange interactions, exist as organisational conventions because the commercial entities involved carry the practice of child caring. The analysis thus illustrates, not only how practices as entities are performed in embodied and individual ways, but take on institutional qualities of a more-than-human kind (Pyhhtinen 2016), including post-social technologies (Knorr Certina and Bruegger 2002). If the practice field was not characterised by precious infants, who are conceived of as innocent and vulnerable, it may well be that the organisational orchestration of the business of child caring would be quite different.

Bibliography

Barnett, C., P. Cloke, N. Clarke, and A. Malpass. 2005. Consuming ethics: Articulating the subjects and spaces of ethical consumption. *Antipode* 37 (1): 23–45.

Beckert, J. 2009. The social order of markets. *Theory and Society* 38 (3): 245–269.

Bergmann, J.R. 1993. *Discreet indiscretions: The social organization of gossip.* Piscataway, NJ: Transaction Publishers.

Brown, B. 2004. The order of service: the practical management of customer interaction. *Sociological Research Online* 9 (4), http://www.socresonline.org.uk/9/4/brown.html.

Callon, M. (ed.). 1998. *The laws of the markets.* Oxford: Sociological Review/Blackwell.

Cook, D.T. (ed.). 2008. *Lived experiences of public consumption: Encounters with value in marketplaces on five continents.* Basingstoke: Palgrave Macmillan.

Crewe, L., and N. Gregson. 1998. Tales of the unexpected: Exploring car boot sales as marginal spaces of contemporary consumption. *Transactions of the Institute of British Geographers* 23 (1): 39–53.

Everts, J., and P. Jackson. 2009. Modernisation and the practices of contemporary food shopping. *Environment and Planning D: Society and Space* 27 (5): 917–935.

Fourcade, M., and K. Healy. 2007. Moral views of market society. *Annual Review of Sociology* 33: 285–311.

Giddens, A. 1990. *The consequences of modernity.* Cambridge: Polity Press.

Gregson, N., and L. Crewe. 2003. *Second-hand cultures.* Oxford: Berg.

Hochschild, A.R. 2003. *The commercialization of intimate life: Notes from home and work.* Berkeley: University of California Press.

Knorr Cetina, K.K., and U. Bruegger. 2002. Traders' engagement with markets: A postsocial relationship. *Theory, Culture & Society* 19 (5–6): 161–185.

Kjaernes, U., M. Harvey, and A. Warde. 2007. *Trust in food: A comparative and institutional analysis.* Basingstoke: Palgrave Macmillan.

Luhmann, N. 1982. *Trust and power.* London: Wiley.

Martens, L. 2009. Creating the ethical parent-consumer subject: Commerce, moralities and pedagogies in early parenthood. In *Critical Pedagogies of Consumption: Living and Learning in the Shadow of the "Shopocalypse"*, ed. J.A. Sandlin and P. McLaren. New York: Routledge.

Martens, L. 2014. Selling infant safety: Entanglements of childhood preciousness, vulnerability and unpredictability. *Young Consumers* 15 (3): 239–250.
Martens, L., and S. Scott. 2006. Under the kitchen surface: Domestic products
and conflicting constructions of home. *Home Cultures* 3 (1): 39–62.
National Toxicology Program, National Institute of Environmental Health,
National Institutes of Health Audit of literature cited and fidelity of
requested changes to draft Bisphenol A expert panel reports. Released July
24, 2007. Available at: http://cerhr.niehs.nih.gov/chemicals/bisphenol/
bisphenol-eval.html.
Pyyhtinen, A. 2016. *More-than-human sociology*. London: Palgrave Macmillan.
Sayer, A. 2006. Approaching moral economy. In *The moralization of the mar-
kets*, ed. N. Stehr, C. Henning, and B. Weiler, 77–100. New Brunswick,
NJ: Transaction Publishers.
Vogel, S.A. 2009. The politics of plastics: The making and unmaking
of Bisphenol A "safety". *American Journal of Public Health* 99 (S3):
S559–S566.
VOICE Group. 2010a. Buying into motherhood? Problematic consumption
and ambivalence in transitional phases. *Consumption, Markets and Culture*
13 (4): 373–397.
VOICE Group. 2010b. Motherhood, marketization, and consumer vulnerability. *Journal of Macromarketing* 30 (4): 384–397.
vom Lehn, D. 2014. Timing is money: Managing the floor in sales interaction at street-market stalls. *Journal of Marketing Management* 30 (13–14):
1448–1466.

10

Conclusion

This book has advanced analyses of children, childhood and consumer culture through a focus on the youngest of children. The work on which it draws has entailed adopting an approach that is substantially different to those that are commonly used when researching older children and consumption practices (Martens 2005). When thinking, for instance, about the ethnographic work conducted by Allison Pugh (2009) with children who live and move in social networks made up of families, friends, peers, schools and clubs, the study turns into an investigation of the interactions between children, and between children and parents, and other groups of adults (teachers, grandparents, marketers). Parents and parenting are important in such accounts, as the interactions and negotiations over the food, toys and technologies that come to appeal to children are part of the work of child caring and the intimate relations of family life (e.g. Gram 2015; Martens et al. 2004). In this study on young children, negotiations and discussions of this kind were absent, and the focus turned to the ways in which 'the young child' is rendered 'silent' when adults, grouped in different ways, and situated in institutionalised practices with more-than-human elements, speak and act on behalf of this child. Adults make the interactional sales events

© The Author(s) 2018
L. Martens, *Childhood and Markets*, Studies in Childhood and Youth,
https://doi.org/10.1057/978-1-137-31503-8_10

that mediate exchanges of goods and services in this field, and adults lead the conversations about young children. These conversations are punctuated by ways of knowing the young child, and I have argued that these knowledge practices converge in a discourse of childhood, that highlight certain qualities of the young child, whilst absenting other possible qualities. The qualities of the young child that came to the forefront, again and again, through 'their' performance and entanglement in unremarkable narrative performances, feed the teleoaffectivity of the practice of child caring. The practice of child caring has served as a key focal point for the arguments I have presented in this book, and there are several reasons for this.

First, this practice brings together the everyday concerns of caring for young children with the tools, objects and services that facilitate this work and responsibility. The commercial practitioners who target new families clearly do so in an important way by inventing, producing and selling these tools and services as commodities. One of the main arguments this book has developed is that child caring is a major locus for practices of pecuniary value creation, and commercial practices were examined for the ways in which these perform child caring 'as an entity' through knowledge practices of 'the young child'. Second, whilst child caring suggests the primacy of the entity of 'the young child', it does so through the idea that this child is in need of care. The practice of child caring is suggestive of generational practices that speak to the intimate relationship between parent and child, and to broader generational saliences, including the entity—or discourse—of childhood. In scholarship on children, childhood and consumer culture, academic reflexivity has been challenged especially by the strong moralities that dominate the ways in which 'the issues' are framed and voiced (Buckingham 2011). One cultural practice that facilitates moralisation is to position specific entities into the foreground—in this field, *the child consumer* and *the market* are two such entities—followed by an outline of a set of immutable characteristics that render these entities incompatible. Discursive practices of this and other kinds are effective at hiding the more complex relations that undergird child caring, not just between differently positioned people, but also between people, their institutions, more-than-human elements and common cultural categories.

It is right to recognise in scholarly debate that engages in these kinds of discursive practices the broader generational saliences that characterise the field, and this study has shown the importance of keeping this visible. Another central argument I have made is therefore that shifting the scholarly focus to the practice of child caring—crucial as it is in its own right as a terrain for value creation and for highlighting the generational and intimate qualities of caring for children—makes it possible to look behind these conceptual façades and *their* practices. Moreover, when foregrounding the practice of child caring, morality and moralisation become elements that are 'internal' to the practice, through the normativities that characterise it (Halkier 2010, 2013), and thus outcomes of repeated performances in a range of settings. The moralities that many feel and see when thinking about children and consumer culture, certainly when considering young children, are part of the normativities of the practice of child caring, and can be studied as such.

I have made use of theories of practice to develop the analysis of child caring this book has presented. Practice theories have gained popularity as theoretical tools in social science research and the field of consumption and consumer culture over the past years, and are appealing to sociologists of consumption because they allow the scholarly gaze to move to everyday life, and the mundane consumption that happens there, as a matter course, in routine accomplishments and performances that are practical, embodied and conceptual (e.g. Halkier et al. 2011). The popularity of the work of Reckwitz (2002) and Schatzki (1996, 2002) in applications of theories of practice in the sociology of consumption is suggestive of the search for a different theoretical language for everyday practical performances; one that places less emphasis on cultural *explanations* and that challenges common assumptions made about human action in theories of behaviour (Shove 2010; Warde 2014). Warde has recently argued that practices-as-entities need more explicit attention in consumption research, and that this requires both methodological fine-tuning and the development of more 'convincing' case studies (2014: 295). Related to this is the question how practices-as-entities are related to institutions and institutionalisation.

In this book, I have used Schatzki's ontology of social practices (1996, 2002), as it offers a set of tools for thinking through practices as social entities. He locates 'the social' in the ways practices are organised around three interconnecting social structures: a teleoaffective structure, a set of rules and principles, and different kinds of understandings. The arguments presented in this book offer a case study in how the practice of child caring 'as an entity' is performed in the interactive spaces of the commercial world of young children and new families. More specifically, Chapters 5, 6 and 7 considered how the teleoaffective structure of child caring becomes a structure through repeated enactments of specific qualities of young children. The inclusion and consideration of the performances of market actants has been important, not only because these give insight into pecuniary value creation practices and how these are organised, but also because these sales practices contribute towards shaping the practice of child caring. Chapters 4, 7, 8 and 9 provided food for thought on how the teleoaffective structure of child caring, and the interconnected rules and principles of this practice, organise this commercial world—and therefore also the interactional practices with prospective and new parents when they engage with the commercial world of early childhood. The analysis thus shows how, through repeated performances and *specifically* organised performances of the practice of child caring, the interactional space of the market takes on institutionalised qualities. These were already evident in my discussion in Chapter 4 on the business of child caring, and include the techno-medical-science density in sales practices, the marketization of child caring pedagogy (Chapter 8), and the specific management of 'the face' in interactional organisation (Chapter 9).

The institutionalised qualities of this market space are also recognisable in very real material forms and formats. Whether consisting in the material organisation of exhibition displays or in the shape and material that make up infant feeding tools, these have not only been included in my analysis as 'data', but have also pointed to the value of merging the elements of theories of practice used here with insights from science and technology studies. I have consequently argued that analyses of practices-as-entities can benefit from the adoption of methodological horizontality. In my analysis, I have focused on the ways in which the practice of child caring as a socio-cultural entity is performed in situated contexts other than family life and the isolation of the domestic setting, and by practice carriers other than parents or mothers, and indeed, other than human (Pyyhtinen 2016). Following trains of thought from science and technology studies and feminist theory (e.g. Knorr Cetina and Bruegger 2002; Nimmo 2011; Taylor 2013; Woolgar 1988), I have argued that the teleoaffective qualities of child caring, through enactments of the young child, are performed in the discursive performances of new and prospective parents when they agreed to talk with me (Martens 2012), in the face-to-face interactions I had with sales staff, in the varied range of textual sales materials I collected and analysed, and in the very fabric and design of exhibition stands and products (Verbeek 2006). I have listened into the cacophony of these performances without prioritising one form of evidence over others, whilst certainly maintaining attentiveness to variations in performances. Such variations are a consequence of different factors, two of which are the fact that performing entities are usually multi-practice-ing and are thus negotiating between the priorities of more than one practice at any one time. In addition, as witnessed in the analysis of discussions with new and prospective parents, and the business of child caring, performing 'entities' are typically 'internally' diverse. Such variations demand scholarly attention because these reveal the diverse politics and interests that shape performances of the practice of child caring (Halkier 2010). In these ways, this analysis of young children and the business of child caring makes a useful contribution to theoretical advancement in the sociology of consumption (Cook 2008; Martens et al. 2004).

Childhood and Markets

Despite their everyday obviousness, childhood and markets are complex cultural entities. Childhood has been a theoretical puzzle in children and childhood studies, where *its* generative and generational qualities are not always fully recognised, resulting in analyses that confuse the different structural properties of childhood (Shanahan 2007). My argument has been that such confusions are a consequence of the performativity of the discourse of childhood. To address these challenges of childhood, Prout (2005) has led the way by criticising the method of social constructionism (see also Woolgar 2012), which proposes that childhood is unreservedly varied, flexible and malleable. As it insists that children and their experiences differ, over time and across cultures, 'varied childhoods' arguments have been popular and support the political agenda of children and childhood studies. But social constructionist arguments can be harnessed to do other work. Witness, for instance, the idea of the voiceless child, who cannot defend 'itself' against the shifting cultural meanings that adults impose on childhood (Honeyman 2005). The latter has entered debate on children, childhood and consumer culture, where it has served to sustain a critique of an all-powerful market, which is said to be at liberty to define 'what a child is' 'in any number of ways' (Cook 2004: 15). Whilst this presents a critical narrative that suits moral popular debate on children and consumption, does it not simultaneously render childhood culturally ineffective? In this book, I have pursued an investigation that provides insight into how specific understandings of the young child become sedimented as part of an ongoing process of performances. As such, I agree with Sparrman and Sandin (2012: 15) that 'the connection between children and markets is relational in the way that they produce one another rather than defining an assumed hierarchical order.' The analysis offered here has thus closely considered the mutually constituting relations between the culturally generative entities of 'market' and 'childhood', set in broader social relations.

The analysis presented in the book suggests that there is a strong convergence around a limited set of key ideas of 'what a young child is.' Three key childhood qualities—those of loveable, vulnerable and pure—were examined in some detail as interconnected prongs in the teleoaffective quality of child caring. The quality of loveable, and its structuration, was explored in an analysis of the aesthetic conventions of sales practices and products, as well as in ritual practices through which love is practiced and sedimented in family life. Vulnerability was traced through different renditions, with enigmatic embodied vulnerability associated with the youngest of children and unpredictability speaking of the young child who is gaining independent mobility. Child purity brought together a range of tasks that render 'the young child' and the products used in childcare, clean in physical and symbolic ways. I clarified in Chapter 4 that these are not the only key qualities with which the young child is attributed, and around which pecuniary value creation is organised. Nurturing is a fourth quality, which in the young child has two sub-qualities, those of soothing and stimulation. Nurturing, especially in the form of stimulation, sits closest to the theme of child development, which has been highlighted as linked to value creation by researchers of early childhood and consumer culture (e.g. Cook 2004). In the analysis presented in this book, nurturing was discussed only where 'it' was joined with the other key ideas in the specific commercial narratives that were investigated. Those working on theoretical considerations of practices and consumption may find interesting the fact that it is these four child qualities that form the bedrock of the teleoaffective structure of child caring. Regardless of the child caring pathways that are considered, as illustrated in Table 4.2, these same teleoaffective qualities may be found back across the board.

The key understandings of 'what a child is' are not only constitutive of the structuration of the teleoaffective qualities of child caring 'in their own right', in and through 'their' repetitious presence in commercial narratives, products and parental talk. The entanglement of these qualities adds an additional dimension to the process of teleoaffective structuration. I have argued that the child quality of loveable is foundational to the practice of child caring, in that 'it' comes before other key qualities of 'the young child' as stimulus for action. Child vulnerability gains its salience through entanglement with the love for the young child, for if the child was not recognised as important in this emotional way, its proposed vulnerability would unlikely stimulate action. The emotional importance of the young child is demonstrated by the abundant presence of techno-medical-science narratives in describing infant vulnerability. To know the young child through techno-medical-science narratives underwrites 'its' emotional importance: children cannot be known in just any one way, only 'the best' knowledge is acceptable precisely because they are so precious.

The business of child caring suggests that there is no such thing as 'the market'. This analysis has gone some way towards opening the 'black box' of the market, challenging the assumption that market practitioners group together under one heading: that of 'the market' assumed to be all-powerful in its very presence, and in the furtherance of a consumer culture in which consumers and meanings are tied up and commercially driven. The business of child caring has been shown to consist of multiple and varied commercial enterprises, some of which are very small; others taking on rather larger proportions and presenting themselves and their ware behind brand names and imposing websites. Companies group together around pathways of child caring, where they compete with one another to sell virtually the same products— whether these be products for personal hygiene and cleanliness, baby and infant foods, or nappies. In view of this, as explained in Chapter 6, techno-medical-science borrowing has a number of benefits, not least of which is that it offers ways of writing elaborate and diverse stories about young children and, for instance, their embodied vulnerability, which in turn can support a range of products rather than only one, and opens avenues for niche market positioning in relation to 'similar' product categories. Whilst the techno-medical-science density in sales narratives may be taken as evidence of the freedom assumed by commercial organisations to image the young child in whatever way is chosen, my analysis illustrates that this is in fact not the case, as such sales narratives always referred back to the key understandings of childhood discussed above.

This business is not solely guided by the teleoaffective qualities of commercial practices, and in particular, the need to make profit. The argument presented here was that, in order to operate in this field, commercial practitioners also have to carry the practice of child caring. Rather than letting 'the market' off the hook, so to speak, the critical purchase of an approach like this one, which works through practices, is that the generative qualities of commercial performances are recognised as located at the intersections of different priorities and saliences. In this sense, Fourcade and Healy's (2007: 286) argument that markets are 'intensely moralized, and moralizing entities,' rings true in my analysis. This has shown that market actants are moralising entities, especially in and through the persistent work that is done on the meanings of 'what a young child is', thus contributing in the specification of 'what it means to care for young children'. As argued in Chapter 3, such cultural work is a form of political practice not only because of the profit making motives that are pursued, but also because, as pointed out above, participating in teleoaffective structuration is a form of 'interest positioning' in a broader sense, in relation to other market actants, in relation to customers (parents and children), and in relation to other organisations who carry this practice (e.g. those specialising in health, education and social care). That market actants are moralizing entities was also shown in Chapter 8, where I discussed how commercial practitioners have become increasingly active as pedagogues of child caring, designing instructional content that sketches this practice in specific ways and that normalises the information-seeking culture that characterises the world of new families (Fuentes and Brembeck 2017).

So, have market forces in affluent societies come to occupy a more influential societal location in matters concerning young children and child caring? The process of alignment between the commercial and the techno-medical-science complexes that my analysis demonstrated certainly seems to suggest this. As has been explored in relation to education (Kenway and Bullen 2001; Buckingham 2011), here too is evidence of the marketisation of domains of practice that are traditionally thought of as outside economic life. My analysis also revealed that the teleoaffective narration of child caring varies between commercial and parental carriers. In particular, parents, even those whose babies have yet to be born, give voice to the idea of the market as profane. The idea of keeping market forces 'in check' as one of the responsibilities of parenting may be read as an expression of greater commercial presence and pressure. Yet some have argued that such cultural responses are certainly not new or limited to affluent consumer worlds (Kopytoff 1986; Zelizer 1985). And, as was seen in Chapter 8, new parents also spoke out against the contradictory nature of the medical advice they received. Even so, the very fact that the business of child caring is not happy just with selling products, but in doing so has taken on a prominent role in the narration of child caring as a social entity, certainly warrants attention.

As shown in Chapters 7 and 9, the business of child caring is also 'intensely moralized'. This is illustrated not only in the sense that substantial effort goes into the moralisation of products (see Chapters 6 and 7), for, as argued in Chapter 9, the very interactional sales environment is organised in accordance with the priorities and principles of this practice. The analysis presented in these chapters shows commercial practitioners engaging with the question of care in child caring, resulting in various forms of commercial care-full-ness, whether this is through the display of child safety consciousness or in the measured responses to the Bisphenol-A scare. And there are other examples of the generative qualities of childhood! When first studying the business of child caring, I was struck by the 'busyness' of this commercial field. As recognised in discussions on markets and the social nature of the interactions that take place there (e.g. Beckert 2009), continuous innovation and competition are the hallmarks of this activity, with new products and ideas always celebrated and seen as particularly newsworthy at the trade and consumer exhibitions I visited. Yet, underneath this ruse of novelty and innovation is a world that is probably more accurately characterised by constancy. My analysis has illustrated the limits of cultural creativity in a field of commerce where key understandings of 'the young child' are repeatedly rehearsed. The value-creation strategies that my analysis gives insight into are interesting for creating innovation, not by rethinking the main axis around which the teleoaffective structure of child caring is organised, but by mixing elements of this teleoaffective structure in apparently novel ways, and by thinking up new narratives that confirm rather than challenge the key meanings of childhood. The question that should follow, then, is not how the meanings of childhood are forever shifting and greatly flexible, fuelled, perhaps, by the assumption that this is directly driven by the ceaseless commercial need for product innovation and competition, but how and why childhood acquires 'its' sedimented understandings, in which innocence continues to hold sway (Davis 2011; Higonnet 1998; Meyer 2007; Taylor 2010), what the consequences are, whether there is a need for a way out of this stasis, and how that might be achieved (see e.g. Taylor 2013)?

Another concerns the question how easy it is in commercial narrating to sketch a child with desires and needs for goods and services. Where understandings of the young child are sedimented around innocence, commercial practitioners will find it hard to push *the child consumer* into the forefront. Yet, this very image may be actively performed elsewhere, for instance, in the narratives of the new and prospective parents and grandparents interviewed in this study when they expressed their concern about 'the market' in relation to their young offspring. Whilst Cook (2004) and Cross (2002, 2004) provide examples of the portrayal of relatively young children with preferences and tastes in the historical marketing literatures they examined, I have found little evidence of contemporary sales narratives that imagine 'the young child' in this way. At best, young children are described as being quick in becoming set in their ways, creating preferences for the 'taste' of some materialities (e.g. nipple or teat) over others. Through their emplacement in close proximity with the myriad of products and services that are on offer in the business of child caring, it may be argued that 'the needs' of young children are actively scripted. This study has shown that these are needs for *care* rather than *commodities*. Commodities take on a secondary location as aids in practices of care, rather than as objects of children's desires and tastes. Of course, this is not to say that commodities may not be objects of parental desires and imaginations. Simultaneously, it is hard to distinguish the needs of the young child from those of its carers. Baby slings and wraps alternatively suggest the young child's need for sleep, the need for embodied closeness between humans, and the need for families to be 'on the move' when small children do not yet have the physical or mental capability to 'keep up'. Organic foods speak a language of the need by young children for clean sustenance, but such concerns easily co-exist with adult concerns about broader environmental issues, or, more cynically, their class-bounded dispositions and tastes. Meanwhile, Sophie the Giraffe (discussed in Chapter 5) may suggest children's needs to develop their embodied mobility and coordination skills, whilst adults may get a kick from buying Sophie because she is cute and provides a melancholic reminder of the squeaky toys that they had in their own childhood (Cross 2002, 2004). Of course, as the marketing narrative of Sophie the Giraffe demonstrates, the multiplication of such 'appeals' is good for business. These examples demonstrate the generative qualities of childhood, and suggest that market actants do not 'operate' alone, nor have the freedom to sketch childhood anew, from a clean slate and as 'they' choose.

Young Children, Older Children, No Children

What other ramifications does this analysis of young children and new families have for analyses of children, childhood and consumer culture? I here briefly return to the question of age, and how age is linked to value creation work. The categorisation of cohorts of people on the basis of their biological age has been identified as a strategy for expanding markets in relation to the young and the old (e.g. Cook 2004; Phillipson et al. 2008). Visiting the websites of a range of companies who operate in the market for pregnancy, birth and early childhood years, reveals the ubiquitous commercial practice of 'staging' the life course transition when expecting a child, and the weeks, months and years following birth. Staging on the basis of the smallest 'life course' or 'developmental' 'step' is translated into specific sets of associated child caring concerns, alongside the offer of a range of associated products. The descriptive practices found in commercial culture in relation to age, but also in relation to the three key child qualities discussed in Chapters 5, 6 and 7, also underwrite the youthfulness of 'the child'.

One overriding emphasis in the sales narratives I explored is an understanding of the young child's need for care as manifested in embodied ways. Here, I discussed examples linked to the bodily closeness sketched in images of embodied care, of the enigmatic embodied child whose vulnerabilities are real, but nevertheless elusive, and that can therefore be realised in a myriad of ways, and of the young child whose body is kept pure through cleanliness rituals. I argued that it is this emphasis on the embodied child that renders 'the child' *young*, and, following Brownlie and Leith (2011), in some respects not quite human.

Future research could focus more closely on the young child's 'ageing.' In a way, of course, much that is written about children, childhood and consumer culture engages with child 'age' and 'ageing', but this is mostly done in implicit ways, through engagement with the manifold contradictions that scholars encounter and vocalise; not least in the juxtaposition between the competent and incompetent child (Sparrman and Sandin 2012), and through the selection of specific case-studies that focus on children of different ages (e.g. Freeman 2009, 2012; Plowman et al. 2010), rather than in and through accounts that compare and contrast children of different ages. There are some indications that such an analysis would need to consider the shift from the young child's embodied needs to that of their 'personal' development, perhaps unearthing the psychological 'awakening' of the young embodied child, as innocence starts to make way for degrees of agency that are symbolised, for instance, by shifts such as those identified in Chapter 6, where infantile vulnerability moved from the category of enigmatic to that of unpredictable. As pointed out by Lawler (2000), the mothers in her study defined their childcare by foregrounding the psychological needs of the child. The distinction between the embodied young child and the psychologically involved child, who speaks and is socially active, is likely important in the way the ageing of young children is understood, in the commercial world as well as beyond. Following the argument of McNamee and Seymour (2013), also in relation to research on children, childhood and consumer culture it would be useful if more attention was given to how 'the child,' 'age' and 'ageing' are connected in value creation practices, and what these mean for how children grow up in contemporary affluent consumer worlds.

The arguments presented here on child caring invite further thought regarding whether and how such a focus may be worthwhile keeping hold of when considering consumer culture and older children. I have also argued that 'the market' is made up of many commercial entities, all trying to realise a profit, and doing so in different and, not infrequently, contradictory ways. In seeking avenues for financial gain, any and every social and cultural concern can become a target. And the observations just made suggest that what child caring is seen to entail changes over time. In relation to older children, scholars could usefully pursue questions related to how children's tastes are nurtured as they grow older, and where this process comes to contradict with the principles of responsible parenting and the enculturation of forms of family-based distinction (Martens et al. 2004; Pugh 2009).

Whilst my focus has been on the business of child caring, I am well aware that this is not the only avenue through which profit is made in relation to the experiences of the life course this book has focused on.

The consumer exhibition, for instance, was as much an event for families visiting together, as an avenue for the sale of the products of child caring (Karsten et al. 2015; Lindsay and Maher 2013). In addition, the commercial field that was explored did not pursue pecuniary value creation solely through the foregrounding of 'the young child' and child caring. By talking a language of getting on with life 'despite' the fact that the care of children had been added to the mix, one commercial sector seems equally keen to understand prospective and new parents as *individual* and *adult* consumers, and in which the concerns of caring for children apparently comes second place (e.g. Bettany et al. 2014; O'Donohoe 2006). It would be useful to see future research explore these diverse ways in which for-profit motives are aligned with the diverse priorities, concerns and interests of personal lives (Smart 2007).

Love, Intensification and Neo-liberalisation

In Chapter 2, territorialisation was described as the process of scholarship converging into disparate research fields focused on primary entities. I highlighted the growing scholarly terrains of markets, consumption, mothering/parenting, and children and childhood as examples of territorialisation that relate to the subject matter explored in this book. Whilst the development of these research pathways may be acknowledged as having distinct benefits, I also argued that there is a problem with investigative segregation that, for instance, Zelizer (2012) speaks of, and that impedes the visibility of cultural practices as complex and nuanced. Territorialisation around entities also runs the risk of confirming the importance of explanations that are directly related to the specific research agendas that are explored, to the exclusion of other agendas and explanations, and indeed, to accounts that move beyond this. One example of this is the different conclusions that scholars reach when examining childhood and motherhood in consumer culture. The argument of the generational saliences of childhood has, for instance, been used to think through how parents and adults 'consume' 'the child', or perhaps more accurately, childhood innocence (Buckingham 2000; Cross 2002, 2004; Honeyman 2005) as a coping mechanism of living life in a hard adult world. By contrast, in the recently expanding literature on motherhood and consumer culture, scholars borrow from motherhood/parenting studies to argue that consumer culture contributes to an experience described as the intensification of parenting or motherhood. This, in turn, is marked as indicative of neo-liberalisation for bringing together the quintessential features of individualisation, responsibilisation and choice (e.g. Cairns et al. 2013). Meanwhile, in the sociology of consumption, especially that which engages with the practice turn, neo-liberalisation is recognised as an ideology and a specific way of thinking about, and performing, the salience of the individual and individualism (Warde 2014). The practice turn, it is argued, helps scholars distance themselves from this. In relation to this, one has to ask the question why parents come to feel responsible for caring for children in the first place, and what makes the choices that they make in the market place seem so very important (Warde 1997)? Surely, underlying the instrumentality of the neo-liberalist ethos, such as it exists in new parents (see Chapter 8), sits the loving quality of 'the young child' and the importance of intimate relations?

I am in no a position to offer a 'measurement' of the changing emotional value of the young child in recent decades. Explaining such a shift, if there is one, would need to be done by looking into a range of different factors, one of which is certainly the declining birth rate and changes in the life course, like the delay in starting families (Brusdal and Frønes 2013; Thomson et al. 2011). This analysis has shown that market actants are active in upvaluing the young child by structuring the teleoaffective qualities of child caring, and, as illustrated, this structure 'hangs' on the furtherance of the loveable qualities of the young child. Commercial carriers therefore confirm rather than reject the emotional salience of young children. On the basis of accepting that consumer culture has become more pronounced in its presence in personal lives, it may even be suggested that this drives, at least in part, this understanding of children. But let me consider how this connects with the theme of intensification that dominates the sociology of mothering and parenting. If it exists, intensification is arguably a condition of child caring, not only of parenting or motherhood. It may be argued that the emotional importance of the young child, through this practice's normativities, drives the dynamic of intensification. If practice carriers strive towards greater perfection, in becoming 'good' child carers, market actants as well as parents must be acknowledged as the agents and subjects of intensification. This is so when new mothers struggle with the imperative to breastfeed their babies (Keenan and Stapleton 2013), and when 'innovation' is announced as delivering 'better' products and services.

Bibliography

Beckert, J. 2009. The social order of markets. *Theory and Society* 38 (3): 245–269.

Bettany, S.M., B. Kerrane, and M.K. Hogg. 2014. The material-semiotics of fatherhood: The co-emergence of technology and contemporary fatherhood. *Journal of Business Research* 67 (7): 1544–1551.

Brownlie, J., and V. Leith. 2011. Social bundles: Thinking through the infant body. *Childhood* 18 (2): 196–210.

Brusdal, R., and I. Frønes. 2013. The purchase of moral positions: An essay on the markets of concerned parenting. *International Journal of Consumer Studies* 37 (2): 159–164.

Buckingham, D. 2000. *After the death of childhood*. Hoboken: Wiley.

Buckingham, D. 2011. *The material child*. Cambridge: Polity.

Cairns, K., J. Johnston, and N. MacKendrick. 2013. Feeding the 'organic child': Mothering through ethical consumption. *Journal of Consumer Culture* 13 (2): 97–118.

Cook, D.T. 2004. *The commodification of childhood: The children's clothing industry and the rise of the child consumer*. Durham, NC: Duke University Press.

Cook, D.T. 2008. The missing child in consumption theory. *Journal of Consumer Culture* 8 (2): 219–243.

Cross, G. 2002. Valves of desire: A historian's perspective on parents, children, and marketing. *Journal of Consumer Research* 29 (3): 441–447.

Cross, G. 2004. Wondrous innocence print advertising and the origins of permissive child rearing in the US. *Journal of Consumer Culture* 4 (2): 183–201.

Davis, R.A. 2011. Brilliance of a fire: Innocence, experience and the theory of childhood. *Journal of Philosophy of Education* 45 (2): 379–397.

Fourcade, M., and K. Healy. 2007. Moral views of market society. *Annual Review of Sociology* 33: 285–311.

Freeman, O. 2009. "The Coke side of life"—An exploration of pre-schoolers' constructions of product and selves through talk-in-interaction around Coca-Cola. *Young Consumers* 10 (4): 314–328.

Freeman, O. 2012. 'I do like them but I don't watch them': Preschoolers' use of age as an accounting device in product evaluations. In *Situating child consumption: Rethinking values and notions of children*, ed. A Sparrman, B Sandlin and J Sjöberg, 157–175. Lund: Nordic Academic Press.

Fuentes, M., and H. Brembeck. 2017. Best for baby? Framing weaning practice and motherhood in web-mediated marketing. *Consumption Markets & Culture* 20 (2): 153–175.

Gram, M. 2015. Buying food for the family: Negotiations in parent/child supermarket shopping: An observational study from Denmark and the United States. *Journal of Contemporary Ethnography* 44 (2): 169–195.

Halkier, B. 2010. *Consumption challenged: Food in mediated everyday lives.* Farnham: Ashgate.

Halkier, B. 2013. Contesting food—Contesting motherhood? In *Motherhoods, markets and consumption: The making of mothers in contemporary Western cultures,* ed. S. O'Donohoe, M. Hogg, P. Maclaran, L. Martens, and L. Stevens, 87–102. London: Routledge.

Halkier, B., T. Katz-Gero, and L. Martens. 2011. Special issue on "Applications of practice theory in consumption research." *Journal of Consumer Culture* 11 (1): 3–13.

Higonnet, A. 1998. *Pictures of innocence: The history and crisis of ideal childhood.* London: Thames & Hudson.

Honeyman, S. 2005. *Elusive childhood: Impossible representations in modern fiction.* Columbus, OH: Ohio State University Press.

Karsten, L., A. Kamphuis, and C. Remeijnse. 2015. 'Time-out' with the family: The shaping of family leisure in the new urban consumption spaces of cafes, bars and restaurants. *Leisure Studies* 34 (2): 166–181.

Keenan, J., and H. Stapleton. 2013. 'It won't do her any harm' they said, 'or they wouldn't put it on the market'. In *Motherhoods, markets and consumption: The making of mothers in contemporary Western cultures*, ed. S. O'Donohoe, M. Hogg, P. Maclaran, L. Martens, and L. Stevens, 71–87. London: Routledge.

Kenway, J., and J. Bullen. 2001. Consuming children: Education-entertainment-advertising. Michigan: Open University Press.

Kopytoff, I. 1986. The cultural biography of things: Commoditisation as process. In *The social life of things: Commodities in cultural perspective*, ed. A. Appadurai. Cambridge: Cambridge University Press.

Knorr Cetina, K.K., and U. Bruegger. 2002. Traders' engagement with markets: A postsocial relationship. *Theory, Culture & Society* 19 (5–6): 161–185.

Lawler, S. 2000. *Mothering the self: Mothers, daughters, subjectivities*. London: Routledge.

Lindsay, J., and J. Maher. 2013. *Consuming families: Buying, making, producing family life in the 21st century*. London: Routledge.

Martens, L. 2005. Learning to consume—Consuming to learn: Children at the interface between consumption and education. *British Journal of Sociology of Education* 26 (3): 343–357.

Martens, L. 2012. Practice 'in talk' and talk 'as practice': Dish washing and the reach of language. *Sociological Research Online* 17 (3): 1–11.

Martens, L., D. Southerton, and S. Scott. 2004. Bringing children (and parents) into the sociology of consumption: Towards a theoretical and empirical agenda. *Journal of Consumer Culture* 4 (2): 155–182.

Martens, L., and S. Scott. 2017. Understanding everyday kitchen life: Looking at performance, into performances and for practices. In *Methodological reflections on practice oriented theories*, ed. M. Jonas, B. Littig, and A. Wroblewski, 177–191. Springer International Publishing.

McNamee, S., and J. Seymour. 2013. Towards a sociology of 10–12 year olds? Emerging methodological issues in the 'new' social studies of childhood. *Childhood* 12 (2): 156–168.

Meyer, A. 2007. The moral rhetoric of childhood. *Childhood* 14 (1): 85–104.

Nimmo, R. 2011. Actor-network theory and methodology: Social research in a more-than-human world. *Methodological Innovations Online* 6 (3): 108–119.

O'Donohoe, S. 2006. Yummy mummies: The clamor of glamour in advertising to mothers. *Advertising & Society Review* 7 (3).

Phillipson, C., R. Leach, A. Money, and S. Biggs. 2008. Social and cultural constructions of ageing: The case of the baby boomers. *Sociological Research Online* 13 (3): 5.

Plowman, L., J. McPake, and C. Stephen. 2010. The technologisation of childhood? Young children and technology in the home. *Children & Society* 24 (1): 63–74.

Prout, A. 2005. *The future of childhood*. London: Routledge.

Pugh, A.J. 2009. *Longing and belonging: Parents, children, and consumer culture*. California: University of California Press.

Pyyhtinen, A. 2016. *More-than-human sociology*. London: Palgrave Macmillan.

Reckwitz, A. 2002. Toward a theory of social practices: A development in culturalist theorizing. *European Journal of Social Theory* 5 (2): 243–263.

Schatzki, T. 1996. *Social practices: A Wittgensteinian approach to human activity and the social*. Cambridge: Cambridge University Press.

Schatzki, T. 2002. *The site of the social. A philosophical account of the constitution of social life and change*. Pennsylvania: Pennsylvania State University Press.

Schatzki, T., K. Knorr-Cetina, and E. von Savigny (eds.). 2001. *The practice turn in contemporary theory*. Routledge: London.

Shanahan, S. 2007. Lost and found: The sociological ambivalence toward childhood. *Annual Review of Sociology* 33: 407–428.

Shove, E. 2010. Beyond the ABC: Climate change policy and theories of social change. *Environment and Planning A* 42 (6): 1273–1285.

Smart, C. 2007. *Personal life*. Cambridge: Polity Press.

Sparrman, A., and B. Sandin. 2012. Situated child consumption: Introduction. In *Situating child consumption: Rethinking values and notions of children, childhood and consumption*, ed. A. Sparrman, B. Sandin, and J. Sjöberg, 9–32. Lund: Nordic Academic Press.

Taylor, A. 2010. Troubling childhood innocence: Reframing the debate over the media sexualisation of children. *Australasian Journal of Early Childhood* 35 (1): 48–57.

Taylor, A. 2013. *Reconfiguring the natures of childhood*. London: Routledge.

Thomson, R., M.J. Kehily, L. Hadfield, and S. Sharpe. 2011. *Making modern mothers*. Bristol: Policy Press.

Verbeek, P.P. 2006. Materializing morality design ethics and technological mediation. *Science, Technology and Human Values* 31 (3): 361–380.

Warde, A. 1997. *Consumption, food and taste: Culinary antinomies and commodity culture*. London: Sage.

Warde, Alan. 2014. After taste: Culture, consumption and theories of practice. *Journal of Consumer Culture* 14 (3): 279–303.

Woolgar, S. (ed.). (1988). *Knowledge and reflexivity: New frontiers in the sociology of knowledge*. Thousand Oaks, CA, US: Sage Publications, Inc.

Woolgar, S. 2012. Ontological child consumption. In *Situating child consumption: Rethinking values and notions of children, childhood and consumption*, ed. A. Sparrman, B. Sandin, and J. Sjöberg, 33–52. Lund: Nordic Academic Press.

Zelizer, V.A.R. 1985. *Pricing the priceless child: The changing social value of children*. New York: Basic Books.

Zelizer, V. 2012. A grown-up priceless child. In *Situating child consumption: Rethinking values and notions of children, childhood and consumption*, ed. A. Sparrman, B. Sandin, and J. Sjöberg, 71–80. Lund: Nordic Academic Press.

Index

Printed by Printforce, the Netherlands